Coastal Defence and Earth Science Conservation

Coastal Defence and Earth Science Conservation

Edited by

Janet Hooke
Department of Geography, University of Portsmouth, UK

1998
Published by The Geological Society

THE GEOLOGICAL SOCIETY

The Society was founded in 1807 as The Geological Society of London and is the oldest geological society in the world. It received its Royal Charter in 1825 for the purpose of 'investigating the mineral structure of the Earth'. The Society is Britain's national society for geology with a membership of around 8000. It has countrywide coverage and approximately 1000 members reside overseas. The Society is responsible for all aspects of the geological sciences including professional matters. The Society has its own publishing house, which produces the Society's international journals, books and maps, and which acts as the European distributor for publications of the American Association of Petroleum Geologists, SEPM and the Geological Society of America.

Fellowship is open to those holding a recognized honours degree in geology or cognate subject and who have at least two years' relevant postgraduate experience, or who have not less than six years' relevant experience in geology or a cognate subject. A Fellow who has not less than five years' relevant postgraduate experience in the practice of geology may apply for validation and, subject to approval, may be able to use the designatory letters C Geol (Chartered Geologist).

Further information about the Society is available from the Membership Manager, The Geological Society, Burlington House, Piccadilly, London W1V 0JU, UK. The Society is a Registered Charity, No. 210161.

Published by The Geological Society from:
The Geological Society Publishing House
Unit 7, Brassmill Enterprise Centre
Brassmill Lane
Bath BA1 3JN
UK
(*Orders:* Tel. 01225 445046
        Fax 01225 442836)

First published 1998

British Library Cataloguing in Publication Data
A catalogue record for this book is available from the British Library.

ISBN 1-897799-96-9

Typeset by Bath Typesetting, Bath, UK
Printed by The Alden Press, Osney Mead, Oxford, UK

Distributors

USA
  AAPG Bookstore
  PO Box 979
  Tulsa
  OK 74101-0979
  USA
  (*Orders:* Tel. (918) 584-2555 Fax (918) 584-2652)

Australia
  Australian Mineral Foundation
  63 Conyngham Street
  Glenside
  South Australia 5065
  Australia
  (*Orders:* Tel. (08) 379-0444 Fax (08) 379-4634)

India
  Affiliated East-West Press PVT Ltd
  G-1/16 Ansari Road
  New Delhi 110 002
  India
  (*Orders:* Tel. (11) 327-9113 Fax (11) 326-0538)

Japan
  Kanda Book Trading Co.
  Tanikawa Building
  3-2 Kanda Surugadai
  Chiyoda-Ku
  Tokyo 101
  Japan
  (*Orders:* Tel. (03) 3255-3497
          Fax (03) 3255-3495)

Contents

List of Contributors

Russell Arthurton
British Geological Survey, Keyworth, Nottingham NG12 5GG

Max Barton
Department of Civil & Environmental Engineering, The University of Southampton, Southampton SO17 1BJ, UK

Alan H. Brampton
Coastal Group, HR Wallingford, Howbery Park, Wallingford, Oxon, OX10 8BA, UK

Malcolm Bray
Department of Geography, University of Portsmouth, Buckingham Building, Lion Terrace, Portsmouth PO1 3HE, UK

Nick Cooper
Department of Geography & School of Civil Engineering, University of Portsmouth, Portsmouth, UK

Brian Daley
Department of Geology, University of Portsmouth, Burnaby Building, Burnaby Road, Portsmouth PO1 3QL, UK

Vincent Dubreuil
URA 1687 CNRS, Université de Rennes 2, 35043 Rennes, Cedex, France

John Gordon
Scottish Natural Heritage, 2 Anderson Place, Edinburgh EH6 5NP, UK

David Harlow
Coastal Engineer, Bournemouth Borough Council, Bournemouth, UK

Janet Hooke
Department of Geography, University of Portsmouth, Buckingham Building, Lion Terrace, Portsmouth PO1 3HE, UK

Thomas A. Hose
Faculty of Leisure and Tourism, The Buckinghamshire College, Wellesbourne Campus, Kingshill Road, High Wycombe, Buckinghamshire HP13 5BB, UK

Simon Jennings
Department of Geography, University of North London, London, N5 2AD, UK

Richard Leafe
English Nature, Northminster House, Peterborough PE7 1BJ, UK

Mark Lee
Rendel Geotechnics, Norfolk House, Smallbrook Queensway, Birmingham B5 4LJ, UK (*Now at*: Department of Marine Sciences and Coastal Management, University of Newcastle, Newcastle upon Tyne, UK)

George Lees
Scottish Natural Heritage, 2 Anderson Place, Edinburgh EH6 5NP, UK

Loïc Lemasson
URA 1687 CNRS, Université de Rennes 2, 35043 Rennes, Cedex, France

Robin G. McInnes
Engineering and Technical Services, County Hall, Newport, Isle of Wight, Hants PO30 1UD, UK

Alan McKirdy
Scottish Natural Heritage, 2 Anderson Place, Edinburgh EH6 5NP, UK

John McManus
Department of Geology, University of St, Andrews, Fife, Scotland, UK

Julian Orford
School of Geosciences, Queen's University, Belfast BT7 1NN, UK

Kevin N. Page
Environmental Impacts Team, English Nature, Northminster House, Peterborough, PE1 1UA, UK

Hervé Regnauld
URA 1687 CNRS, Université de Rennes 2, 35043 Rennes, Cedex, France

Elisabeth M. Saiu
Cartograph Ltd, 13–15 Newmarket Road, Cambridge CB5 8EG, UK

Part One

Frameworks for conservation and defence

In this part the context is set for the debate as to how far our coasts should be protected and how the needs of geological and geomorphological conservation can be met. The arguments for earth science conservation are introduced. The way in which attitudes and policy have altered in the last ten years is outlined and the administrative and decision-making frameworks in Britain are explained. The current situation in relation to coastal earth science conservation and the role and actions of the conservation agencies are presented.

1 Issues and strategies in relation to geological and geomorphological conservation and defence of the coast

Janet Hooke

Summary
- Conservation is required for scientific, educational, ecological, aesthetic and engineering reasons.
- Coastal defences protect economic assets from erosion and flooding.
- Major developments in policy and practices have taken place over the past 10 years in the UK including establishment of coastal groups, construction of Shoreline Management Plans based on coastal cells, and adoption of the policy of working with nature.
- The themes and structure of this book are introduced.

Context

Tremendous changes in attitude, policy and practice in relation to coastal defences have taken place in Britain over the past 10 years but considerable conflicts between the interests of protection and those of conservation still remain. There is a need for each group of interests to understand the other viewpoint, for the processes and landforms to be understood, for the consequences of action (including doing nothing) to be rigorously examined and for new methods and techniques to be developed, especially if these could offer a satisfactory compromise. Difficult decisions have to be made but these should be informed by a full awareness of the various interests, the possible strategies and activities and the outcomes of each, in so far as they are known, and by advice on the uncertainties. The particular concern here is how the needs of earth science conservation, that is the conservation of geological exposures and geomorphological features, can be reconciled with the needs and wishes for protection of people and assets from erosion and coastal flooding. These are highly topical issues, receiving much publicity, but they are also important in a wider context of whether and how we espouse policies of sustainability in environmental management.

Conservation

The conservation pressures arise for a number of reasons. First is the scientific need to have sites and opportunities to study the origin and characteristics of rocks and their interrelations, and to study coastal landforms and the processes by which they evolve, so that we understand the earth better and can manage resources effectively. This scientific need is recognized in the existence of statutory nature conservation bodies in Britain [English Nature (EN), Countryside Council for Wales (CCW), Scottish Natural Heritage (SNH), Joint Nature Conservation Committee (JNCC)] and in the designation of statutory sites as Sites of Special Scientific Interest (SSSIs). Many SSSIs occur on the coast because of the advantages of geological exposure of strata by marine processes and because of the dynamic landforms created by the active processes. Continued availability of sites is essential to advance our knowledge and understanding of both the past and the present. Secondly, is an educational need to have sites available for teaching people about the origins and dynamics of the earth. This is to satisfy intellectual curiosity but also to provide the understanding for caring stewardship of the earth, an issue of increasing prominence at the close of the second millennium. Another reason for coastal conservation is that physical variety provides the basis for ecological variety through the range of habitats associated with different landforms and rock types. Again, a public and popular desire for greater efforts of nature and wildlife conservation has been very evident in recent years. Less easily and clearly articulated is also the wish for access to 'natural' places and the opportunity to visit aesthetically pleasing locations. As the lengths of undeveloped and unprotected coast become less then those still remaining become more greatly valued. Lastly, reasons for conservation are arising now not because of the intrinsic value of the coast but because of the utility of unprotected parts of the coast in a strategy of holistic and sustainable management. Conservation has become a necessity and an integral part of the coastal defence with which it seemed in conflict.

Defence

The need for coastal defence has long been accepted and taken priority over conservation interests in Britain. It has been general policy to protect valuable economic assets such as houses and buildings or other infrastructure. Structural solutions have been agreed as a way to ensure stability and even to enhance assets, for example in the form of sea walls and promenades at resorts. There have also been issues of safety, particularly in relation to eroding cliffs, both for those venturing below them as well as those living on the top. Once investment has been made and activities engaged then it is difficult to break a commitment to protect. For many years the procedure for approval of new capital constructional schemes of coastal protection has involved cost–benefit analysis and therefore it has not been usual for agricultural land to be protected unless it had some other consequences, e.g. in preventing flooding. However, loss of environmental benefits or assets and intangible benefits have not been included which, to many, has meant an undervaluing of the conservation needs outlined above. This is beginning to change now with much research and experimentation in testing contingent and intangible benefit valuation. Until recently the attitude was predominantly one of being able to control nature and this was incorporated in policy and practice. The attitude was that if coastal defence was needed then it could and should be carried out. It was also not possible to prevent development on the coast on the grounds of coastal erosion or instability and thus cases arose of construction of new buildings in hazardous locations which then prompted demands for protection. Decisions on coastal defence in Britain are taken by local authorities and sent to central government for approval and grant-aiding. Therefore, until recently, these decisions were taken in isolation and by each separate authority managing a part of the coast, leading to piecemeal schemes.

Changes in policies and practices

Marked changes in policy and practice have taken place in the last 10 years, partly because of the change in environmental attitudes and values, but mainly because of the difficulties in maintaining a policy of stability and protection on the coast. It was becoming increasingly apparent that the piecemeal management of the coastline of Britain was having detrimental consequences on neighbouring locations. The establishment of coastal groups, led by SCOPAC (Standing Conference on Problems Associated with the Coastline) on the south coast, created the format and pressure for increased cooperation and for more strategic and integrated planning and management of the shoreline (Hooke & Bray 1995). The need for longer time perspectives and for wider spatial perspectives in making decisions on and designing coastal defences was becoming appreciated. This led eventually to the explicit recognition of these requirements in the Shoreline Management Plans in which strategic decisions on whether to defend the line of the coast, advance the line, retreat the line or do nothing are to be made, for lengths of coast based on cells and involving several local authorities (MAFF 1995). The recommendations are to be based on physical processes and characteristics and historical evolution of the coastline as well as assessment of the economic, social and cultural attributes of the coastal margin.

As well as these changes in strategic management, major changes in practices and techniques have occurred. There has been an accelerating trend away from conventional structural or hard engineering solutions to coastal defence problems and a turn towards 'soft' engineering. This has become explicit in adoption by the government of the policy of 'working with nature' rather than the previous attitude of believing that nature could be controlled and dominated. Of course, a consequence is that it becomes even more imperative that coastal managers and advisors have a thorough understanding of the natural components and systems.

In spite of the adoption of these principles and declarations in support of them from many bodies, there are still some real difficulties with individual decisions. There are still not the mechanisms in place which facilitate decisions in favour of long-term strategies and wide public benefit. Because of the political pressures locally on decision-makers to protect their citizens, the cost–benefit basis of evaluation, the difficulty of the wider communal voice being heard, and the lack of any compensation mechanisms for those having to endure loss for the wider benefit, the weight of decisions is still in favour of coastal defence.

Sustainability has now become a key concept in developing environmental management strategies. It shifts the focus from the short-term to consideration of the long-term consequences of actions and to ensuring that these are not of net detriment to all involved. However, even if a policy of sustainability is fully accepted in management of the coast then there are still some problems of what the actions should be. As pointed out by Pethick (1996) we cannot go back to a completely 'natural' state and therefore we have to decide what is a realistically acceptable situation and try to identify what is a sustainable strategy from there. This may include designing landforms and locating infrastructure in self-sustaining forms, 'It is suggested that the goal of coastal management is to design a coast which tends towards the reproduction of its natural functions.' (Pethick 1996).

Structure

This book arises from a conference which brought together coastal defence engineers, local authority coastal managers, professional conservationists, geologists and geomorphologists, decision-makers and landowners. The aim is to expand understanding of the differing viewpoints and to explore possibilities of conflict resolution, consensus and compromise. The problem with a search for such a middle ground may be that it satisfies no one. However, one issue which emerges from the papers and discussion is the desire specifically to find techniques and methods of cliff protection which provide partial defence but still allow some erosion such that exposures are maintained and supply of sediment to the coastal system is continued, albeit at a lower level. This is the focus of much research at present. Another issue that emerges is that attitudes and practices in coastal management, as in much else, follow fashions and thus what seems all the rage now becomes unacceptable shortly, but at the time of the fashion alternatives seem unthinkable. Of course, in this field the fashions are based on genuine beliefs and states of understanding and knowledge at the time.

The book is divided into sections based on a number of themes. As part of this introduction on the issues and the present situation, in Chapter 2, Richard Leafe sets out the conservation context and the developments which have taken place within and by the conservation agency, English Nature. The second theme is that of the methods and techniques available for defence and conservation and the extent to which practices can be found to meet different situations and requirements. Alan Brampton (Chapter 3) outlines methods specifically designed to help meet conservation needs while providing some protection. Both Max Barton (Chapter 4) and Mark Lee (Chapter 5) likewise address the issues of what rates of cliff erosion would achieve the various aims and how these might be attained. The latter paper tackles the question of methods of prediction of rates of recession and both demonstrate the need to have a thorough understanding of the processes and evolution of cliffs and historical data of changes. The scale of change that can possibly occur is demonstrated by the study from Fife (Saiu and McManus, Chapter 6) but it also raises this question of what state and what attributes of the coast we wish to conserve.

The third theme is that of strategic planning and decision making. The possibilities of implementing strategic planning to suit conservation interests while still protecting valuable assets are demonstrated by Robin McInnes (Chapter 7) for the Isle of Wight, an island very rich in its earth science heritage where that is now being regarded as an asset. The difficulties of specific management decisions though are exemplified by Orford and Jennings (Chapter 8). In an elegant scientific study they examine the evidence for the evolution and behaviour of a gravel barrier and the nature of flooding and wetland behind the barrier. Their evidence leads them to conclude that periodic breaching of the barrier has been a normal part of the development, is necessary to maintenance of the marshes and is the only viable strategy in the long term. In spite of this, the decision was made to maintain the barrier and to prevent overtopping and breaching. Even conservation itself can sometimes lead to conflicts of interest. One dilemma is illustrated by Regnauld *et al.* (Chapter 9) from sites in Brittany where cliffs are rapidly eroding thus exposing new stratigraphy and providing sediment to the beach and coastal system. However, the erosion is destroying and depleting an archaeological resource in the form of implements and artefacts exposed by the erosion and this source is finite. A similar dilemma arises at Hengistbury Head on the south coast of England and also at Hurst Castle Spit (Bray & Hooke, Chapter 10). There the conflict is between maintenance of the dynamism of a mobile spit and the danger of it breaching and thus destroying ecologically valuable salt marsh. The pressures of development and the incidence of soft rock cliffs or zones subject to sea flooding are not nearly as great in Scotland as in England but, as Lees et al (Chapter 11) demonstrate the pressures still exist and are increasing. They outline SNH's policies and strategies for conservation.

A fourth theme is that of resources and evaluation. The coast and its materials can be regarded as a resource in many different ways. Beach and cliff materials have themselves been used as mineral resources in the past. Now, a major concern is actually with finding the mineral resources with which to meet the defence requirements using the methods which are more acceptable to conservationists, that is practices such as beach replenishment. Russel Arthurton (Chapter 12) considers the availability of sources of material. The understanding that is needed in order to use the material most effectively and to design schemes, where they are necessary, most efficiently is demonstrated by Cooper and Harlow (Chapter 13) in their analysis of the performance and longevity of the Bournemouth beach replenishment schemes. A different aspect of the geological resource is that of its value in educational and leisure terms and how geotourism can become an economic asset. This is something which the Isle of Wight has specifically recognized in its strategy and is exploiting, but Hose (Chapter 14) has researched the type of visitors and the impact of information on visitors which should help in the design and enhancement of such assets. Kevin Page (Chapter 15) concludes this part with a summary of the arguments in favour of geological conservation.

The final part of the book focuses on the central south coast of England, in particular Poole and Christchurch Bays, to exemplify some of the issues and conflicts which arise and the ways in which they are being resolved or decisions are being taken. The problems in that region are severe due to the high pressures of development from the density of population and the degree of investment in facilities and infrastructure on the coast. It is also a stretch of coastline containing key world rock stratotypes, beds with rare and highly significant fossils, eroding cliffs demonstrating processes and dynamics of landslides and mass movement, and a mobile spit landform which is a classic of its type. Added to this, it is now recognized that the cliffs are the major source of supply of material for the beaches. It is also the location in which some of the most notorious coastal defence schemes have been carried out but is the location of the pioneering attempts at revised management frameworks in the form of SCOPAC and where various innovative methods of defence have been tried or are being evaluated. It can thus be considered a microcosm of the issues addressed in this volume. Thus the final two chapters examine the geological value of this part of the coast (Daley, Chapter 16) and the geomorphology and management of the Bays (Bray and Hooke, Chapter 17), giving specific detail which may provide valuable background to field visits as well as an illustration of the arguments. The viewpoints of the local authorities and of the conservation agency are juxtaposed.

Conclusion

The challenges for the future include the problem of prediction. This is at the fundamental level of uncertainty and variability of dynamical systems, and at the level of assuming predictability but identifying the relevant conditions, especially given the changed frequencies of storms over recent decades and the probability of global warming in the future. Further development of techniques that accommodate conservation and defence must take place, but we should not always compromise. Often, the best decisions will be ones that promote conservation in a suitable location but allow defence in others. The challenge of dealing with private loss for the sake of public good must also be faced. Above all we must seek greater understanding of the coastal system, its processes and landforms by careful measurement, monitoring and analysis such that informed decisions can be made.

References

Hooke, J. M. & Bray, M. J. 1995. Coastal groups, cells, policies and plans in the UK. *Area*, **27**, 358–368.

MAFF, 1995. Shoreline Management Plans: A Guide for Coastal Defence Authorities. *Publication PB 2197*, Ministry of Agriculture, Fisheries and Food, London.

Pethick, J. 1996. Understanding coastal processes and morphology. Paper presented at Conference on Coastal Defence and Earth Science Conservation, University of Portsmouth, March 1996.

2 Conserving our coastal heritage – a conflict resolved?

Richard Leafe

Summary

- England's coastline, with its highly varied geology and diverse range of coastal process, gives rise to one of the best coastal environments for Earth heritage conservation in the world.
- The most valuable sites for geology and geomorphology in England have now been designated as Sites of Special Scientific Interest by English Nature and its predecessor bodies.
- For many years this precious resource has been under pressure from coastal development and particularly coastal defence.
- The need to maintain clean exposures, best achieved by marine erosion, has been in direct conflict with the aims and, until recently, the methods of the coastal defence engineer.
- This paper explores the ways in which the conflict has been addressed over recent years, including development of 'softer' engineering techniques, Shoreline Management Plans and Earth heritage sites.
- Recent English Nature initiatives, particularly Natural Areas, and their role in advancing Earth heritage conservation are emphasized.

Introduction

English Nature are the Government's advisers on nature conservation in England. As well as providing advice on nature conservation, which includes Earth heritage conservation, English Nature selects and designates land as Sites of Special Scientific Interest (SSSI) and designates and manages National Nature Reserves.

Geological and geomorphological conservation have long been a part of statutory conservation in Britain. In 1990 the Nature Conservancy Council (NCC) consolidated the previous work into a national strategy for Earth Science Conservation in Great Britain (NCC 1990). The Strategy provided, for the first time, a cohesive focus for geological and geomorphological site conservation in Britain. Over the past five years English Nature, along with sister agencies in Scotland and Wales, have led the implementation of the strategy. Through this process, approaches to the subject have broadened and the new name of Earth heritage conservation adopted to reflect this. English Nature has recently published a re-defined strategy that continues to build on the themes and principles of its predecessor (English Nature 1996). The new strategy embraces English Nature's commitment to sustainable development and the delivery of conservation goals through the concept of Natural Areas.

Within this overall approach the coast has a pivotal role to play, hosting some of the finest exposure sites in the geological SSSI series, and of unique value for coastal geomorphology and mass movement. This precious resource has been damaged by the construction of coastal defences and still, albeit hopefully to a lesser degree, remains threatened.

Threats from coastal defence

Coastal defence threats to Earth heritage sites fall into three broad categories; obscured exposures, sterilization of soft cliff environments and interference with sediment dynamics.

Placing coastal defence structures over designated exposures, although perhaps not actually destroying those features, effectively renders the site useless from a research and teaching view point. Although re-exposure may be possible at the end of the design life or useful purpose of the defence, in practice, such works often result in permanent damage to a site. Porthleven cliffs in Cornwall illustrate this well with a considerable loss of a valuable section of the Porthleven Cliffs East SSSI under a mass concrete sea wall (Fig 2.1).

The soft cliff resource of England is important not only for the

Fig. 2.1. Sea Wall at Porthleven, Cornwall.

exposures of soft rock geology but also the movement of the cliffs and their role in the geomorphological system of the coast. Of the 256 km of unprotected soft cliffs in England, some 70% has a geological/geomorphological SSSI designation, 30% of which is of recognized international importance (Leafe & Radley 1994). The recent MAFF Coast Protection Survey highlighted that approximately 10% of this resource may require some coastal defence measures within the next ten years, representing an obvious threat to Earth heritage sites (MAFF 1994).

Many types of defence, by design, interfere with movements of material along the shore. Ultimately, this often severely impacts upon the most sensitive of sites, those selected for their active process coastal geomorphology, such as spits and nesses, often formed at the end of a coastal unit or cell, downdrift of defence works. Hurst Castle spit in Hampshire, for example, shows all the symptoms of transport path disruption. The landform is now fossilized, dependent on beach replenishment to prevent a total loss of the integrity of the feature. More recently the extension of gabion mattresses on the crest of Chesil Beach at Portland, Dorset, as part

Fig. 2.2. Gabions on Chesil Beach, Dorset.

of an ill-conceived coastal defence scheme, has damaged the structure, function and appearance of the upper beach (Fig. 2.2).

Conflict resolution

Recent years have seen a progression of developments in the policy and practice of the coastal defence engineer that have gone a considerable way to reducing conflict. Much of this is based on the desire of both parties to understand the positions of others, share objectives and communicate more effectively. Key developments in this process are briefly reviewed.

Alternative engineering solutions
A recognition of threats to conservation of Earth heritage sites, and the untenable position of preventing any defences from being constructed, led the Nature Conservancy Council to commission HR Wallingford to appraise the use of alternative and novel solutions to coastal defence problems (HR Wallingford 1991). The

Fig. 2.3. Logo of the Campaign for a Living Coast.

approach involved categorizing the interests of the site and erosion mechanisms and cross referencing to the most suitable form of defence. The result was a tendency to promote erosion reduction techniques rather than those which sought to completely stop erosion. Although the site classification developed remains useful today, there is a continuing need to refine the techniques and better understand their impact on processes of erosion and conservation interests.

Campaign for a Living Coast

The intricate relationship between coastal process, Earth heritage and wildlife sites on the coast, together with conclusive evidence of a general decline in the conservation value of the English coast, prompted English Nature to launch its Campaign for a Living Coast in 1992 (Fig. 2.3). The campaign had at its heart the objective of achieving no net loss of habitats and natural features and actively sought to produce objectives for coastal management that would not differentiate between Earth heritage and biological conservation (English Nature 1992). A broad publicity campaign, aimed at coastal decision-makers, notably coastal engineers, proved highly successful in raising awareness and challenging long held attitudes.

MAFF Flood and Coastal Defence Strategy

A strong partner in the greater integration of conservation requirements in coastal defence is MAFF's Flood and Coastal Defence Division. The 1993 Strategy for Flood and Coastal

Defence in England and Wales (MAFF 1993) set environmental acceptability as one of three key criteria for judging suitability of defence schemes for exchequer support. This emphasized English Nature's position in scheme consultations and should result in improvements to the environmental performance of schemes. The strategy also outlined a mechanism for the planning of defences. Based on the concept of sediment cells (Motyka & Brampton 1993), and encouraging the formation of regional Coastal Defence Groups, a more holistic approach to coastal defence planning is evolving. English Nature, generally a core member of Coastal Groups, endorses this approach and is devoting resources to the delivery of the strategy through the production of Shoreline Management Plans.

Shoreline Management Plans
The main aim of a Shoreline Management Plan (SMP), the delivery of sustainable coastal defences, is highly consistent with conservation aims. A sustainable defence, by definition, is unlikely to result in the kind of disruptions to natural processes that have characterized the past. The approach, based on an understanding of coastal processes and morphological change within a sediment cell, or sub-division of it, facilitates the integration of Earth heritage objectives, as a component of objective setting for the natural environment, with those for coastal defence. In this way it is hoped that the process of conflict resolution can start long before the promotion of any individual scheme (Swash *et al.* 1995). SMPs for the whole coast of England are currently under development, to a format outlined by MAFF (MAFF 1995), completion of this first generation of plans is anticipated by 1998 (Hutchison & Leafe 1995).

As part of its contribution towards this initiative, English Nature has developed an Environmental Objective setting methodology (English Nature 1997). The methodology follows the stages of resource evaluation, change predictions and objective specification. In evaluating environmental assets, English Nature is exploring the concepts of Critical Natural Capital and Constant Natural Assets. Critical Natural Capital (CNC) is defined as 'those elements of the natural environment whose loss would be serious, or which would be irreplaceable, or which would be too difficult or expensive to replace in Human timescales'. Constant Natural Assets (CNA) is defined as all environmental resources that do not qualify as CNC. The aim with CNA is to maintain the overall stock of assets although not necessarily in the same place. In using this concept in shoreline management planning we are attempting to develop a readily employable tool for the definition of environmental assets who depend for their existence on the continuation of coastal defences and those that do not. As most coastal conservation assets fall into the CNA category, the amount of CNC defined that requires artificial protection is low, for example some floristically diverse coastal grazing marshes behind the sea wall in Essex and North Kent fall into this category. The definition of Earth heritage sites that qualify as CNC requires a different approach, it is proposed that sites must meet one of the following criteria:

- it is a geological integrity site (as defined in the NCC Strategy);
- there is no opportunity to replace the feature elsewhere within the Natural Area (see next section);
- the feature cannot be replaced for either technical or financial reasons within an acceptable timescale.

It is hoped that the definition of Earth heritage CNC within SMPs will provide added protection to this group of sites whose interests are extremely susceptible to damage by coastal defences. It should be stressed that the concept is in the early stages of development and does not in anyway replace the existing mechanisms for site safeguard.

English Nature's Maritime Natural Areas
In order to provide a geographic context to conservation policy, English Nature is developing the concept of Natural Areas. Although not a formal designation, it enables English Nature and others to take account of all aspects of land use that affect the conservation resource, rather than identifying specific scientific attributes of individual sites. The initiative is being used to focus resources to ensure the maximum environmental gain. Twenty four Maritime Natural Areas have been defined based on coastal process

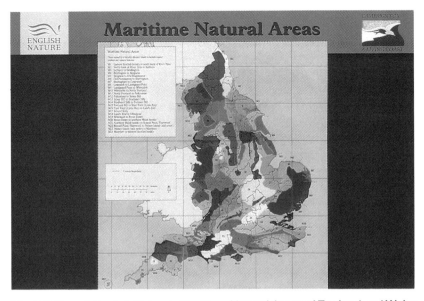

Fig. 2.4. Map of English Nature's Maritime Natural Areas of England and Wales.

cell divisions and habitat types (Fig 2.4). We are currently in the process of developing Maritime Natural Area profiles, supported by a large database, that characterise each area and will aid the development of objectives. Earth heritage interests form a key component of these profiles. English Nature is developing a significance rating for the Earth heritage interests within MNAs. Early results indicate that one third of all MNAs can be regarded as of outstanding interest for Earth heritage (Littlewood 1995).

Objective setting for Earth heritage sites at this geographical level is compatible with SMP areas, providing this initiative with pre-existing objectives for conservation. The further development of this concept will facilitate the integration of Earth heritage and wildlife conservation, and in the process, strengthen both.

Conclusions

There will always be an element of potential conflict between the aims of the coastal defence engineer and conservation. This paper has outlined some of the ways in which this conflict can be resolved.

Throughout the various initiatives is the recurring theme of the need to communicate effectively. The movements towards strategic planning of coastal defences, based on a sound understanding of the earth science process operating, and the spread of best environmental practice, provide the Earth heritage community with a real opportunity to ensure future defence works are constructed in a sustainable fashion and do not compromise the outstanding Earth heritage value of the English coast. English Nature will continue, through the Natural Areas initiative, to place the existing Earth heritage site network in a broader context to ensure maximum benefits from emerging strategic management initiatives.

References

English Nature. 1992. *Coastal Zone Conservation, English Nature's Rationale, Objectives and Practical Recommendations.* English Nature, Northminster House, Peterborough.

English Nature. 1996. *Conserving England's Earth Heritage – a New Strategy.* English Nature, Northminster House, Peterborough.

English Nature. 1997. *Nature Conservation Objectives in Shoreline Management Plans – A suggested approah.* English Nature, Northminster House, Peterborough.

HR Wallingford. 1991. *A Guide to the Selection of Appropriate Coast Protection Works for Geological Sites of Special Scientific Interest.* Report to English Nature, Peterborough. Report EX2112.

Hutchison, J. & Leafe, R. N. 1995. Shoreline Management: A view of the way ahead. *Institute of Civil Engineers Coastal Management '95: Putting Policy into Practice, 12–14 November 1995, Bournemouth.* Proceedings.

Leafe, R. N. & Radley, G. P. 1994. Environmental benefits of soft cliff erosion. *1994 MAFF Conference of River and Coastal Engineers, 4–6 July.* Proceedings.

Littlewood, A. 1995. Earth science conservation management in the coastal zone: The Natural Areas Concept. Bournemouth University, School of Conservation Sciences unpublished thesis, and report to English Nature, Peterborough.

MAFF/Welsh Office. 1993. *Strategy for Flood and Coastal Defence in England and Wales*. MAFF publications, PB 1471.

MAFF. 1994. *Coast Protection Survey of England*. MAFF publications.

MAFF/Welsh Office. 1995. *Shoreline Management Plans – a Guide for Operating Authorities*. MAFF publications.

Motyka, J. M. & Brampton, A. H. 1993 *Coastal Management, Mapping of Littoral Cells*. HR Wallingford Report SP328.

NCC. 1990. *Earth Science Conservation in Great Britain – A Strategy*. Nature Conservancy Council, Northminster House, Peterborough.

Swash, A. R. H., Leafe, R. N. & Radley, G. P. 1995. Shoreline Management Plans and Environmental Considerations. In: Healy & Doody, P. (eds.) *Directions in European Coastal Management*. Samara Publishing, Cardigan. pp 161–167.

Part Two

Methods and techniques of defence and conservation

In this section the methods and techniques which might be used to accommodate both the needs of defence and of conservation are explored. The discussion focuses on cliffs since these are valuable areas for geological exposures and they are ones where problems arise from rapid erosion. Certain methods which may offer partial protection while still allowing some erosion and exposure are illustrated. Prediction of rates of cliff recession is a key to effective management and developments in this field are described. Rates of change of coasts and complexity of issues arising from a rapidly changing situation are demonstrated in a case study.

3 Cliff conservation and protection: methods and practices to resolve conflicts

Alan H. Brampton

Summary

- Coastal cliff recession is seen in very different lights by different interest groups. A protection scheme to protect cliff-top properties may have a variety of adverse impacts on conservation interests, and on other parts of the coast.
- Past protection works have stabilized many of the soft cliffs in England and Wales, and many of those that remain are designated Sites of Special Scientific Interest.
- Alternatives to 'traditional' defences, such as concrete seawalls, may offer the option of slowing cliff recession to an acceptable rate, whilst limiting the adverse environmental effects of a scheme. Mitigation works, such as periodic beach nourishment, will also have a role in modern cliff management techniques.
- In the future, it may be economically prudent to alter or replace existing cliff protection schemes using such techniques.

The conflict

Coastal communities, and the engineers they employ, have generally tended to regard an eroding cliff as at best an inconvenience, at worst a hazard both to those living on top of it and to those wishing to use the shoreline beneath it.

From other viewpoints, however, coastal cliffs form an important ecological habitat, and an important component of the aesthetics of a coastline. By their erosion they both provide a valuable insight into the geology, and contribute to the dynamic evolution of a coast.

Over the last few centuries, the various stimuli for managing the

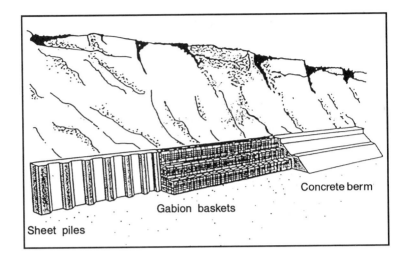

Fig. 3.1. Typical sea wall types.

coastline (e.g. trade, transport, recreation and preventing land loss) have favoured attempts to stabilize cliffs, preventing or greatly reducing their recession. As a consequence, the vast majority of geologically 'soft' cliffs in England and Wales have now been defended. In many cases, the defence has taken the form of a seawall or revetment at the toe of the cliff (often extended downwards and outwards several times in response to chronic scour problems at the toe of the structure). A variety of the methods used is presented diagrammatically in Figs 3.1 and 3.2. Some erosion of the cliffs above the defences then continues, although the rate of recession is reduced.

At some sites, however, the face above such defences is also protected, so no (visible) evidence of the once-eroding cliff remains. While some cliffs, with complex geotechnical characteristics, will periodically collapse despite the defences installed (e.g. the recent spectacular land-slip at the Holbeck Hall Hotel, Scarborough), generally the protection effectiveness of cliff defence schemes is good. While such successes may be short lived on a geological timescale, they have been to the profit of a number of coastal resorts (including Bournemouth and Blackpool) that would otherwise have lost major investments to the depredations of the sea.

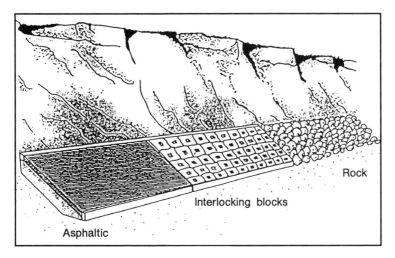

Fig. 3.2. Typical revetment structures.

There is a reverse side to this view of coastal management. Biologists will point to the loss of habitat, of the specialized flora that flourish on eroding coastal cliffs, and the associated fauna. Geologists lament the obscuring of interesting rock strata, and the reduced number of sites where active erosion and land-sliding provide an opportunity for teaching and research and where key stratotypes are exposed. There is now a serious concern about the scarcity of naturally eroding cliffs in England and Wales, and many have been designated as Sites of Special Scientific Interest to help preserve them.

Coastal engineers and geomorphologists know the adverse consequences of 'fixing' one part of a coastline on adjacent stretches. There are many examples of beach erosion attributable to defence works in front of coastal cliffs depleting the supply of 'fresh' beach sediment to feed a longshore drift. A good example is provided by the cliff stabilization works at Bournemouth. The prevention of cliff recession led to a shortfall in the sediment budget (subsequently remedied by beach nourishment). The integrity of some landforms, such as Hurst Castle spit, is also being destroyed by the diminution of supply.

It is worth pointing out, in this context, that a very substantial percentage of beach sediments in England and Wales is derived from cliff erosion. Other sources of sediment are now small in comparison. Protecting cliffs is therefore very likely to bring about a noticeable change in the dynamic behaviour of beaches in their vicinity.

Future cliff management strategy

It can be appreciated that one person's ideal cliff erosion rate is likely to be another person's poison. The balancing of conflicting interests in coastal management has never been an easy task, partly because the reasons for such management themselves vary considerably over time. Many sea defences built along the east coast of England between 1950 and 1960, for example, are uneconomic by today's standards. But in the context of food shortages after World War II, and as a response to the unexpected and disastrous flooding in the 1953 storm surge, such decisions can be more kindly judged. The emergence in recent years of a strong impetus for conservation has arrived at the same time as a stringency in public expenditure, and a better understanding of the dynamics of the coastline, and the impacts that ill-planned human intervention can cause. In common with other aspects of coastal defence management, a new look is being taken at the methods used in cliff protection schemes, and at their overall impacts on the coastline. Research commissioned by MAFF (Flood Defence Division) is currently underway into the management of soft cliffs; many of the ideas in this paper stem from this project (although they are the views of the author, and not necessarily of the Ministry).

This research reviews methods for protecting cliffs that have not previously been defended, or for changing defences already in place. Increasingly, however, consideration will need to be given to removing or abandoning existing defences, and coping with the effects of the subsequent cliff recession.

Preserving a balance between financial prudence, the conservation of a natural environment and the protection of property on cliff tops, is a challenge to coastal managers and engineers. Hengistbury Head in Dorset is an interesting example. Further erosion of the cliffs on the southern side of this peninsula will result in the loss of public open space (popular with tourists), of heathland and archaeological remains on the cliff top, and could eventually expose Christchurch Harbour to a greatly enhanced wave climate. This would threaten properties on the shoreline of the harbour (which presently need little or no coastal defence), and would radically alter the ecological character of the harbour, an SSSI. A defence scheme, however, would involve an initial expenditure and subsequent maintenance works, would reduce the supplies of fresh material to the beaches and would reduce or destroy the interesting exposures of rock strata from the Tertiary era, as well as arguably altering the aesthetic qualities of the beach.

The eventual outcome of the debate on this, and similar dilemmas, on whether or not to protect a cliff is not the primary responsibility of coastal engineers. They should, however, have a role in discussions on defence strategy, advising on the costs and practicability of different defence schemes. This leads on to the main topic of this paper, namely alternative methods to manage coastal cliffs, to achieve reduced recession rates, or to have lesser impacts on adjacent coastlines.

Mitigation of defence works

Any scheme which reduces the erosion of soft cliffs will bring about a reduction in the supply of beach-forming sediments, with possible detriment to beaches elsewhere. It has been argued that the reduction should be not only calculated, but economically valued, and added to the costs of a proposed scheme. The calculation would be complicated, since some of the material would be too fine to remain on the beaches; whether it will eventually contribute to the sediment budget of a distant estuary would be almost impossible to prove. In addition, cliff-top house-owners may wish to know why, if the sediment eroded from their property is valuable to down-drift authorities, they have received no payment for it over the years.

A practical and constructive alternative, beneficial to the overall sediment budget of the coastline, is to carry out artificial nourishment of the beach in front of the cliffs (as at Bournemouth). The costs of such nourishment operations would need to be included with the costs of the defence scheme. Nourishment may even replace the need for 'built' defences.

The disadvantage is the reasonable division of the costs between neighbouring authorities. There are difficulties, at present, in accounting for benefits 'at a distance' when applying for a coastal defence scheme. This is an area where co-operative defence management within a coastal 'cell' will hopefully bring about improved methods in the future.

Other mitigation methods are also possible. A cliff that has been defended is less valuable as a habitat for some species. Perhaps management of the cliff face might reduce this type of adverse impact. This might include clearing and pre-drilling a vertical bluff for Sand Martins and importing sand/soil to form a new 'bed' for plants that rely on regular fresh exposures. These mitigation works would also need to be included in the defence scheme costs. While well intentioned, however, such ideas for (literally) superficial mitigation schemes will not compensate for the loss of the dynamic behaviour of a coastal cliff.

Methods to reduce cliff recession rates

Until recently, decisions made about managing cliff erosion have been stark; either a cliff was allowed to evolve naturally, or its toe was defended by a solid defence structure, and erosion limited to the face above these structures. (Fig. 3.3). With the increased emphasis on demonstrating (financial) value in undertaking coastal defence schemes, however, this situation has now changed. Compromise solutions are being sought, either on financial grounds, or for environmental reasons. Broadly speaking, the idea is to *reduce* the cliff recession rate, by installing less expensive defences. If the recession rate is slowed (but not stopped) then many of the environmental objections to a scheme can be overcome (e.g. land-sliding and consequential exposures of rock strata will still occur and some sediment will be supplied downdrift).

Some methods include control of groundwater seeping into the

Fig. 3.3. Conventional cliff toe protection, Isle of Wight.

cliff from the landward side (e.g. improving drains and sewers, eliminating soakaways), or for controlling the flow of groundwater through the cliff (e.g. by installation of various types of drainage systems). This is an area where a closer combination of geotechnical and coastal engineering skills is required. Another idea is to install less effective coastal defence structures beneath the cliffs, limiting but not totally eliminating wave attack at its toe. In the UK, the Nature Conservancy Council took an active role in promoting such methods, and commissioned research into alternative types of cliff protection schemes. Figs 3.4–3.7 are taken from the report arising from that research (as are Figs 3.1 and 3.2) (Nature Conservancy Council 1991). Some of these defence types have now been employed to try to control the erosion of cliffs designated as an SSSI because of their active erosion processes.

Rock sills and timber palisades aim to slow erosion over a long length of cliff by reducing the intensity of wave action at the beach crest. (Figs 3.5–3.6). Other methods aim to control cliff erosion, trying to prevent erosion in some (critical) areas, while allowing erosion to proceed elsewhere. This will clearly result in a more

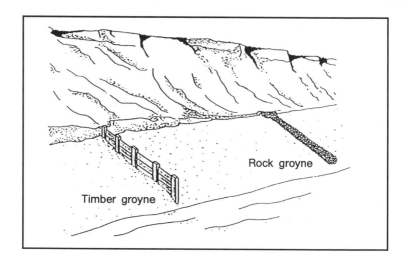

Fig. 3.4. Beach control structures – groynes.

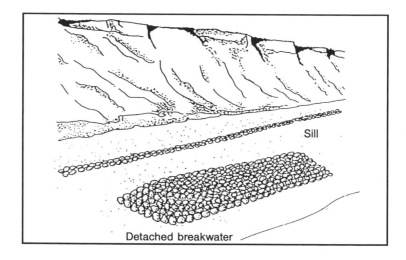

Fig. 3.5. Attenuation structures.

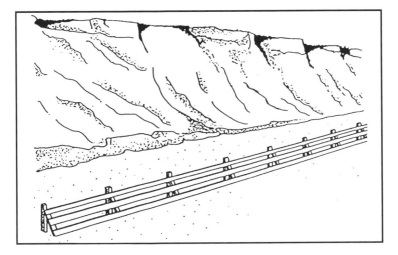

Fig. 3.6. Typical timber palisade.

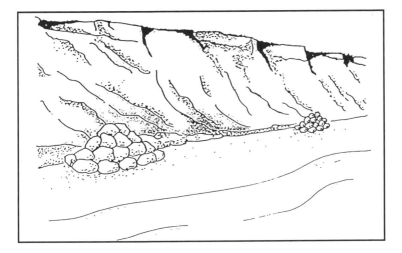

Fig. 3.7. Strongpoints with intervening cliff eroding at a controlled rate.

Fig. 3.8. Rock sill protecting sandy cliffs, Norfolk.

irregular plan shape of the cliff line, which may alter the wave and sediment dynamics, and perhaps reduce the overall erosion rate. The use of a technique involving 'Strongpoints', as sketched in Fig. 3.7, to protect isolated cliff-top properties is clearly likely to be cheaper than more conventional solutions illustrated in Figs 3.1 and 3.2. The use of groynes to produce a wider beach at critical points along a coastline (for example at the base of an eroding cliff) is not a new idea; exactly this technique was used to control erosion at Hengistbury Head before World War II. The challenge lies in predicting the effects of such 'partial' protection techniques, both on the adjacent coastline, and on the morphological development of the cliffs themselves. On the latter point, for example, the cessation of wave attack and toe erosion does not immediately bring an end to cliff top recession. Similarly, even if a scheme produces, as desired, an embayed coastline which is more slowly changing than the original, will the cliff-top line follow the new shoreline, or will landslips occur laterally (i.e. parallel to the old shoreline)?

Conclusions

The present 'green' lobby, together with a need for stringency in public spending, have produced an interest in novel methods of cliff management. These methods may allow a compromise to be struck between conservation of the natural environment and conservation of land and property on the cliff tops. The main challenges are:

1. to bring together the skills of a range of specialists, to specify objectives and then design appropriate 'intermediate' defence options;
2. to develop and validate predictive methods that can predict their effectiveness; and
3. to monitor the methods used, and refine both the design and prediction methods.

Reference

Nature Conservancy Council. 1991. *A Guide to the Selection of Appropriate Coast Protection Works for Geological SSSI's.* Nature Conservancy Council, Northminster House, Peterborough.

Fig. 4.2. The Naish Farm cliffs looking east from the Chewton Bunny outfall and showing the effects of rapid marine erosion during the 1980s. The lowest scarp face, below the well-defined preferred bedding plane shear surface at the base of zone A3, is well exposed with only small amounts of talus at the back of the narrow beach. The intermediate level scarp is much obscured in the photographed section by recent scarp slumps. The characteristically well-exposed top scarp, with exposures of the Plateau Gravel, is seen at the cliff top.

geology, consider the conservation attitude to be flawed (if the site is so important, why is it allowed to be washed away?).

The compromise solution: engineering to reduce erosion rates

A compromise between the conflicting viewpoints is the proposal that partial toe protection be installed in a way that allows some erosion to occur but at a reduced rate (Powell 1992). The proposal assumes that this limited erosion will still allow soil movement on the cliffs and prevent the exposures being obscured by accumulating talus. At the Naish Farm site of the Barton Clay cliffs such partial protection could take the form of either an offshore breakwater or partial beach replenishment. This compromise solution poses two main problems: firstly, the difficulty of designing such partial protection measures and secondly, predicting the influence such works will have on the state of the geological exposures.

The first problem, the engineering design, stems from the intermittent nature of the erosion, depending as it does on the vagaries of winds, tides and beach profile. The incidence of suitably erosive conditions is difficult to predict and the risk is of providing either too much or too little protection. With too little protection, one severe storm may nullify the previous period of protection and return the cliffs to the status quo. With too much protection, the conservation benefits may be reduced unnecessarily. It appears most reasonable that the design should be empirical (i.e. by trial and error). In geotechnical parlance this would be called the 'observational method' which is where the design is modified according to the observations made during and after the initial installation.

The second problem, the influence of partial toe protection on the geological exposures, is the subject of this paper. To examine this problem it is necessary to evaluate the character and extent of the exposures. This will be most effectively done by introducing a measure of the extent to which a cliff profile possesses geological exposures (the 'exposure ratio' as defined below).

The exposure ratio

Degrading cliffs normally show a pattern of scarp faces with exposed strata and masses of colluvium derived from landslides and other mass transport processes. With a benched cliff profile controlled by preferred bedding plane shear surfaces, such as that at Naish Farm, the general appearance is as shown in Fig. 4.3. The exposure ratio (ER), see Fig. 4.4, may be defined as

$$\text{Exposure ratio (ER)} = \left(\frac{\text{sum of exposed strata height}}{\text{total cliff height}} \right) \times 100\%$$

Current (as at May 1996) values of exposure ratio in the best exposed portions of the Naish Farm Cliffs are shown in Table 4.1.

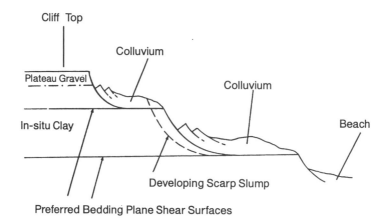

Fig. 4.3. Diagrammatic representation of the benched cliff profile at Naish Farm. In the characteristic sections there are three well-defined scarp faces with exposures of the *in situ* strata. The pattern of degradation is controlled by the preferred bedding plane shear surfaces which act as the basal surface to each successive new scarp slump.

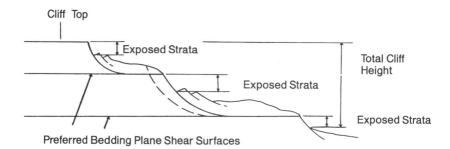

Fig. 4.4. Definition of exposure ratio which is the ratio of the sum of the exposed strata heights to the total height of the cliff. In the example shown, the exposure ratio is approximately 50%.

The lateral continuity of the benched profile makes these values typical of particular stretches of the cliff-line. The values are markedly reduced over short sections where large mudslides have cut through and obscured the scarp faces. In all cases the exposure ratio quoted includes the exposure of the Plateau Gravel in the cliff-top scarp (accounting for between 5 and 15% of the cliff height).

Table 4.1. Approximate values of exposure ratio in the Naish Farm area (May 1996)

No.	Eastings range (N.G.R.)	Recession rate (m a^{-1}) (1982–1993)	Exposure ratio (%) (maximum value)
1	2182–2183	0.74	34
2	2186–2190	1.14	39
3	2215–2225	1.14	54
4	2230–2235	1.71	55
5	2245–2250	0.94	47
6	2260–2270	0.60	23

The height of each individual exposure was estimated by observation only. Values of recession rates during the period shown are from Bates *et al.* (1995). Accumulations of colluvium now cover the basal scarp at location Nos 1 and 2 as a result of the influence of the strong point at the outfall of Chewton Bunny. Previous to the construction of the latter, the exposure ratio at both these locations would have been larger.

It should be noted that owing to the character of the bench slides, there are zones within the sequence which are rarely, if ever, exposed (Fig. 4.5). In the Barton Clay cliffs, sliding on the preferred bedding planes occurs irrespective of their elevation within the cliff, continuing to below beach level (Barton 1977). Only very short sections just below the Plateau Gravel may sometimes be seen but more often obscured by talus. Thus at Naish Farm, despite its stratigraphical importance, it is highly probable that particular levels (of around 0.5–1.0 m above the preferred bedding plane shear surfaces) have never received the stratigraphical and palaeontological study such has been devoted to the rest of the sequence. From the stratigraphical viewpoint, the colluvium never makes up this deficiency since the solid strata are completely remoulded within the interior of the benches by the intense shearing suffered by the softened material as it accommodates to the markedly non-circular slip surfaces.

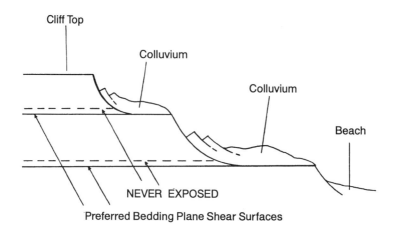

Fig. 4.5. The pattern of degradation, when controlled by preferred bedding plane shear surfaces, is such that certain thicknesses of the strata are virtually never exposed. At Naish Farm these are zones of about 0.5–1 m thickness above the preferred bedding planes.

The exposure ratio can prove a useful index for two purposes:
(a) as a measure of the value of a cliff in its current state, for research and teaching; and
(b) as a measure of the stage of degradation reached by the cliff processes.

The variation in exposure ratio can be most profitably examined in relation to the intensity of toe erosion, using Hutchinson's tripartite classification (Hutchinson 1967, 1973) which may be summed up as follows:
(i) abandoned cliffs (i.e. no toe erosion);
(ii) cliffs with moderate toe erosion;
(iii) cliffs with rapid toe erosion.

Abandoned cliffs

The cessation of toe erosion allows talus to accumulate at the foot of the slope and the degradation processes gradually to reduce the overall slope angle β to the ultimate stable value β_u (Fig. 4.6). For London Clay cliffs, Hutchinson (1973) has shown an exponential

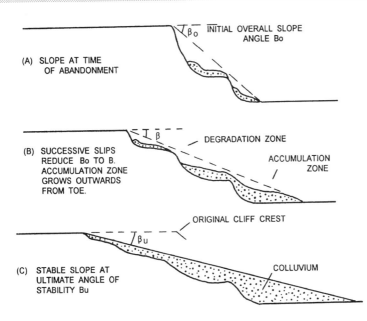

(A) SLOPE AT TIME
    OF ABANDONMENT

INITIAL OVERALL SLOPE
ANGLE Bo

(B) SUCCESSIVE SLIPS
    REDUCE Bo TO B.
    ACCUMULATION ZONE
    GROWS OUTWARDS
    FROM TOE.

DEGRADATION ZONE

ACCUMULATION
ZONE

ORIGINAL CLIFF CREST

(C) STABLE SLOPE AT
    ULTIMATE ANGLE OF
    STABILITY Bu

COLLUVIUM

Fig. 4.6. The evolution of abandoned cliffs (based on Hutchinson 1967 and Ingold 1975).

relation involving considerable movement over the first decade with the final stability being reached only after several thousand years. However, the rate at which the stability is reached must be highly dependent on the groundwater conditions, significant seepage would certainly allow a faster rate of accumulation of colluvium. When the slope is fully covered by the latter, the exposure ratio is zero. The changes in slope angle β and exposure ratio (ER) with time may be represented as in Fig. 4.7. ER can be expected to vary within limits but to reduce rapidly during the initial highly active stage, becoming close to zero during the long final stage with only small and very intermittent movements.

When cliff stabilization works are incorporated as well as toe protection, the run-down to stability is accelerated: such is the case at Highcliffe (Mockridge 1983; Tyhurst 1996) where the exposure ratio is now mostly zero (having been helped in this direction by earth moving, drainage and boarding of the top scarp). Before the

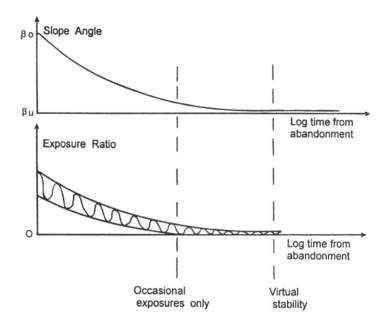

Fig. 4.7. General trend of reducing overall slope angle (β) and exposure ratios with time in abandoned cliffs. The exposure ratio can be expected to fluctuate with time but the range of fluctuation is also likely to decrease with time.

stabilization works, but after toe protection, the ER value at Highcliffe was about 30% (Barton 1973), and before any of these works (in the early 1960s) was probably around 40% (the Plateau Gravel scarp face accounting for between 5 and 20%). The most notable effect of the construction of the revetment on the beach was the rapid coverage of the cliff foot by the accumulation of uneroded colluvium (see Fig. 4.8).

Cliffs with moderate toe erosion

In London Clay cliffs, Hutchinson (1973) equated this class with cliffs in which the rate of removal by the sea was broadly in balance with the rate of supply by 'weathering' (an inappropriate term but by which Hutchinson clearly implied the degradational processes). While most of the eroded material will be colluvium, it must be

Fig. 4.8. The accumulation of colluvium at the foot of the Highcliffe cliffs (just west of Chewton Bunny) following cessation of marine erosion due to the construction of the steel sheet pile and timber revetment in the late 1960s.

assumed (in contradiction to Hutchinson 1973) that some erosion of the *in situ* clay will occur or else the slope will no longer recede but merely flatten its profile. With moderate erosion, recession rates are typically in the range of 0.25–0.8 m a^{-1} (Hutchinson 1973). With moderate toe erosion it has been noted that cliff slopes tend to maintain a fairly constant angle (Edil & Vallejo 1977; Vallejo & Degroot 1988). In the benched cliffs at Naish Farm, the cliffs also tend to have fairly regular profiles with the overall slope angle β ranging over a small interval.

With the continuity of the benched profile, the same pattern of exposure is maintained over time but with a fluctuation in exposure ratio due to the periodic build-up of talus at the foot of the scarp slopes before further bench sliding allows more of the scarp face to be exposed. Fresh scarp slumping (either of the internal or of the top scarp) reduces the exposure ratio but scarp slumping (see Fig. 4.3) is usually accompanied (synchronously or soon after) by bench sliding which allows the slump block to move away from the scarp face. It is important to note that it is always the same stratigraphic levels which will receive maximum exposure: the 'hidden' levels (Fig. 4.5) remaining deeply buried.

Cliffs with rapid toe erosion

In this category significant erosion of the *in-situ* toe occurs (the mechanisms of which are discussed by Hutchinson 1986). Typical recession rates are in the range of 0.9–2.1 m a^{-1} (Hutchinson 1973). For London Clay cliffs, Hutchinson (1973) and Bromhead (1979) recognized a cyclic pattern with deep-seated landslides followed by a period in which the latter are degraded by mudslides before further *in-situ* toe erosion occurs. A cyclic pattern has also been recognized elsewhere (Edil & Vallejo 1977; Vallejo & Degroot 1988). The frequency of the cycle must depend on the rate of marine attack.

In the Barton Clay cliffs at Naish Farm, the rate of marine erosion markedly increased from a moderate value in the 1940s and 1950s to a rapid rate in the 1960s (following depletion of the beach) and to a yet more rapid rate in the 1970s following the construction of the Highcliffe sea defences and the concomitant development of scour on their downdrift side (Barton & Coles 1984). Although steeper overall slope angles were produced, the benched form of the cliff was maintained so that the cyclic pattern as recorded in the London Clay cliffs is not seen. The reason for this lies in the presence of the frequent preferred bedding plane shear surfaces. Increased rates of toe erosion encourages faster rates of movement along these surfaces. In the case of the London Clay cliffs, the slope angle can be steepened to the point where the static forces can produce a massive failure involving the whole cliff in one very large rotational slip.

The exposure ratio figures of Table 4.1 are those produced by the current rapid rates of toe erosion. In the best exposed sections these reach a maximum value of 55%. The exposure ratio is reduced towards the east where the recession rate is less (although still some distance from the western end of the Barton-on-Sea defences) and also at the extreme western end where the cliffs now come under the influence of the strongpoint protecting the stream outfall of Chewton Bunny.

Exposure ratios with reduced erosion rates

Prediction of the likely exposure ratio of benched-form clay cliffs following partial toe protection will need to encompass the following factors.

(i) The objective is to avoid both the high rates of recession associated with *rapid toe erosion* and the eventual slope coverage associated with *zero toe erosion*. The aim therefore is for the state of *moderate toe erosion* (perhaps aiming at a value of about 0.3–0.6 m a^{-1} although this would be subject to negotiation).

(ii) The ideal condition would allow not only the colluvium accumulating at the cliff base to be readily eroded and thus provide an exposure of *in situ* clay in the lowest scarp, but also some erosion (albeit limited) of the *in situ* toe to prevent flattening of the cliff profile in the longer term. The beach replenishment or toe protection works will need continuous monitoring and adjustment to achieve this desired result.

(iii) By definition, the frequency with which erosion occurs and/or the amount at any one time must be reduced. While the aim will be for the rate of removal of colluvium to be slightly in excess of the rate of supply, the latter is fairly continuous while the marine erosion is intermittent. This will result in the lower scarp being more usually covered by colluvium and only infrequently exposed for study.

(iv) The exposure of the internal (middle level) scarp faces will be subject to variation. Since the trend for degrading slopes is an accumulation of talus at the foot, the internal scarps will tend to have the longer periods of exposure. The best exposures will occur in the top scarp – at Naish Farm, this will be in the Plateau Gravel and not the Barton Clay.

(v) Many more observations of exposure ratios over time and with varying rates of toe erosion are required before accurate predictions can be made. The currently available evidence for the Barton Clay cliffs at Naish Farm suggests that the range in exposure ratios resulting from partial toe protection will be considerably reduced from the current maximum values, perhaps to a maximum of 40% and perhaps as low as 20% in the typical benched profiles (sections with lobate mudslides will continue to have only minimal exposures).

(vi) The actual exposure ratios will reflect the actual toe erosion rates. The longer the time interval between bouts of toe erosion, the more the pattern will tend in the intervening periods to that shown by abandoned cliffs. It is for the conservation interests to consider whether the conditions obtained with moderate toe erosion are acceptable from their standpoint. Higher exposure ratios can only be obtained at the expense of increased recession.

Conclusion

The arguments presented here apply to clay cliffs where the engineering work is purely in terms of toe protection. The engineering work could be extended, of course, to creating exposures by a programme of excavation on the cliff area itself. However, such work entails a host of other problems and must be the subject of further research. While this could produce an exposure at the time it is required, the cliff ceases to be a natural entity and its longer term response would need study in respect of the location and frequency of, and volumes removed and disturbed by, the excavation programme.

References

Barton, M. E. 1973. The degradation of the Barton Clay cliffs of Hampshire. *Quarterly Journal of Engineering Geology* **6**, 423–440.

Barton, M. E. 1977. Landsliding along bedding planes. *Bulletin International Association Engineering Geology* **16**, 5–7.

Barton, M. E. & Coles, B. J. 1984. The characteristics and rates of the various slope degradation processes in the Barton Clay cliffs of Hampshire. *Quarterly Journal of Engineering Geology* **17**, 117–136.

Bates, J., Herbath, Y. & Tresidder, D. 1995. *Cliff Erosion in*

Christchurch Bay. MEng Group Design Project Report, University of Southampton.

Bromhead, E. N. 1979. Factors affecting the transition between the various types of mass movement in coastal cliffs consisting largely of overconsolidated clay with special reference to Southern England. *Quarterly Journal of Engineering Geology* **12**, 291–300.

Edil, T. B. & Vallejo, L. E. 1977. Shoreline erosion and landslides in the Great Lakes. *Proceedings of the 9th International Conference on Soil Mechanics & Foundation Engineering* **2**, 51–57.

Hutchinson, J. N. 1967. The free degradation of London Clay cliffs. *Proceedings of Geotechnical Conference*, Oslo, **1**, 113–118.

Hutchinson, J. N. 1973. The response of London Clay cliffs to differing rates of toe erosion. *Geologia Applicata e Idrogeol, Bari, Italy*, **8**, 221–239.

Hutchinson J. N. 1986. Cliffs and shores in cohesive materials: geotechnical and engineering geological aspects. *Proceedings of the Symposium on Cohesive Shores, Burlington, Ontario*. National Research Council, Canada 1–44.

Ingold, T. S. 1975. The stability of highways in landslipped areas. *The Highway Engineer*, **22**, 14–21.

McKirdy, A. D. 1987. Protective works and geological conservation. *In*: Culshaw M. G. *et al.* (eds) *Planning and Engineering Geology*. Geological Society, London, Special Publications **4**, 81–85.

Mockridge, R. G. 1983. Highcliffe Cliffs – the maintenance of coastal slopes. *Proceedings of the Conference Shoreline Protection, Southampton*. Institution of Civil Engineers, 235–242.

Nature Conservancy Council 1983. Barton Cliffs SSSI, Hampshire. *Earth Science Conservation* **20**, 49–50.

Powell, K. A. 1992. Engineering with conservation issues in mind. *In*: Barrett, M. G. (ed.) *Coastal Zone Planning and Management*. Thomas Telford, London, 237–249.

Tyhurst, F. 1996. Highcliffe-on-Sea: the local authority perspective. *Field guide, Conference on Coastal Defence and Earth Science Conservation*, University of Portsmouth.

Vallejo, L. E. & Degroot, R. 1988. Bluff response to wave action. *Engineering Geology* (Elsevier) **26**, 1–16.

5 Problems associated with the
prediction of cliff recession rates for
coastal defence and conservation

E. M. Lee

Summary

- Cliff recession can provide important sources of littoral sediment and is essential for maintaining some wildlife habitats
  and geological features.

- It is a complex and uncertain process, difficult to predict in
  the short term.

- Predictions of recession rates are best based on an analysis
  of the historical record and an understanding of the geomorphological evolution of the cliff.

- Partial coast protection schemes, which reduce rather than
  prevent marine erosion, can result in considerable process
  variation and can lead to the development of new cliff forms.
  This may lead to problems in predicting the effectiveness of
  such schemes in providing an acceptable compromise between risk reduction, supply of littoral sediments and conservation interests.

Introduction

On many soft cliffs it is desirable to slow down rather than stop
marine erosion. This is particularly so where the cliffs are important
sources of littoral sediment or of great conservation value for their
scenic value, wildlife habitats or geological features (Leafe &
Radley 1994). However, although a wide range of techniques are
available that could reduce rather than prevent erosion, their use is
constrained by the difficultly in identifying erosion rates and
recession scenarios which could provide an acceptable compromise
between risk reduction, sediment supply and maintaining conservation value. Prediction of cliff recession is not without its problems,
primarily because of the complexity and uncertainty inherent in the

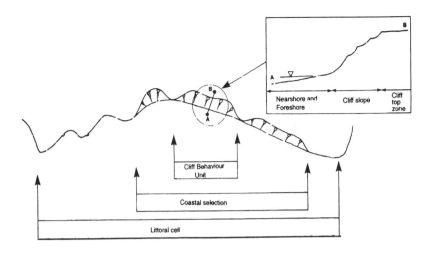

Fig. 5.1. A simple cliff behaviour unit (CBU).

recession process. This is of particular importance to the conservation debate as by attempting to modify cliff behaviour through the use of partial erosion control techniques coastal engineers are trying to design cliffs with a new and hopefully less dynamic recession character.

Cliff behaviour units

To understand cliff recession something must be known of the conditions and processes operating on the nearshore and foreshore and on a cliff (and, in many cases, behind the cliff). It is for this reason that the concept of a 'cliff behaviour unit' (CBU) provides an important framework for cliff management. These units span the nearshore to the cliff top and are coupled to adjacent CBUs within the framework provided by littoral cells (Fig. 5.1).

In trying to explain or understand cliff behaviour it is useful to consider cliffs as open process–response systems characterized by inputs, throughputs and outputs of sediment. In this way a range of system types can be recognized:

(i) **Simple cliff face systems**, comprising a single sequence of inputs and outputs with limited storage. Examples include:

- 'soft' unconsolidated sands and gravels, e.g. the Suffolk coast;
- 'soft' tills, e.g. the Holderness coast; and
- 'hard' rock cliffs, e.g. Chalk cliffs.

(ii) **Simple landslide systems**, comprising a single sequence of inputs and outputs with variable amounts of storage within the failed mass. Examples include:

- rotational failures on the London Clay cliffs; and
- mudslides on the North Norfolk and Dorset coasts.

(iii) **Complex systems**, comprising strongly coupled sequences of *sub-systems*, each with their own inputs and outputs of sediment. The output from one sub-system forms the input for the next. Such systems are often characterized by a high level of adjustment between process and form, with complex feedback mechanisms. Examples include:

- landslide complexes with high rates of throughput and removal of sediment, e.g. the Barton Clay cliffs of Christchurch Bay;
- seepage erosion dominated cliffs, e.g. the Chale Cliffs on the Isle of Wight; and
- relict landslide complexes with relatively low rates of throughput and removal of sediment, e.g. the Isle of Wight Undercliff, the Landslip Nature Reserve, East Devon.

(iv) **Composite systems**, comprising a partly coupled sequence of contrasting simple sub-systems. The output from one system may not necessarily form an input for the next. Examples include:

- the Durham cliffs comprising mudslide systems developed in till over Magnesian Limestone cliffs prone to rockfalls;

and
- the West Sussex cliffs formed of Wadhurst clay and sandstones.

Cliff recession

Cliff recession is a four stage process, involving:

- detachment of blocks of material from the cliff face;
- transport of this material through the cliff system;
- deposition of the material on the foreshore;
- removal of the material by marine action.

The process is the result of the complex interaction of a number of destabilizing factors over time (Fig. 5.2). Marine erosion is of obvious importance and involves foreshore lowering, undercutting of the cliff and removal of debris. These lead, in turn, to instability and mass movement in the cliff slopes which eventually results in the loss of cliff top land. Even when marine erosion has ceased, as on naturally abandoned and some protected cliffs, cliff instability and loss of cliff top land can persist as the cliff slope continues to degrade towards a long-term angle of stability.

Preparatory and triggering factors

When a cliff fails the displaced material moves to a new position so that equilibrium can be re-established between the destabilizing forces and the strength of the material. Landsliding, therefore, helps change a cliff from a less stable to a more stable state with a *margin of stability*. No subsequent movement or recession will occur unless the cliff is subject to processes which, once again, affect the balance of opposing forces. In many inland settings landslides can remain dormant or relatively inactive for thousands of years. However, on the coast, marine erosion removes material from the cliff base, reducing the margin of stability, and promotes further recession. Thus, on any coastal cliff the margin of stability will vary through time; from a peak immediately after a recession event to progressively lower levels as marine erosion or other slope processes

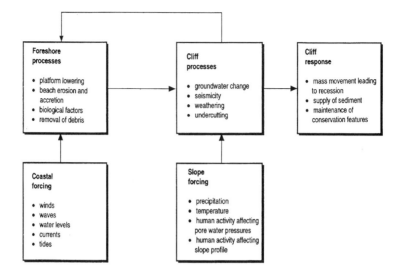

Fig. 5.2. A summary of the cliff recession process.

(e.g. weathering) affect the cliff stability (Fig. 5.3).

This perspective makes it possible to recognize two categories of factors which are active in promoting cliff recession:

(i) **preparatory factors** which work to make the cliff increasingly susceptible to failure without actually initiating recession; and

(ii) **triggering factors** which actually initiate recession events.

As the margin of stability is progressively reduced by the operation of preparatory factors, so the minimum size of triggering event required to initiate recession becomes smaller. Thus triggering events of a particular magnitude are redundant (i.e. do not initiate cliff recession) until preparatory factors lower the margin of stability to a critical value. It follows that cliff recession is usually the variable interaction of a range of destabilizing forces. As Fig. 5.3C indicates, this can mean variable time periods (epochs) between recession events, depending on the sequences of storm or rainfall events. In addition, the same size triggering events may not

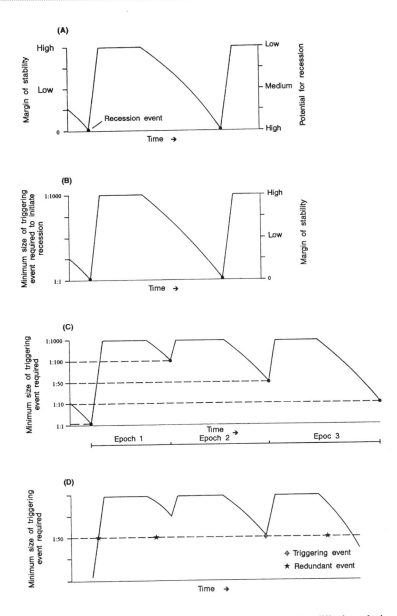

Fig. 5.3. The relationship between the margin of stability of a cliff, size of triggering factors and redundant events.

necessarily lead to recession events. The response of a cliff to storms of a particular size is controlled by the antecedent conditions. This is graphically illustrated in Fig. 5.3D which shows the occurrence of a sequence of 1 in 50 year storms, only one of which initiates a recession event. The rest are redundant.

Timescales for predicting and measuring cliff recession

A fundamental concept in cliff behaviour is that for any given geological setting, climate and exposure to wave attack a characteristic set of cliff and foreshore features will develop which define individual CBUs. However, although characteristic forms can be recognized which persist through time, individual components will be evolving and the pattern and interrelationships of these features will be continuously changing. Indeed, in active systems this repetition of characteristic forms will persist through time even though the cliff profile has retreated and the CBU comprises new components.

However, cliff recession is a complex process. It involves small scale losses associated with water and wind erosion, weathering and spalling off a cliff face, and episodic events associated with the periodic failure of cliffs in response to preparatory factors, such as slope profile steepening, and triggering factors, such as large storms or periods of heavy rainfall. For example, at Black Ven, Dorset there is an estimated 56 year cycle of major activity associated with gradual increases in slope angle (Chandler & Brunsden 1995). Other cliffs are highly sensitive to major storms; for example, the 15 m loss of cliff at Covehithe during the 1953 east coast storm surge.

Cliffs are an enigma. Their behaviour is often characterized by two apparently contradictory states: a complex and uncertain sequence of recession events and the establishment and maintenance of a characteristic set of landforms within a CBU which persist through time. These conditions highlight a fundamental problem for the prediction and measurement of cliff recession – the need to relate highly variable records or observations of recession events to the overall trend operating within a CBU. Here, it is convenient to view cliff recession over a range of relevant timescales: short, medium and long term.

Short term behaviour
When viewed from this perspective recession appears to be a highly variable process, with marked fluctuations in the annual recession rate around an average value. This type of behaviour is characterized by periods of no activity punctuated by short phases of recession.

Medium term behaviour
Over this timescale the fluctuations smooth themselves out as there is a tendency for CBUs to maintain a balance between process and form through negative feedback and self regulatory mechanisms (e.g. storage of debris). When viewed from this perspective the recession rate will be relatively constant, often with no observable trend. This medium term condition can be regarded as reflecting steady state behaviour, characterized by maintenance of CBU form, parallel retreat of the cliff profile and a balance over time in the sediment budget, i.e. the overall rate of detachment equals the overall rate of removal from the foreshore, with minimal changes in the volume of material stored within the cliff system.

The timescales over which steady state behaviour may be expected to become apparent will vary accordingly to the nature of the CBU, especially the sensitivity to triggering events of different magnitudes. Typical timescales are:

- simple cliff CBUs in rapidly eroding materials (e.g. the Holderness coast): 5–10 years;
- simple cliff CBUs in slowly eroding materials (e.g. Chalk Cliffs): 10–100 years;
- simple landslide CBUs: 10–100 years;
- composite CBUs: 10–100 years;
- complex CBUs with high rates of throughput and removal of sediment (e.g. Black Ven): 50–250 years; and
- complex CBUs with low rates of throughput and removal of sediment (e.g. the Isle of Wight Undercliff): 100–10 000 years.

For the overwhelming majority of cliffs, equilibrium behaviour can develop over 10–100 years. It is fortunate, therefore, that historical records provide excellent coverage over this period and beyond. In many instances the historical records will cover more than one 'cycle' of activity and, thus, can shed considerable light on how the system has evolved.

Long term behaviour
Over this timescale the characteristics of the CBU may gradually change, reflecting the progressive evolution of the cliffline in response to major environmental changes, e.g. the Holocene climate and sea level changes.

It is clear that the medium term behaviour characterized by a steady state equilibrium between CBU form and processes, is of major importance to cliff management. This timescale provides a framework within which recession is a regular and predictable process and enables the significance of individual major events to be evaluated in terms of the contribution of the overall pattern of cliff recession. It follows that the most reliable predictions of recession can be made for medium-term timescales during which the CBU achieves steady state. This is also the timescale for planning requirements.

Prediction of recession rates

There are three broad approaches to prediction:
    (i) those based on the historical and contemporary behaviour of a CBU (i.e. historical assessment, geomorphological assessment; Moore *et al.* 1995);
   (ii) those based on simple empirical relationships between CBU form and process (e.g. the Brunn Rule; see Bray & Hooke, 1997);
 (iii) those which model CBU behaviour in response to the past, present and future forcing processes (process–response models).

In all cases it is essential that the predictions are based on an historical data set and an understanding of cliff behaviour. However, it should be noted that such predictions are based on a number of key assumptions: the past and present are the key to the future, that the CBU achieves steady state over a medium term timescale and that this timescale is covered by the historical record.

The assumption of steady state behaviour is valid so long as the forcing regime remains stable or that the CBU's self-regulatory mechanism (i.e. sediment flux and storage) can compensate for any changes. It is widely recognized that coastal defence works will result in significant changes to a CBU. Under total protection schemes this usually leads to a cessation or major reduction in the previously dominant cliff processes. For partial protection schemes the effects of reducing the wave attack at the cliff foot can be manifest by a period of process variation (nonsteady behaviour), the development of temporary forms and, in some cases, new characteristic forms. The development of non-steady state behaviour under partial protection schemes is a significant constraint to predicting reliably short and medium term recession rates and scenarios. Other than looking for natural cliffs in similar materials experiencing only partial wave attack at the base, coastal engineers can be left in the realms of speculation, as there is no historical record that can help judge what will happen and there is rarely an understanding of how the change in wave attack will affect the magnitude and frequency of recession processes.

Here it is important to stress that large-scale dramatic events do occur on protected cliffs. For example, the 1993 Holbeck Hall landslide, Scarborough, led to the destruction of the hotel and sea walls below with a loss of around 100 m of land (Clark & Guest, 1994) and the landslide at Overstrand, Norfolk led to loss of around 100 m of cliff top during a three year period between 1990 and 1993. The slope toe at Overstrand had been largely protected by wooden breastwork defences.

Conclusion

Cliff recession is a complex and uncertain process which is generally best predicted over medium-term timescales during which the CBU achieves a steady state condition. This steady state is characterized by a smoothing out of the highly variable short term recession rates and balance between process and form that is reflected by the development and maintenance of a characteristic cliff form which persists through time. However, not all cliffs achieve or maintain this steady state. Coastal defences, especially partial protection schemes, can result in significant changes to the CBU which are manifest by non-steady behaviour, considerable process variation and, in some cases, the development of a new characteristic form. This non-steady behaviour in response to defence works cannot be readily predicted from the historical record or an understanding of the past geomorphological evolution of the CBU, nor can it be predicted by existing mathematical models.

There are also problems relating to the choice of erosion control technique. It is difficult to design a scheme which allows a predetermined rate of erosion that is acceptable to both property owners and conservationists. This is because there is no simple relationship between wave attack and erosion rate. It is difficult to design a scheme which would deliver the target reduction in recession rate with any degree of confidence. In addition, it is generally assumed that erosion reduction will maintain the conservation interest. But many soft cliffs are very sensitive to wave attack and there could be a significant reduction in landsliding even when only a limited amount of protection is provided. Once a slope is no longer seasonally active it can become heavily vegetated and degraded.

By way of conclusion, it is clear that the middle way between coast protection and conservation is not an easy choice. It should not be viewed as a cheap and mutually beneficial compromise where a bit of defence will give a bit of heritage and a bit of risk reduction. Coastal engineers and managers should remember that it is still coastal engineering–but designing landforms with less foresight into how the final product may behave.

Acknowledgements

This paper is based on research carried out for the Ministry of Agriculture, Fisheries and Food: 'Soft Cliffs: Prediction of Recession Rates and Erosion Control Techniques'. The research was undertaken by Rendel Geotechnics and HR Wallingford, in association with the Cambridge Coastal Research Unit and the River and Coastal Environments Research Group of Portsmouth University.

References

Bray, M. J. & Hooke, J. M. 1997. Prediction of soft-cliff retreat with accelerating sea level rise. *Journal of Coastal Research*, **13**, 453–467.

Chandler, J. H. & Brunsden, D. 1995. Steady state behaviour of the Black Ven mudslide: the application of archival analytical photogrammetry studies of landform change. *Earth Surface Processes and Landforms*, **20**, 225–275.

Clark, A. R. & Guest, S. 1994. The design and construction of the Holbeck Hall landslide coast protection and slope stabilization emergency works. *Proceeding of the MAFF Conference of River and Coastal Engineers.*

Leafe, R. N. & Radley, G. P. 1994. Environmental benefits of soft cliff erosion. *Proceedings of the MAFF Conference of River and Coastal Engineers.*

Moore, R., Clark, A. R. & Lee, E. M. 1995. Coastal cliff behaviour and management: Blackgang, Isle of Wight. *In: Geohazards and Engineering Geology*, Engineering Group of the Geological Society, London, preprints volume.

6 Impacts of coal mining on coastal stability in Fife

Elisabeth M. Saiu & John McManus

Summary

- Twentieth century development of collieries along 15 km of coast in SE Fife led to dumping of mine wastes on the unprotected shorelines. Coastal dynamics ensured a westward spread of the detritus, leading to the burial of beaches, blocking of harbours and the development of new headlands.

- The demise of the mines between 1967 and 1984 led to the cessation of dumping and commencement of coastal erosion. Coastal defences were installed to protect oil-related harbour installations and a housing development. Elsewhere, erosion continues and locally threatens archaeologically important caves.

- GIS techniques enabled precise comparison of OS plans of the coast constructed during the past century. This has permitted identification of zones in which High or Low Water Marks have shown stability or instability since 1894.

- Locally, segments of the coast have been lowered so that LWM and HWM have moved landward. Each overlies an actively mined area, and computation of mining subsidence from mining plans yields estimates compatible with topographically determined sinking rates.

History of mining and coastal change due to mine wastes

Coal has been extracted in Fife, Scotland for over 700 years. The earliest workings were entirely from outcrop mining, but as technology advanced at the end of the nineteenth century deep mining became widely practised and mining extended beneath the Forth (Cunningham 1907, 1922).

Underwater mining began at the Wellesley colliery during the

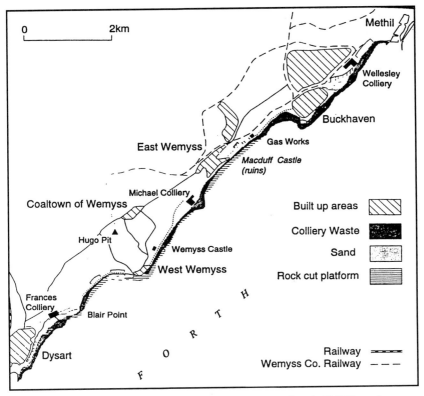

Fig. 6.1. Principal localities referred to in the text, based on 1:10 560 scale maps and showing the extent of the shoreline waste-built terraces in 1950.

1890s (Fig. 6.1). Excess wastes were deposited to form a bing beside the mine, 1 km east of a small fishing harbour at Buckhaven and the recreational beach at Silver Sands. The harbour remained operational until the 1920s after which the harbour became silted up.

By the 1950s the Wellesley wastes (redd) had built an apron of deposits reaching over 100 m seaward of the former coastline, and extended beyond Buckhaven harbour, which had filled with coarse sediments. The Silver Sands beach and tidal swimming pool had been buried beneath the redeposited mine wastes. At the Michael Colliery 4 km to the west the redd deposited on the shoreline had created a headland which extended 150 m out to sea beyond the former coastline. A further 8 km to the west a second similar headland had developed from the wastes derived from the Frances colliery. The entire coastal stretch was buried beneath a mantle of colliery waste.

The closure of the Wellesley and Michael collieries in the mid 1960s led to cessation of dumping of new material on the bings, but the unprotected wastes continued to undergo erosion from the dominant waves approaching from the southeast. An oil-rig construction yard and graving dock were developed on the site of the former Wellesley colliery, and rip-rap was installed along the foot of the bing to prevent wastes migrating into the new dock facility. In the absence of the supporting sediment supply from the bing, cliffs were eroded in the recently deposited sediments along the coast west of the bing, and the released sediments migrated towards the buried Buckhaven Harbour. Freshly reclaimed recreational areas began to disappear, and a housing development was threatened. After 30 m of cliffline retreat had taken place in a six month period heavy rip-rap protection schemes were constructed. Beyond the coastal protection, however, fresh erosion was taking place.

The coastal terrace of wastes which had accumulated in front of the old cliffline became subjected to wave attack due to the reduction of migrating sediment from the Wellesley area, and the former cliffs became again exposed to the sea. The archaeologically important Wemyss caves were actively threatened and conservationists and Fife Regional Council became concerned to maintain access and protect the heritage assets.

At the Michael colliery the headland remained unprotected. Most of the Michael wastes moved westwards towards West Wemyss, and continued to provide supplies for the western redd-built terrace.

A preliminary survey in 1992 of the changing coastal equilibrium of the southeast Fife coastline suggested that mining subsidence was significant in reshaping the coastline (Saiu 1993). With the exception of the Wemyss Castle, almost the entire area had been undermined during the period 1850–1970, with a total of 19 separate seams having been worked beneath some parts of the coastal strip between Buckhaven and Dysart (National Coal Board archives). In order to quantify the effects of mining subsidence on the coastline and determine whether the former coastal strip had been lowered significantly an investigation was undertaken using three approaches:

(a) comparison of Ordnance Survey plans of the coast, particularly changes in marked positions of High and Low Water Marks
(b) comparisons of Ordnance Survey bench mark heights between 1896 and 1996; and
(c) calculation of potential mining subsidence using mining plans supplied from the National Coal Board.

Recognition of coastal changes

High and Low Water Mark migration
Ordnance Survey 1 : 2500 scale plans of the coastline for 1894, 1914, 1960 and 1994 were used to provide detail of the history of changes. Using the Smallworld GIS software precise measurement of changes of the positions of High and Low Water Marks (HWM and LWM) at 100 m intervals along the coast were taken.

On the approximately 5000 m of coast immediately west of Buckhaven harbour between 1894 and 1914 HWM migrated landwards by 20 m on average, while LWM was stable in position. By 1956 the coastline had undergone radical changes (Fig. 6.2). HWM had moved seaward by an average of 60 m as the terrace of wastes built out, while LWM migrated landwards by a mean of 90 m. The distance between HWM and LWM (beach width) had decreased from over 200 m to less than 50 m, making the beach significantly steeper (gradient 0.1 compared with 0.025 before). By 1994 the wastes no longer featured on this part of the coast, LWM had moved seawards by 45 m presumably as the sediments accumulated offshore, but it remained 40 m landward of its 1894 position. (All distance values have a margin of error of ±10%).

Between Silver Sands Bay and East Wemyss HWM retreated 10 m landwards between 1894 and 1914, advanced seawards by 25–70 m, according to position by 1956, but by 1994 had retreated to 20 m landward of its 1914 position. Today, as in earlier times,

uninhabitable. Any variation of up to ±0.3 m for any bench mark can be attributed to natural error (Advice from Ordnance Survey). However, the preliminary results show that over 12 benchmarks have subsided between 0.41 and 2.0 m during the period 1896–1960.

Mining subsidence

Potential maximum subsidence has been calculated using NCB 1:2500 mine plans (scale 1:2500) and the influence function method. A computer program, the Surface Deformation Prediction System (Karmis & Agioutantis 1989) was used, which could adjust for irregular workings and multiple seams. Subsidence values were calculated at 10 m intervals on the surface for each seam, using real grid co-ordinates. The data were then transferred into IDRISI GIS where the subsidence values were superimposed to produce a total value of subsidence for the area. At least 19 coal seams have been worked beneath the coast between Methil and Dysart, using a combination of pillar and room workings, and later longwall workings which involved backfilling. Whereas subsidence associated with longwall workings is predictable and relatively swift, subsidence resulting from pillar and room operations may occur a century and more after working ceased (National Coal Board 1975).

The calculated potential subsidence for the coastal zone between Buckhaven and West-Wemyss is indicated in Fig. 6.3. The pattern is artificially constricted both landward and seaward as computations have been restricted to those seams and areas which impact the coastal zone itself. The amount of subsidence varies greatly along the coast from zero in totally protected areas beneath the estate buildings to a maximum calculated figure of 5.5 m to the west of the area shown in Fig. 6.2, between Buckhaven Silver Sands Bay and the former East Wemyss gasworks. Over most of the area the subsidence is much less, generally in the range 0.5–2 m. In the area of the significant caves it is between 1 and 2 m.

Conclusions

During the last hundred years the coastline of southeast Fife has experienced a number of changes which can be related directly to mining activity.

1. The southeast Fife coastline was submerged in a blanket of colliery waste as a direct result of the dumping of bing material onto the beach at the three sites along the-coastline, at the Wellesley (1890–1967), Michael (1890–1968) and the Frances (1850–1984) collieries.

2. Closure of the Wellesley and stabilization of the bing margin produced sediment starvation and coastal erosion towards Buckhaven harbour. The erosion was eventually deflected into Silver Sands Bay and towards East Wemyss.

3. Analysis of Ordnance Survey plans shows that the removal of the protective terraces which had built up during the mining era has revealed that the cliff is no longer at its former level. The archaeological remains are now more vulnerable to coastal erosion than at the end of last century.

4. Mining subsidence, hitherto concealed by the built terraces, has been calculated. It is not uniform in distribution, and although commonly 1–2 m, some areas are little affected. The area with greatest estimated subsidence (5.5 m) lies northeast of the former East Wemyss gasworks, where today there is broken ground with substantial landsliding on the cliffs. There is a 10% margin of error for each mining subsidence value calculated (National Coal Board 1975), together with a further 10% incurred from the GIS-processing. The results, however, still remain significant.

5. The mining subsidence is non-uniform along the coast, but reflects the irregular workings which underlie the coastline. Those areas where most coal was extracted are now experiencing the greatest amount of erosion, i.e. Wemyss Caves and Silver Sands of Buckhaven. At these sites the LWM, which is located on rock, has migrated shorewards, illustrating the fundamental role the mining subsidence has played in reshaping the coastline of southeast Fife.

Acknowledgement

The Carnegie Trust for the Universities of Scotland is thanked for their support of the publication of the colour figures within this chapter.

References

Cunningham, A. S. 1907. Mining in the Kingdom of Fife *Leven Advertiser and Wemyss Gazette*, Leven, Fife.

Cunningham, A. S. 1922. Fife Coal Company Limited: the Jubilee Year 1872–1922 *Leven Advertiser and Wemyss Gazette*, Leven, Fife.

Karmis, M. & Agioutantis, Z. 1989. Mining subsidence prediction using the influence function method. *Coal* **26**, 4–61.

National Coal Board 1975. *Subsidence Engineers Handbook*. Mining Department, NCB, Hobart House, London.

Saiu, E. M. 1993. Destabilisation of coastal equilibrium by industrial growth and decline in eastern Scotland Unpublished BSc Thesis, University of St. Andrews.

Part Three

Strategies and decision-making

The purpose of this part is to explore and
demonstrate how decisions on conservation
and defence have and can be made and to
discuss strategies for reconciling defence and
conservation requirements. The policies and
strategies developed by one area, the Isle of
Wight, which has a particularly rich earth
science heritage are outlined. In a case study
from Somerset the value of understanding the
longer-term history of processes and landforms
is demonstrated but also how decision-making
may ignore scientific advice. The dilemmas set
by conflicting interests of preservation against
new exposure of sediments and of artefacts in
coastal cliffs are presented in a case study from
Brittany. The way in which application of the
ideas and information on coastal sediment cells
can provide a strategy for coastal defence and
conservation decisions is discussed. Finally, the
situation with regard to coastal features and
their conservation in Scotland is described.

7

Practical experience in reconciling conservation and coastal defence strategies on the Isle of Wight

Robin G. McInnes

Summary

- The coastline of the Isle of Wight is of international importance with respect to its range of geological exposures.
- In addition, the geomorphological features arising from the
  complex geology, and the natural processes that have been
  acting upon the geology, have resulted in much of the coastline receiving specific designations and protection.
- It is the superb range of coastal scenery that has, to a
  considerable degree, resulted in the development of the
  Island's very successful tourist industry. Against this background the Isle of Wight has tried to address coastal defence issues involving protection of life and property in
  vulnerable locations where there is economic justification.
- By developing coastal policies through dialogue and in close
  consultation with the conservation organisations,
  it has been possible to achieve a balance between the
  requirements of coastal defence and earth science conservation. Practical examples are given where apparently conflicting demands have been reconciled satisfactorily.

Geology

The Isle of Wight forms part of the geological structure known as
the Hampshire–Dieppe Basin. On the Island sedimentary rocks of
early Cretaceous to early Oligocene age are exposed below some
Quaternary gravel and alluvium cover. Compressional earth
movements during the Cenozoic folded the solid geology deposits.
As a result, the oldest rocks, the Wessex Formation, are brought to
the surface in the cores of the Sandown and Brixton anticlines,
whilst the narrow belt of vertical Chalk and Palaeogene beds extend
across the Island from Whitecliff Bay to Alum Bay.

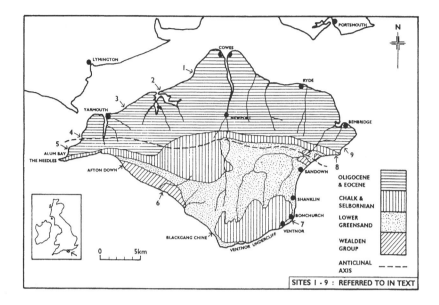

Fig. 7.1. Isle of Wight coast – Earth Science Conservation.

The Island was previously linked to mainland England by a chalk ridge which extended westwards to the Dorset coast. At the end of the last Pleistocene glacial period or 'ice age', sea levels began to rise as the great ice sheets melted. At some point in time, believed to be 8–10 000 years ago, the sea flooded the river valleys, cutting through the Chalk ridge and creating an island. Subsequent erosion has created a breach over 30 km wide and the Island as it is today. Prior to the breach of the Chalk ridge, the area to the north formed the drainage basin of the Solent River with the Test, Stour, Avon and Itchen flowing in from the north and the Western Yar, Medina and Eastern Yar from the south. The magnificent scenery of the Island is the result of the interaction of erosional processes and the underlying geological structure.

The chalk ridge which extends across the Isle of Wight from Alum Bay in the west to Culver Cliff in the east is interrupted in three places where the northward flowing Western Yar, Medina and Eastern Yar have cut valleys. North of the ridge, the area underlain by the Palaeogene sands and clays slopes gently down from 30 to 60 m to the Solent shore.

South of the chalk ridge is a broad valley, the 'bowl of the Island' extending from Brook to Sandown Bay. This valley is underlain mainly by early Cretaceous sands which produce light, well-drained and easily cultivated soils.

Along the southern corner of the Island rise the Southern Downs, a second area of Chalk downland. The northern edge of these downs is deeply indented by a number of stream valleys, whilst the southern face is precipitous. The particular geological structure of this area has produced a coastal landslide complex between Blackgang and Luccombe (Fig. 7.3). The end-product of the processes which have operated over the last 2000 years is the terraced landscape of the Undercliff, backed by an inland cliff of Upper Greensand above which are steep Chalk downs.

A distinctive feature of the southern coast of the Island are the chines. These are deep, often steep ravines incised through soft sandstones or clays by streams on their way to the sea. The chines owe their origin to intermittent erosion of the coast which promotes continual rapid stream down-cutting. The rapid recession of the cliff line means that the streams adjust to the new sea-level position by incision.

Coastal geomorphology

The coastline of the Isle of Wight is subject to various processes of coastal erosion, weathering and coastal instability. This has resulted in an extraordinary range of textbook examples of coastal features including sea stacks, wave cut platforms, landslide features, salt marsh and dunes. On account of the completeness of the geological succession and the variety of geomorphological features large sections of the Isle of Wight coast have received national designation both in terms of their scientific interest as 'Sites of Special Scientific Interest' (SSSIs) and as 'Areas of Outstanding Natural Beauty' (AONBs). In addition to this, various sections of the coastline are also designated as Heritage Coast, Local and National Nature Reserves and Special Protection Areas and Special Areas of Conservation; the sites of geological interest referred to in this paper are indicated on Fig. 7.1.

Fig. 7.2. Greensand cliff at Gore cliff, Niton.

Fig. 7.3. Coastal landslide due to marine erosion and high groundwater levels, Castlehaven, Niton.

Coastal sites of earth science conservation importance

In order to appreciate the value and range of exposures of earth science conservation interest on the Isle of Wight it is necessary to summarize briefly information on key sites around the coast of the

Isle of Wight. Starting with the northwest coast of the Isle of Wight and moving anti-clockwise around the coastline, sites of importance are described.

1. Gurnard Ledge to Saltmead Ledge SSSI

This site includes some 3 km of undeveloped and little disturbed coastline on the northwest coast of the Island. It includes a considerable area of soft maritime cliffs with large expanses of inter-tidal sand and shingle interspersed with outcrops of Bembridge Limestone. This section is of particular geological importance because of the rock sequence which occurs and the range of fossil plants and insects which have been recovered over the years. At Thorness Bay it is possible to see a full succession of rocks from the upper part of the Headon Hill Formation down to the lowest beds of the Bouldnor Formation. The exposures of the Bembridge Limestone and Bembridge Marls are also of particular importance in understanding the geological history of this area.

Towards the base of the Bembridge Marls is a thin limestone known as the 'Insect Limestone'. This is a particularly important source of Tertiary fossil insects and is one of the best sites for finding these species in Britain. Over 250 species have been found within the Limestone and for 39 species this is the 'Type' locality; 20 species are unique to the Isle of Wight. In terms of fossil plants which also occur at other levels in the Bembridge Limestone and Bembridge Marls, this site is of critical importance for studies of European Tertiary palaeobotany.

2. Newtown Harbour SSSI

Newtown Harbour, which has now been designated as a National Nature Reserve, includes an extensive system of estuarine saltmarsh and mudflats that form a dendritic pattern of tidal creeks making up the Newtown Estuary. The site is bordered to the north by the Solent shore and consists of rapidly eroding cliffs, sand and shingle banks and beaches and large areas of inter-tidal mud, sand, shingle and rocky ledges. The spits at the entrance to the harbour are particularly important in protecting habitats for a wealth of saltmarsh flora and habitats for breeding birds. A shingle bank at the mouth of the estuary reveals a rich source of Quaternary mammals including elephant, bison, deer and hippopotamus.

3. Bouldnor and Hamstead Cliffs SSSI

This section of the northwest coast of the Island is of particular importance to geology because of the complete succession which it provides through the series of rocks of Oligocene age (some 30 million years old) known as the Hamstead Beds. Within this site is also the 'Type' section of the Bouldnor Formation, the youngest Tertiary strata developed in the Hampshire Basin.

Bouldnor Cliff is the principal site in the UK for fossil mammals of Oligocene age, having yielded an extensive fauna of over 24 species; it is the only known mid-Oligocene fauna anywhere in Britain. The site is also the best locality in Britain for fossil reptiles of Oligocene age, including turtles, crocodiles and snakes.

The cliff and foreshore section is also of great importance for studies of Tertiary fossil plants from the Bembridge Marls and the Hamstead Beds, and contains the 'Type' locality for a species of Sequoia tree. This is the only locality in Britain to yield fossil plants from the Middle and Upper Hamstead Beds and is also the only locality in Britain at which detailed studies of the palaeoecology and sedimentology of Oligocene fossil plant-bearing rocks have been undertaken.

Fig. 7.4. Alum Bay and Headon Hill from the Needles Headland.

Fig. 7.5. Cliff top developments at Brambles Chine, Colwell Bay.

4. Colwell Bay SSSI

Colwell Bay is situated between Fort Albert and Cliff End to the north and Warden Point to the south; the frontage includes two chines known as Linstone and Brambles Chine, respectively (Fig. 7.5). This is a particularly important geological section of the Headon Formation, Lower Oligocene and Lower Eocene and contains a rich molluscan fauna. The area provides 'Type' exposures for various locally named rock groups including the fossil rich Colwell Bay member.

5. Headon Warren and West High Down SSSI

The dramatic scenery of this world famous site comprises parallel Tertiary and Chalk ridges. The former, Headon Warren, is an important ecological site. The cliffs at Alum Bay to Totland Bay are geologically important as a classic section of Lower Tertiary strata. The Chalk ridge terminates in the sea stacks known as the Needles and the eroded Chalk formations here are of great geomorphological interest (Fig. 7.4).

The cliff section from Alum Bay to Totland Bay is one of the most well-known geological sites in the world and has been studied by geologists for over 170 years; it includes such important visits as that of the British Institution in 1851 which was accompanied by geologists including Fitton and Murchison as well as the Prince Consort. This area is of great importance in understanding the geological evolution of the Isle of Wight and the Hampshire Basin, and is complementary to the sites at Whitecliff Bay at the eastern end of the Isle of Wight, and Hordle on the mainland. Within this site is a complete sequence of rocks from the Chalk to the Bembridge Limestone, containing important faunas of fossil vertebrates, invertebrates and flora.

The rock sequence provides a complete section from the Reading Clay, which rests unconformably upon the Chalk, up through the Oldhaven Formation, London Clay, Alum Bay Sands, Barton Clay, Barton Sands, Headon Hill Formation and into the Bembridge Limestone. A study of these sediments reveals the continually changing sequence of environments which existed in the western Isle of Wight during Eocene times, and significant environmental differences between this section and sections of similar age at Whitecliff Bay and Hordle can be recognized.

The rocks of the Headon to Bembridge interval are a particularly important source of fossil mammals, 46 species having been recorded. This is therefore one of the most important localities in the Tertiary rocks of Europe. Beds within the Headon Hill Formation are of particular importance as a source of fossil turtles, crocodiles, lizards and snakes and this is, therefore, also an important site for several types of Tertiary reptiles. Fossil plants occur on several horizons within the site and the flora assemblage which occurs is important for reconstructing the vegetation history of the Hampshire Basin.

6. Hanover Point to St Catherine's Point SSSI

The whole of the southwest coast of the Island is of extraordinary interest from a geological aspect (Fig. 7.6). The entire length comprises steep slopes formed in Wealden and Lower Greensand Beds and is subject to continuous slipping resulting from the differing strengths and permeabilities of the various marl, shale and sandstone strata. The coastline is dissected by a series of deeply incised chines or ravines. Towards Chale there is an impressive Upper Greensand cliff formed at the inland extremity of the

Fig. 7.6. The southwest coast of the Isle of Wight from Afton Down.

landslips. The complex mass movement features, including the Undercliff and the contemporary active coastal landslips and mud flows are of great geomorphological interest.

This long coastal expanse provides a complete geological sequence passing chronologically from the Wealden Group, the Lower Greensand Group, the Gault Clay, and Upper Greensand and into the Lower Chalk, in a cliff section unrivalled anywhere in Britain. The site is of great importance for studies of the Cretaceous rock sequence, interpretation of the environments in which the rocks were laid down and the fossils they contain. Of particular note are the fossil reptile faunas which occur in the Wealden Group, and which make this site the richest source of Lower Cretaceous dinosaurs in Europe.

The coastal section between Atherfield and Rocken End near Chale (Fig. 7.7) constitutes the finest Lower Greensand exposure in Britain, with the complete thickness of the formation being clearly visible. There are richly fossiliferous horizons throughout this sequence and thus the section is particularly important for Lower Cretaceous palaeontology and stratigraphy. The Wealden sediments between Brook and Atherfield have yielded abundant fossil remains including fine specimens of dinosaurs, and several new genera have been discovered here.

Fig. 7.7. Blackgang Cliffs viewed from Chale Terrace.

7. Bonchurch Landslip SSSI

The Undercliff landslide complex which extends from Blackgang in the west to Luccombe in the east is well-known worldwide as a spectacular geomorphological feature; the Undercliff is the largest urban landslide complex in northwestern Europe. At the eastern end of the Undercliff between Bonchurch and Luccombe is an area known as the Landslip. This undeveloped area is of great interest for the complexity of mass movement features including the coastal landslips and mud flows beneath it.

8. Bembridge Down SSSI

Situated at the eastern end of the Isle of Wight this site includes the 85 m vertical face of Culver Cliff which forms the eastern limit of the Chalk ridge which extends across the Isle of Wight. South of the Chalk ridge there is a geologically important continuous succession of the Wealden Group to the Upper Greensand occurring in the cliff section. This is the entire Cretaceous sequence found on the Isle of Wight.

The Yaverland to Culver section provides a complete sequence through the Wealden Group, Gault and Upper Greensand, together with the basal part of the Chalk. The Wealden Group, exposed at Yaverland, has been known as a source of large fossil dinosaur bones since 1829 and 11 genera of turtles, crocodiles and dinosaurs have been described. These finds include the oldest known 'Type' specimen of the dinosaur Yaverlandia bitholus: Yaverland is therefore a very important dinosaur site with good potential for further finds. In addition to its importance as a source for dinosaur remains and other fossils, the Culver section is particularly important for the stratigraphical aspects of the Lower Chalk sequence.

9. Whitecliff Bay and Bembridge Ledges SSSI

This site comprises an extensive area of intertidal sand, rock and shingle and includes the actively eroding low cliff line (Fig. 7.8). The site includes the important exposures of the Upper Chalk to the Bembridge Marls as well as containing important horizons of fossil faunas and floras.

Whitecliff Bay provides the most continuous exposures of Palaeogene sediments in western Europe, with a near complete series of Upper Palaeogene to Lower Oligocene strata exposed.

It is clear from the short descriptions of the geologically important sites above that the Isle of Wight coastline has a wealth of geological and geomorphological interest. Without doubt the coastline of the Isle of Wight is one of its greatest assets and this, of course, has been recognized nationally by the designation of the many important sites. In a popular holiday region like the Isle of Wight there are considerable pressures on the coastline both natural and human and it is necessary to reconcile all these in developing an effective coastal strategy including the need to protect sites of earth science conservation interest.

Development of a coastal policy for the Isle of Wight

The Isle of Wight Council, following local government reorganization, has inherited and is developing the coastal policies produced

Fig. 7.8. Whitecliff Bay and Bembridge Ledges SSSI viewed from Bembridge Down.

by its predecessors. South Wight Borough Council introduced *A Management Strategy for the Coastal Zone* (1993) which covered three-quarters of the Isle of Wight coastline. The aims of this strategy can be summarized as follows:

1. To develop a sustainable strategy to ensure that people and property within the coastal zone are protected as far as possible from the hazards of coastal erosion, flooding and instability.
2. To provide a basis for understanding coastal processes taking place around the Island's coast and the relationship with adjoining authorities coastlines.
3. To encourage closer links between all the disciplines involved within the coastal zone including economic and environmental and heritage interests, to their mutual benefit, and encourage public participation.
4. To examine and to try and improve the amenity, aesthetics, conservation, environment and enjoyment of the coastal zone through a more co-ordinated approach to problems.
5. To encourage research, plans and projects leading towards a sustainable strategy for the coastal zone founded upon sound

ecological, environmental and economic principles and practices.

With these aims and objectives in mind, a strategy for the Isle of Wight coast is being developed taking account of the full range of views of consultees and making use of documents such as English Nature's 'Campaign for a Living Coast' and 'A Guide to the Selection of Appropriate Coast Protection Works for Geological SSSIs' (1991). At a number of important sites around the Isle of Wight coast the possibility of conflict between the interests of earth science conservation and coastal defence have arisen historically. Efforts have been made to reconcile these interests taking account of the advice mentioned above and noting which operations would be likely to damage the special scientific interest of these sites.

In recent years the Isle of Wight has developed a close partnership with English Nature and other conservation organizations who can provide coastal engineers with expert advice on earth science conservation interests. This advice and dialogue has assisted in ensuring that where it is has proved essential for economic and safety reasons to carry out works, these have been undertaken in a manner that would be least detrimental to, or in harmony with the scientific interest of particular coastal sites.

Reconciling coastal defence and earth science conservation interests

Where coastal defence works have been required in areas of earth science conservation interest, a number of methods of resolving possible conflict have been adopted and these can be considered through the following examples.

1. Brambles Chine, Colwell
The site at Brambles Chine is developed within a geological Site of Special Scientific Interest. An application submitted to the Isle of Wight County Council in the early 1970s for development of a cliff top site with holiday bungalows was refused by the Council but was subsequently won on appeal; this was against the technical advice

offered by the County Surveyor and Planning Officer at that time. Rates of erosion on this soft cliff line, which are subject to wave action from the west and from deflected waves through the Western Solent, result in cliff retreat of up to 3 m a year after some winters. Coastal erosion together with seepage and weathering has resulted in cliff retreat and the loss of some cliff top properties along this frontage.

As a result of this relatively recent development, pressure was increased to carry out some form of coastal defence works to protect the properties and a scheme was prepared and an application submitted to the Ministry of Agriculture, Fisheries and Food for coast protection grant aid. Following detailed discussions with English Nature, which extended over a considerable period it was agreed that two groynes should be constructed along this frontage in timber with rock stubs at the cliff base together with limited beach nourishment. It was agreed that this particular option would fulfil the coast protection needs by reducing the rate of erosion but nevertheless would still allow some limited cliff weathering and thereby maintaining this very important exposure.

This was a low cost scheme (approximately £70 000) and the site is being monitored to assess the impact of works on the SSSI and on the residential properties. Property owners were advised that, bearing in mind the earth science conservation interests and the benefit costs available for this scheme, this was the minimum option that could be pursued. Following the publication of PPG20 it is most unlikely that a development such as that at Brambles Chine would be approved today.

2. Alum Bay

The owners of Alum Bay Theme Park have been concerned for some time about a lowering of beach levels at Alum Bay, particularly in the vicinity of the foot of Alum Bay Chine where the lower station of the chairlift structure is located on the beach. In recent years the owners have noticed a reduction in beach levels (comprising coarse flint pebbles) of 1–2 m and sought the Council's assistance in identifying a coast protection option for this site. The Council was, of course, fully aware of the international importance of the Alum Bay site and was concerned both about the impact of any potential works as well as the benefit costs that could be achieved for a scheme at this location. It was agreed that the sensible option was to monitor beach levels over a longer period to assess any changes that may be taking place. The development of a Shoreline Management Plan for the Isle of Wight should assist at locations such as this by making recommendations on monitoring so that an effective base for coastal change can be established.

3. Blackgang Chine
The extraordinary geological and geomorphological importance of the southwest coast of the Isle of Wight has been explained elsewhere. At Blackgang a tourist attraction was developed within the Chine in the 19th century and has expanded to become one of the Island's leading theme parks. The hamlet of Blackgang included a number of substantial properties and cottages in the 19th century and over the intervening period, with cliff recession approaching 100 m, many of these properties have been lost. The main economic value of this site is therefore the theme park itself.

Blackgang Chine faces the southwest and the cliffs receive the full impact of southwesterly storm waves, together with processes of landsliding and sub-aerial weathering and seepage erosion of the cliff face. Following the major landslide at Blackgang in January 1994, which was the latest of a succession of major events particularly over the last 40 years, a study was commissioned into the options for management of the Blackgang frontage. Taking account of the scale of ground movements, the earth science conservation importance of this section of coastline and the limited enclave of development in the vicinity of the theme park, it was resolved that no action should be taken or was practically possible, with respect to coastal defence along this frontage; the Blackgang frontage is therefore being regarded as an area of 'managed retreat'. With respect to the southwest coast as a whole the *Management Strategy for the Coastal Zone* published by South Wight Borough Council (1993) included the following recommendations:

i. The special landscape, ecological and environmental value of the southwest coast of the Island is fully recognized.

ii. A policy of managed retreat will be practised along this coastline with the exception of possible works to protect part of the A3055 Military Road between Compton Bay and Afton Down.

4. A3055 Military Road at Afton Down
The important tourist route, the A3055 Military Road, which forms part of the 'round the Island' coastal network, provides spectacular views for motorists and pedestrians close to the summit of Afton Down. The views from this route are impressive both looking westwards towards Freshwater Bay and Tennyson Down, as well as back along the southwest coast of the Island towards Blackgang and St Catherines Down. One particularly vulnerable location along the A3055 was on the eastern flank of Afton Down where a capping of glacial deposits overlay the junction of the Lower Chalk and Upper Greensand. At this particular point the carriageway is within 12 m of the cliff edge. A significant realignment of the carriageway inland proved unacceptable to English Nature due to the important cliff top vegetation habitats. Weathering and erosion has been reducing this distance at the rate of between 0.2–0.3 m a year. Following detailed discussions with the National Trust and English Nature, a limited stabilization scheme has been undertaken recently to extend the life of the carriageway on its existing alignment at this point. The work comprised battering back a short section of the cliff top and anchoring the loose material with netting and with pre-grown turf; it is hoped that these small scale remedial measures will be effective in maintaining the life of the road on its present alignment in the short to medium term and at the same time having a nil effect on the ecological environment and earth science interest of this dramatic section of the Island's coast.

5. The Ventnor Undercliff
The Isle of Wight Council and its predecessor, South Wight Borough Council, has developed comprehensive strategies for management of the Ventnor Undercliff landslide complex. A key element of its landslide Management Strategy has been protection of the coastline. Historically, coastal defences have taken a variety of forms including concrete and masonry walls, an offshore breakwater and rock groynes and rock revetments. Coastal

Fig. 7.9. The coastline of the Ventnor Undercliff landslide complex.

defences are of course confined only to those areas of significant habitation where there is economic justification for carrying out a scheme. The Council recognizes fully the importance of the Undercliff both in earth science conservation and ecological terms and wishes to take these aspects into account when developing future coast protection schemes and when planning refurbishment works.

In order to reduce the visual impact of coastal works wherever possible, a number of schemes have been undertaken involving the provision of rock revetments. An example of this is the Ventnor Western cliffs, a soft cliff line of reconsolidated landslide debris comprising chalk and Upper Greensand debris that had been deposited and consolidated gradually over the last 8–10 000 years. Careful selection of suitable rock armourstone resulted in the use of Carboniferous Limestone from the Mendip Hills in Somerset which blends well with the Lower Chalk and Upper Greensand debris which comprise the cliffs. The result has been the provision of approximately 1.5 km of rock revetment which fulfils the coastal protection needs of this particular frontage but is not detrimental to the visual amenity and maintains the exposure of the upper cliff which is a valuable example of landslide and mass movement processes including solifluction.

Within the Undercliff there are considerable lengths of undeveloped coastline and the natural processes of landsliding and other ground movement types have been able to take place uninterrupted and provide a habitat for a wealth of important invertebrate species. Within the Undercliff itself other sites of earth science conservation interest set slightly further back from the coast, including the rear scarp cliff itself and the Lowtherville graben, have remained undeveloped for stability reasons. This has resulted in their preservation and they represent sites of international importance for the study of the processes of landsliding.

6. Bonchurch to Luccombe Cliff line
This section of cliff is entirely within the Cretaceous, and at the southern end of Sandown Bay comprises rocks principally of the Ferruginous Sands which dip gently southwards. A distinctive feature of Sandown Bay is its wide fine sandy beaches, the sand being derived from the erosion of the cliffs through much of the Bay. Apart from Redcliff near Culver Cliff at the northern end of Sandown Bay and the high cliffs south of Shanklin Chine, much of this source of supply has been cut off as a system of coastal defences was developed. The longshore drift generally carries sand northwards through the bay; a system of timber and concrete groynes maintain beaches to prevent the bulk of sand migration. The cliff line, therefore, south of Shanklin Chine round to Monks Bay at Bonchurch is a valuable source of material for the beaches to the north and is also of considerable conservation interest, forming the seaward flank of the Bonchurch Landslip SSSI. This frontage is regarded as sacrificial coastline in the interests of preserving the Sandown Bay sediment budget. In its coastal management strategy for this section, South Wight Borough Council noted that 'the importance of the cliff line between Monks Bay, Bonchurch and Shanklin Chine as a source of beach material for Sandown Bay is recognised. It is recommended that no coastal defence work should be carried out on this frontage, although a rocktrap fence may be provided south of Shanklin Chine'. This approach, bearing in mind the earth science conservation interest of the frontage, has provided

a sound basis for a decision against carrying out coastal defence works at this location.

Coastal strategies for the future

As part of the development of the Isle of Wight Shoreline Management Plan and the Isle of Wight Unitary Development Plan, specific strategies will be applied to ensure that the earth science conservation and coastal defence interests of vulnerable sections of the Isle of Wight coastline are managed effectively.

The development by the former South Wight Borough council of a management strategy for its coastal zone covering approximately three-quarters of the Island's coastline was a major step forward in terms of management of the coastal zone on the Isle of Wight. The Isle of Wight Council proposes to produce a management strategy for the whole of its coastline taking account of the new Department of the Environment 'Policy Guidelines for the Coast' as well as the 'Best Practice Guide for Coastal Zone Management'. This new unitary document will attempt to reconcile all the interests involved within the coastal zone through a comprehensive consultation process. With respect to coastal defence aspects, these will be addressed through the Isle of Wight Shoreline Management Plan which is currently being prepared and is overseen by a steering group which includes a representative from English Nature.

Whilst the former South Wight Borough Council's *Management Strategy for the Coastal Zone* divided the Isle of Wight coast into six sub-cell units based on the best available knowledge of sediment transport of that time, a Shoreline Management Plan, for which resources have been made available by the Ministry of Agriculture, Fisheries and Food and by the Isle of Wight council, will be able to define management units more accurately in order that strategic policies can be developed for each frontage. The importance of earth science conservation in the Isle of Wight coast from scientific, environmental and economic (touristic) reasons is fully recognized and therefore every effort will be made to ensure that the strategies put in place are acted upon and prove sustainable for the future.

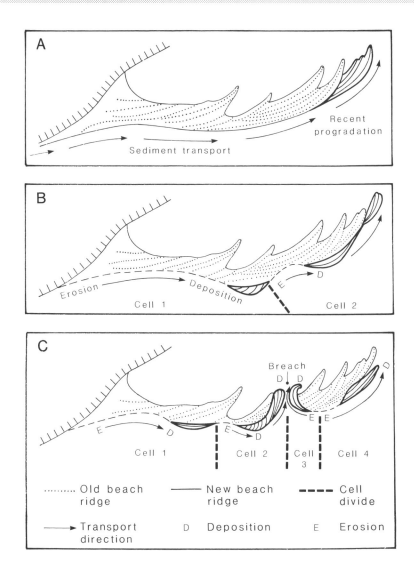

Fig. 8.1. The movement from a drift dominated barrier (A) to a system of barrier longshore reworking (B) and eventually barrier breaching (C) as cannibalization leads to sub-wave sediment cells and washover sites (after Orford *et al.* 1991).

supply fluctuations and incident wave climate, in particular, extreme sea-levels associated with storms. Together these long term macroscale controls set the framework by which barrier types develop. One of the principles now elucidated with coastal gravel deposition is that longshore sediment supply is effectively controlled by the rate of sea-level rise. This is based on an assumption that the sediment source is a thin veneer of readily available sediment resting on a landward rising lithified basement (Forbes *et al.* 1995). As SLR decreases then longshore supply will also diminish. Once longshore sediment supply finishes the available undiminished wave power will start to cannibalize the existing sediment of the barrier. This is seen by perturbations in the longshore barrier continuity, identified with the development of low-order wave sediment cells (Fig. 8.1). The up-drift sediment source areas of such cells are the likely breach positions under storm activity (Orford *et al.* 1991).

Porlock gravel barrier

Porlock barrier is located along the high cliffed coast of Somerset fronting on to the macro-tidal Severn estuary (Fig. 8.2). Burial of the cliffs during periglacial phases created a veneer of unconsolidated heterogenous sized sediment available for toe-slope removal by later wave action. The present cliff shows exhumed features of older cliffs cut into basement rock. There is a current dearth of major sediment supply to the beach zone apart from some recent slides caused by human induced changes in the vegetation of the cliff. Porlock makes a re-entrant trap at the eastern end of the Exmoor Plateau for the longshore drift of gravel moving east under the dominant westerly Atlantic waves. Gravel sediment has been held in the form of a single barrier along the length of the re-entrant. The gravel is breached contemporaneously in one position (Porlock Weir harbour) but is virtually coherent along its length to Hurlestone Point, its eastern terminus.

The barrier is divided into morpho-sedimentary units which indicate the longshore development trend of the barrier (Fig. 8.3). Under a modern reducing sediment supply, the up-drift end is sediment starved such that at Porlockford the barrier has been

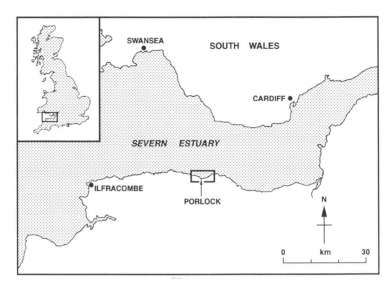

Fig. 8.3. Location of Porlock barrier, Somerset.

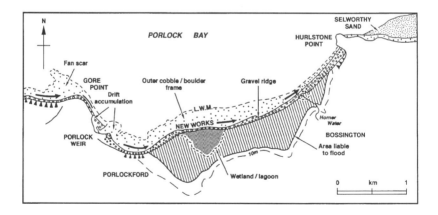

Fig. 8.3. Morpho-sedimentary structure of Porlock barrier.

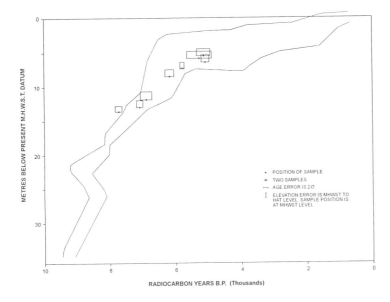

Fig. 8.4. Sea-level curve for the Severn Estuary (after Heyworth & Kidson 1982) in addition with new sea-level index points (Jennings *et al.*, in press) established from a palaeoecological reconstruction of inter-tidal and back-barrier sediments from Porlock.

overtopped and the barrier pushed landwards, while at the down drift end of the system, Hurlestone Point, the sediment is building up in the form of a substantial prograded ridge. This imbalance in sediment supply leads to inevitable problems with retaining the stability of the whole barrier.

Palaeoenvironmental reconstruction and implications for barrier development

Palaeoenvironmental reconstruction (pollen and ^{14}C dating) of core sediment taken from the foreshore and the existing back-barrier seasonal wetlands (Cooper *et al.* 1995; Canti *et al.* 1996) has produced a number of dated sea-level index points that substantiate and extend the relative HW to LW sea-level curve envelope derived

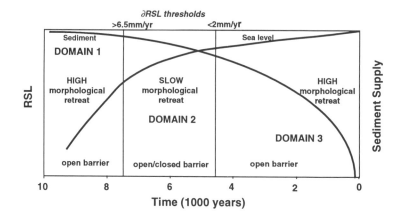

Fig. 8.5. Schematic domains of macroscale control on Porlock barrier through changing sea-level rise and longshore sediment supply during the Holocene.

by Heyworth & Kidson (1982) for the Severn Estuary (Fig. 8.4). We are now in a better position to identify the relative sea-level rise (SLR) over 9×10^3 year BP and assess its effect on sediment supply to the barrier. Of importance is that the organic sediments which provide the dating framework are identified as freshwater deposition and appear only between 5 and 8×10^3 year BP. Before and after this period, sedimentation is essentially inorganic mud. The shape of the relative SLR curve and the net sedimentation rate indicate essentially three phases of sea-level change rate that centre on and bracket this period of freshwater deposition.

This reconstruction distinguishes three domains of varying combinations of SLR and sediment supply (Fig. 8.5), which together control the morphosedimentary nature and response of Porlock barrier. High rates of SLR prior to 8×10^3 year BP would cause the barrier to retreat. Despite the large longshore sediment supply, the barrier would not hold its longshore continuity in the face of rapid horizontal shift in sea-level position, allowing continuous back-barrier flooding from a marine source. Given the high turbidity of the Severn estuary, the high inorganic mud content of this depositional phase is understandable (Allen 1990).

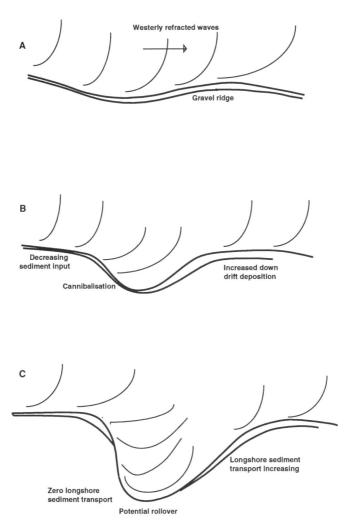

Fig. 8.6. Stages of cell development dependent on wave refraction re-
sponding to shoreline changes caused by variation in longshore transport
rates. (A) Drift-aligned gravel ridge with continuous longshore sediment
supply. (B) Intermittent sediment supply allows cannibalization to start
which perturbs the wave refraction pattern to reinforce the cell structure.
(C) Zero longshore sediment transport within the cell is a function of swash
alignment. Immediately downdrift of the zero longshore supply position is a
potential overwash site leading to barrier rollover.

As the SLR decreased *c.* 6×10^3 year BP ago the spatial translation of the barrier also slowed down. The longshore sediment supply, although reducing under a decreasing sea-level rate of rise, was still sufficient to allow existing barrier breaches to seal and allow the back-barrier area to change naturally to a freshwater situation (similar to the present-day artificially maintained situation). During this phase the freshwater organic deposition was maximized for a very limited period of the barrier history. This dominance indicates periods of barrier sealing in order for the lagoon to be fresh water dominated. At about 4×10^3 year BP ago the SLR had reduced to a point where sediment supply was so substantially reduced that the barrier started to break-up via cannibalization into major sub-cells. This allowed overwashing and barrier breaching that stopped any further major freshwater wetland growth. Further deposition was dominated by marine mud with occasional organic occlusions. Figure 8.6 demonstrates how the first longshore cell may have developed through sediment starvation and cannibalization.

Contemporary barrier and coastal lowlands: a coastal zone managment problem

The development of the contemporary barrier's structure therefore reflects the importance of macroscale status of SLR and longshore sediment supply. It also shows the importance and the modulation effect of mesoscale storminess which sets the modern longshore cannibalization rate and the new cellular structure that produces the stress positions at which the barrier is likely to be breached. Figure 8.7 shows how the present (1994) longshore barrier crest height reflects and helps identification of long-term sediment cells. Low crest positions indicate points of potential overwash. The current cell structure is identified in Fig. 8.8 based on height and morpho-sedimentary structure of cross-barrier profiles (positions 1–12 on Fig. 8.7).

At the present time Porlock has a back-barrier zone that is strongly defended from marine influences by a twentieth century history of groyning to both retard longshore sediment flux, and protect terrestrial drainage sluices. In recent years there have been

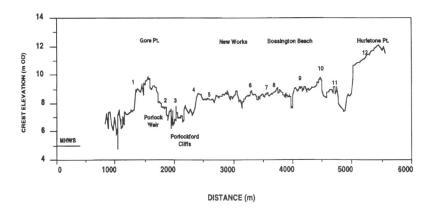

Fig. 8.7. The longshore variation in the crest elevation of Porlock gravel barrier (June 1994).

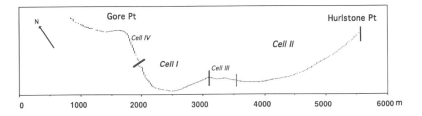

Fig. 8.8. The boundaries of wave-sediment cells recognized along Porlock Barrier. All cells are drift directed towards Hurleston Point.

attempts artificially to control lower stress positions along the barrier where overwashing has occurred, by dumping dredged river mouth deposits to build-up the barrier crest. The result of maintaining the barrier is that Porlock has coastal lowlands with both seasonally flooded pastures (fresh water) and permanent fresh water lagoons lying within the high water limit. Such wetlands are rare in nearby north Devon and thus have been identified as designated areas by English Nature on conservation grounds.

It is important to realize that the artificial stabilization of barrier longshore continuity is a product only of the last few hundred years and has been imposed by humankind. Hence the current seasonal freshwater wetlands and pasture are not the natural landscape of the back-barrier and have been established at the expense of the barrier. The problem is that there is an accelerating urgency of keeping up the protection levels on the barrier to sustain the current agricultural usage of the lowlands. There is, however, a major coastal zone management problem in that there are two landowners of the Porlock barrier. The boundary between a private landowner to the west and the National Trust to the east is approximately at the boundary between cell III and cell II (Fig. 8.8). The increasing sediment starvation and cannibalization of cell I allows the barrier at the southern edge of cell I to be overwashed and breached during severe storms. The rough pasture land behind the barrier is frequently flooded by salt water so that the landowner wants to re-build the barrier to prevent overwash and to this end attempts to bulldoze overwash material back up the back slope of the barrier. He has also augmented the depleted barrier by replenishment of dredged material from the entrance of Porlock Weir. This material is too poorly mixed for a sustainable increment to the barrier and prevents matrix infiltration of backwash from storm wave water on the barrier face. Thus the surface return of backwash quickly erodes into the fill and headward erodes the barrier crest. There is a further problem in this rebuilding of the barrier in that engineered beach profiles are far too steep at the crest relative to stable beach profiles in downdrift areas (cf. profile 4 with profiles 9 and 11: Fig. 8.9).

The source of optimum sediment (type, size and volume) for any future barrier engineering lies in the accumulation found on the down-drift area under National Trust (NT) control. After some considerable internal and external debate NT now recognize the implications of non-sustainable coastal engineering – once started, forever committed, and now are resolved not to undertake engineering of coastal properties unless non-action can be seen as having direct consequences in terms of life and limb. It has a national policy of non-intrusion into the coastal zone and has refused to allow sediment to be taken from their end of the barrier to replenish that of the eastern end. English Nature have designated the lands at the rear of the barrier as a SSSI given that the seasonal freshwater flooding behind a fixed barrier leads to wetlands which

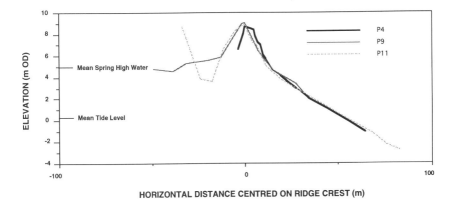

Fig. 8.9. Comparison of rebuilt profile 4 with natural profile 9 and 11. Note the over steepening of the upper barrier area on P4 compared with P9 and P11.

are rare in Devon. They feel that the barrier should be maintained. The people of Porlock village also believe the barrier should be replenished given the threat of increasing coastal flooding. The scene is set for a confrontation as the private landowner wants the Environment Agency to pay for this ongoing barrier replenishment, who in turn are reluctant to spend substantial sums on a structure which under MAFF guidelines should be allowed to retreat naturally. The situation is further distorted by the fact that Porlock barrier sits within the boundaries of Exmoor National Park (AONB) which has guidelines on conserving the landscape. Initially, the scientific lobby which supported the view of NT that the coast should be left alone, was in turn supported by the range of organizations concerned. During the winter of 1994–95 these barrier sections breached again during a severe storm. In the face of public pressure, representatives of the Exmoor National Park, the local water authority, the local MP and MEP thought that the landowner had a justifiable case (despite the scientific view) while the then NRA agreed to spend £5000 on helping to maintain the barrier. Although such defences are only supporting current agriculture, there is a clear perception within Porlock village that such defence of the barrier is ultimately important as flood control for protection of built property, despite the elevation of the village above current flood limits.

Constraints on the future management of Porlock barrier

The morphosedimentary structure of gravel-based barriers essentially reflects longshore sediment supply. This can be seen in terms of barrier development switching from a drift-aligned system with surplus sediment supply to a swash-aligned system where sediment is scarce. Porlock barrier now has swash-aligned status due to the last several thousand years of reducing SLR rise rate. Although swash-alignment is associated with attempts of the morphology to minimize wave energy by transforming the barrier into sub-cells, there is always a problem that reduction of sediment supply leads to barrier instability and breaching. On this basis, swash-aligned gravel barriers should not be viewed as coherent elements persistent over time and space. Their longevity ultimately depends on SLR rate. Barriers under SLR can hold their position only if sufficient sediment is available, they will retreat or fail when sediment supply is reduced. Barriers appear to be able to retain some longshore coherence when retreating, by rolling over themselves through overwash. However, even this process can only continue for a limited time and the spatial consequences of gravel barrier retreat must be recognized in barrier breakdown through breaching and sub-cell development. As a consequence, incursions of marine water and sediments into the back-barrier area and the demise of a dominant freshwater seasonal wetland is probable.

The option taken at Porlock is to attempt to stabilize the barrier at breach positions. The question needs to be posed as to where this course of action will take the barrier. As sea-level rises so the return periods associated with storms capable of overwashing the ridge will decrease. The crest will increasingly reduce in elevation unless artificially nourished. The rate of nourishment needs to increase geometrically if a stable profile is to be held (Dillon 1970). This will be unlikely given the cost benefit of this operation and the economic marginality of protected land. Partial rebuilding of the crest forces the barrier into greater disequilibrium. The longer this support is given, the greater the potential catastrophe to the back-barrier area, because when the barrier finally fails under rising sea-level, the more substantial the inundation will be. If the barrier is allowed to respond to current sediment starvation in a natural way then overwash pushes the barrier further into swash alignment, minimizes longshore sediment transport, allows limited marine incursions and prepares the management of the coastal lowlands for a policy of managed vegetation retreat rather than catastrophic loss.

Conclusion

A pessimist might argue that the coastal management situation at Porlock is only a microcosm of CZM in the UK as a whole! There is no coherent strategy, with national guidelines having been breached and scientific evaluation ignored. A naturally breaching gravel barrier has been artificially managed into an unsustainable fixed feature. A precedent for barrier stabilization has been made which will be recalled increasingly in the future. The stabilization of a barrier out of equilibrium with sediment supply, sea-level change and climate change will, inevitably, leave the barrier needing continuing support to maintain its position in the immediate future, at a cost which is unlikely to be matched by benefit.

Acknowledgements

The work on Porlock barrier was undertaken as part of EU Environment and Climate Programme: No. EV5V-CT93-0266. Discussions with government and NGO representatives on the Porlock Management Group are willingly acknowledged. Interpretations of data and comments on CZM are entirely the responsibility of the authors.

References

Allen, J. R. L. 1990. The Severn Estuary in Southwest Britain – its retreat under marine transgression and fine-sediment regime. *Sedimentary Geology*, **66**, 13–28.

Canti, M., Hea, V., McDonnell, R., Straker, V. & Jennings, S. 1996. Archaeological and palaeoenvironmental evaluation of

Porlock Bay and Marsh. *Archaeology in the Severn Estuary, 1945,* **6**, 49–69.

Carter, R. W. G., Johnston, W. & Orford, J. D. 1984. Formation and significance of stream outlets on the mixed sand and gravel barrier coasts of southeast Ireland. *Zeitschrift fur Geomorphologie,* **28**, 427–442.

Cooper, J. A. G., Orford, J. D., McKenna, J., Jennings, S. C., Scott, B. & Malvarez, G. 1995. *Meso-scale Behaviour of Atlantic Coastal Systems under Secular Climate and Sea-level Rise.* CEC Environment and Climate programme, No. EV5V-CT93-0266. Final Report.

Dillon, W. P. 1970. Submergence effects on a Rhode Island barrier and lagoon and inference on barrier migration. *Journal of Geology,* **78**, 94–106.

Forbes, D. L., Orford, J. D., Carter, R. W. G., Taylor, R. B., Shaw, J. & Jennings, S. C. 1995. Morphodynamic evolution, self-organisation and instability of coarse-clastic barriers on para-glacial coasts. *Marine Geology,* **126**, 63–85.

Heyworth, A. & Kidson, C. 1982. Sea-level changes in southwest England and Wales. *Proceedings of the Geologists' Association,* **93**, 91–111.

Houghton, J. T., Jenkins, G. J. & Ephramus, J. J. 1990. *Climatic Change: The IPCC Scientific Assessment.* Cambridge University Press, UK.

Jennings, S. C., Orford, J. D., Canti, M., Devoy, R. N. J. & Straker, V. The role of relative sea-level rise and changing sediment supply on holocene gravel barrier development: the example of Porlock, Somerset, UK. *Holocene,* in press.

Orford, J. D., Carter, R. W. G. & Jennings, S. C. 1991. Coarse clastic barrier environments: evolution and implications for Quaternary sea-level interpretation. *Quaternary International,* **9**, 87–104.

Orford, J. D., Carter, R. W. G. & Jennings, S. C. 1996. Control domains and morphological phases in gravel-dominated coastal barriers. *Journal of Coastal Research,* **12**, 589–605.

Randall, R. E. 1977. Shingle foreshores. *In:* Barnes, R. S. K. (ed.) *The Coastline,* Wiley, London, 49–61.

9 The mobility of coastal landforms under climatic changes: issues for geomorphological and archaeological conservation

Hervé Regnauld, Loïc Lemasson & Vincent Dubreuil

Summary

- On the coastline of Brittany (Western France) many geomorphological features are exposed to wave erosion. These features are made of periglacial Weichselian slope deposits, covered by Holocene dunes and they include some prehistorical artefacts (flints, ceramics, kitchen middens).

- The response of these features to coastal erosion is retreat, accompanied by many block falls and slides. These falls have two consequences: they destroy some periglacial relics (ice wedges, patterned soils), or storm surge deposits, which are not found again landward; they expose new parts of the cross sections, in which new artefacts are found.

- A conservation policy has to be defined in relation to the specificity of each site.

Introduction

The constant action of the sea on cliff exposures is often considered an easy method to maintain geological exposures in a clean and visible state. Active wave erosion prevents the colonization and growth of vegetation. This point has been mentioned very often on the southern coast of Britain. In France some sites have been specially protected (South of Ile de Groix, for instance) in order to let the sea erode interesting exposures or mineral outcrops. A policy of cliff retreat to maintain conservation interest assumes the exposed geological features are unchanged landward. This is true of many sedimentary layers, deposited over long periods of time under relatively homogeneous conditions. However, many sites are different from this model and coastal retreat may well destroy some information or reveal new geomorphological and geological features. Some examples are discussed below.

Coastal retreat and preservation of exposures: a loss of information?

In some cliff sites, the exposures which are submitted to wave action (and so are retreating) are very discontinuous and the sediment units do not present such a spatial continuity landward. In this case the coastal retreat results in a loss of information. In Northern Brittany most of the coastline is made of gently sloping crystalline cliffs, covered by highly variable periglacial deposits. The usual cross section in these deposits (Clet 1983) presents a basal layer of coarse grained grit and weathered rocks, occasionally organised in sorted bands. A thick cover (1–6 m) of head is frequently observed just above. The top of the section is characterized by aeolian deposits (0.2–1.2 m thick) then by dunes, the most ancient of them being historical.

During the last 10 years wind speed has greatly increased in Brittany and the wave climate has been modified. As a result, many coastal cross sections have receded at a very high and unusual rate (more than 1 m a year) and a considerable length of the coastline has been eroded. Figure 9.1 presents one example on the northern coast (close to St Malo) between 1990 and 1996. New exposures have been created in formerly vegetated areas. Thus, in the beginning of the 1990s a considerable amount of new information was offered to the coastal scientists. The interpretations of Clet (1983) were modified. The new studies have been focused on two periods of time. The first one is the Late Glacial period. The new exposures (and new TL dates) have allowed reinterpretation of the former works. In Baie de St Bieuc, Loyer *et al.* (1995) have shown that the base of the cross section could be dated from stage 7 (instead of 5) and that two glacial periods were superimposed in the so called 'head deposit'. Many different phases are recognized between 5a and 5e, stages 4 and 3 are not showing many signs of periglacial activity, whereas stage 2 is marked by some traces of active permafrost. On the southern coast Van Vliet-Lanoe *et al.*

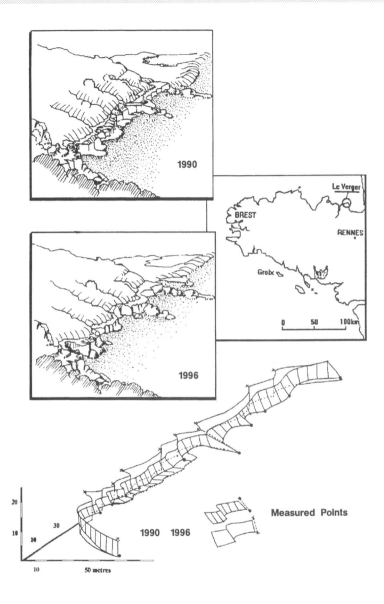

Fig. 9.1. Location of one site in Northern Brittany, the Anse du Verger. Two views of this site, in 1990 and 1996, and associated profiles of the retreating cliffs.

(1995) have taken the opportunity of new erosion in old exposures to demonstrate that some features, formerly attributed to ice were, in fact, due to palaeoseismic activity. These features are discontinuous and unevenly distributed. The cliff retreat would destroy patterns that may not be found again. Coastal retreat, in this case, produces a loss of information.

The second period which was extensively studied after the opening of new cross-sections is the late Holocene. Many ancient dune fields have been discovered and dated, showing that dunes were older than previously thought. In some places (namely Hoedic Island, Groix Island, Le Verger bay) palaeo storm surge deposits were observed in these dunes, as in the Netherlands coastal system (Jelgersma et al. 1995), and dated (Regnauld et al. 1995). Some of them are shells disposed in narrow and discontinuous lines. Most often they are a mixture of broken shells and marine sands, very badly sorted. Grain size analysis and morphoscopy demonstrates that these layers are made of submarine sand washed over the top of former barriers during high energy events.

A tentative correlation of storm surge deposits with the sea level curve is presented in Fig. 9.2. This figure is a compilation of data from Bernard (1995), Bernard & Visset (1992), Gruet et al. (1992, 1994), Visset et al. (1990, 1994), Sommé et al. (1992), Regnauld et al. (1995) and of Pirazzoli (1991). It presents the type of data which were used to construct sea level curves (symbols 1–5) and proposes some possibilities to draw the curve, according to the inferred reliability of the data. Symbol 7 shows some kind of smoothed curve, where extreme points have not been used. It is interesting to note that storm surge deposits are correlated with periods when the data are very much scattered above and under the smoothed curve. A debate is opening about the relative importance of surges and sea level indicators. Some sea level indicators, such as flooded peat bogs, may be indicating occasional floods rather than an actual sea level rise. The only way to resolve this debate is to search for a precise chronology of late Holocene storms. Figure 9.2 is not intended as anything other than a proposal for more discussion. Each time a storm surge deposit is destroyed because of coastal retreat, some information is lost.

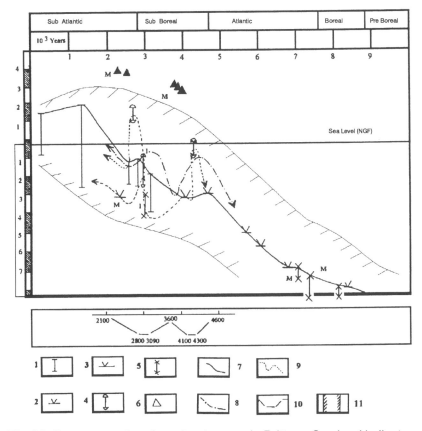

Fig. 9.2. Some examples of sea level curves in Brittany. Sea level indicators are as follows: 1, living amplitude of inter-tidal shells; 2, upper limit of salt water, from plants; 3, upper limit of salt water, from pollens; 4, living amplitude of inter-tidal plants in tidal changes; 6, storm surge deposits; 7, smoothed curve, using only the 1, 2 and 3 symbols, with the higher limit of the ecological amplitude of the shells. This curve is obviously wrong for the last 2000 years; 8, and 9, two possible curves, if all the data points are given the same importance (8, Channel; 9, Atlantic); 10, relative variation of the sea level in Vendée, after bog vegetation and submerged forest (sketch at the base of the figure); 11, proposal for a smoothed area, in which sea 'level' indicators are likely to be found, either associated with mean sea level or occasional floods, or surges. The middle of the Subboreal and the beginning of the Atlantic are supposed to be periods of higher storm activity. Data are compiled from Bernard (1985), Bernard & Visset (1992), Gruet *et al.* (1992), Gruet & Souriau (1994), Visset *et al.* (1990,1994), Sommé *et al.*, (1992), Regnauld *et al.*, (1995) and Pirazzoli (1991).

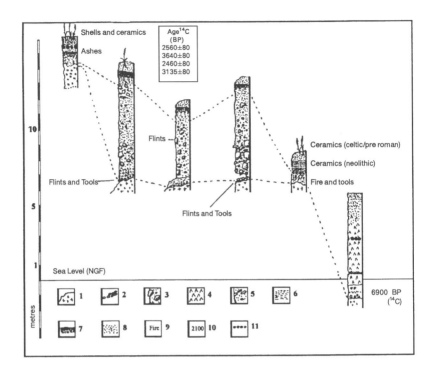

Fig. 9.3. Cross-section in Le Verger: 1, basement; 2, palaeo shingle beach (stage 5? 7?); 3, head, with intercalated periglacial sequences; 4, peat; 5, sorted beds of blocks and fine sediment; 6, aeolian deposits (stage 2?); 7, palaeo dune and soil (pre Boreal); 8, Modern dunes (historical); 9, artefacts: 10, C14 dates of shells in the dune; 11, Storm surge deposits.

Coastal retreat and the discovery of new prehistoric artefacts: more knowledge

Coastal erosion of exposures may also be very useful as it is excavating naturally places where archaeological remains are likely to be found. One of the most famous places with a half submerged neolithic stone circle is a small island in Golfe du Morbihan, Er Lannic. In this site sea action washes away the silt and mud around the stones and keeps them visible. On the northern coast of Brittany the recent retreat of cliffs has revealed many interesting new sites.

Figure 9.3 presents a cross-section (in Anse du Verger) in which many artefacts were found between 1990 and 1996.

At the base of the section, where a palaeo shingle beach is present, two clusters of flint tools were found. They are 55 m apart. The tools were used to pierce, cut and scrape, and analysis of them is still going on. Inside the head deposit (which displays many different facies) many isolated flint tools were located and collected. Some of them were included in fallen blocks and were not *in situ*. Others have been taken into solifluxion lobes. These tools are large pebbles (10 cm across) with a sharp edge and a very rough handle.

At the top of the section, lying on an aeolian bed (symbol 6 of Fig. 9.3) the remains of a camp fire were discovered in March 1996. A storm, associated with a very high spring tide had washed away a large body of beach sand, exposing the top of the aeolian beds, in which the camp fire was found, with some ceramic fragments. Two distinct layers of aeolian sand contain ceramics.

This site is highly fragile. Solutions were proposed in order to protect it from the next high spring tide, but protection was not allowed, as the policy of the local authorities is to let the coastline retreat at its own rate. In April the site was half destroyed and covered by a new layer of beach sand. In May, it was gone. During the few days of the neap tides it had been carefully studied and mapped. Work is still going on, with what is left of the surroundings and with the artefacts that were collected.

A tentative chronology may be proposed, though it is not a definitive one. The palaeo shingle beach, with the two clusters of tools might be associated with an interglacial high stand. If the St Brieuc Baie chronology may be extended here, this could be stage 7. The tools within the head are not dated. The ceramics belong to two different periods. The lower ones are associated with the neolithic period and are probably linked to kitchen middens found 300 m apart and dated from 3800 to 2600 BP. The upper ones are more probably Celtic and pre-Roman artefacts.

More information will appear as the cliff retreats landward, though, this information has to be extracted from the site as soon as it appears, and before it is eroded. The usual behaviour of this cliff is to collapse during high spring tides and to remain stable during neap tides. This allows a 7–10 day period for monitoring the new

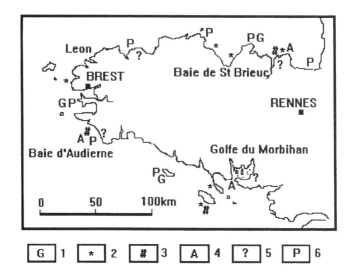

Fig. 9.5. Location of the main sites with geomorphological conservation issues in Brittany: 1, coastal erosion maintains good exposures; 2, erosion destroys Weichselian features; 3, erosion destroys Holocene features; 4, erosion destroys archaeological sites; 5, site where information has been irredeemably lost; 6, protected site.

differentiate the type of information that might be lost or gained in the process. This map tends to prove that no general policy can be defined. Local issues should be considered with local solutions and should not be treated with a uniform rule.

References

Bernard, J. 1995. Palynological studies of coastal peat bogs at la Parée beach (Vendée, France) indicate cyclic variations in the level of the Atlantic Ocean. *Quaternaire*, **6**, 159–166.

Bernard, J. & Visset, L. 1992. Une tourbière interglaciaire sur la plage de la Parée à Bretignolles (Vendée, France): première approche pollenanalytique. *Quaternaire*, **3**, 16–22.

Clet, M. 1983. *Le Plio Pleistocene en Normandie*. Apport de la palynologie. Thesis, University of Caen, 1–135.

Gruet, Y. & Souriau, P. G. 1994. Paléoenvironnements holocènes du marais poitevin (littoral Atlantique, France): reconstitution d'après les peuplements malacologiques. *Quaternaire*, **5**, 85–94.

Gruet, Y., Bernier, P., Meon, H. & Margerel, J. P. 1992. Une vasière intertidale du sub boréal en l'ile de Noirmoutier (Vendée, France). Approche biosédimentologique des variations holocènes du niveau marin. *Quaternaire*, **3**, 23–30.

Jelgersma, S., Stive, M. J. F. & van der Valk, L. 1995. Holocene storm surges in the coastal dunes of the western Netherlands. *Marine Geology*, **125**, 95–110.

Loyer, S., van Vliet-Lanoe, B., Monnier, J. L., Hallegouet, B. & Mercier, N. 1995. La coupe de Nantois (baie de St Brieuc, France): datations par thermoluminescence et données paléo environnementales nouvelles pour le Pleistocène de Bretagne. *Quaternaire*, **6**, 21–34.

Pirazzoli, P. A. 1991. *World Atlas of Holocene Sea Level Changes*. Elsevier, Amsterdam.

Regnauld, H., Cocaign, J. Y., Saliege, J. F. & Fournier, J. 1995. Mise en évidence d'une continuité temporelle dans la constitution de massifs dunaires du Sub Boreal à l'actuel sur le littoral septentrional de la Bretagne: Un exemple dans l'Anse du Verger. *Comptes Rendus de l'Académie des Sciences*, **321**, 303–310.

Regnauld, H. & Kuzucuoglu, C. 1992. Rebuilding of a dune field landscape after a catastrophic storm: beaches of Ille et Vilaine, Brittany, France. *In*: Carter, R. W. G., Curtis, T. G. S. & Sheedy-Skeffington, M. J. (eds) *Coastal Dunes, Geomorphology, Ecology and Management for Conservation*. Balkema, Rotterdam, 379–387.

Sommé, J., Munaut, A. V., Emontspohl, A. F., Limondin, N., Lefevre, D., Cunat, N., Mouthon, J. & Gilot, E. 1992. Weichselian ancien et Holocene marin à Watten (plaine maritime, Nord, France). *Quaternaire*, **3,** 87–90.

Van Vliet-Lanoe, B., Hallegouet, B., Bonnet, S. & Laurent, M. 1995. Evidences d'une activité séismique au Pleistocène moyen et supérieur dans le Massif Armoricain. Implications pour la dynamique du pergelisol européen. *Environnements Périglaciaires*, **2**, 3–22.

Visset, L., Girardclos, O. & Lambert, G. N. 1994. La forêt de

chênes sur tourbe, à l'ile d'Errand, dans les mariais de Brière
(Massif Armoricain – France) Palynologie et premiers résultats
dendrochronologiques. *Quaternaire*, **5**, 69–78.

Visset, L., Voeltzel, D., Maisoneuve, E., Nikodic, J., Margerel, J. P.
& Borne, D. 1990. Paleoécologie holocène des 'Marais du
Rocher' en Mazeillais (Vendée), dans le Marais Poitevin (littoral
Atlantique – France) *Quaternaire*, **1**, 111–122.

10 Spatial perspectives in coastal defence and conservation strategies

Malcolm Bray & Janet Hooke

Summary

- The concept of landform-orientated management based upon geomorphological knowledge is developed here to tackle the coastal defence and conservation problems associated with dynamic landforms. Simple, easily applicable criteria are compiled within a classification system for identifying and understanding the behaviour of 'landform units' within littoral cells.

- Such knowledge should assist the strategic planning of coastal defence so as to avoid adverse impacts.

- Where damaging interventions are already established, examples are presented of ways that landforms and geological exposures may be maintained in semi-natural states through manipulation of processes.

Introduction

The past five years have witnessed significant changes in attitudes towards the planning and practice of coastal defence in England and Wales. Long established piecemeal, site-specific and reactive methods have been replaced by strategic approaches developed within shoreline management plans (SMPs). Furthermore, traditional 'hard' engineering (structural) schemes are being superseded by 'softer' methods that accommodate natural processes. Such changes have special implications for the conservation of dynamic coastal landforms together with their dependent features of geological or ecological value.

Dynamic landforms are important components of open coasts formed as erosion, transport and deposition of sediments produce linked sequences of cliffs, beaches, shingle spits, barriers and nearshore banks. These landforms pose special conservation problems because their continued formation and existence commonly results from the balanced operation of natural processes, yet unrestricted process activity often poses coastal defence problems due to the historical legacy of valuable property and developments in hazardous locations. Inappropriate coastal defence or control measures may not only damage landforms themselves, but also their dependent features. Changes are commonly transmitted between linked landforms so as to create self-perpetuating sequences of adverse impacts extending over various spatial and temporal scales. Bray & Hooke (1995) identified many such problems as being the result of traditional site-focused management methods and they set out a geomorphological approach for understanding and managing landforms as components of dynamic natural process systems. Using examples, this paper demonstrates the practical uses of those methods and evaluates their applications within SMPs.

Classification of dynamic coastal landforms

The conceptual model of Bray & Hooke (1995) is adopted for classifying landforms according to fundamental systems criteria as outlined in Fig. 10.1. Primary differentiation is according to the *spatial dependence* of landforms within defined coarse sediment circulation systems or littoral cells. Degrees of dependence are indicated by the continuity of transport of those sediments that comprise the landform as discussed by Bray *et al.* (1995). Secondary classification into sediment sources, stores and sinks is then undertaken according to *position* and *function* within the cell. A further fundamental property of coastal landforms is their *capacity for self-regulation* which indicates their robustness or tolerance to change. Landforms sustained by, or with access to, abundant sediment can be considered infinite (robust) in terms of their capacity to adjust to forcing factors. Those that have limited sediment supplies, or that have become isolated from fresh sources have a finite capacity for self-regulation and are potentially more sensitive.

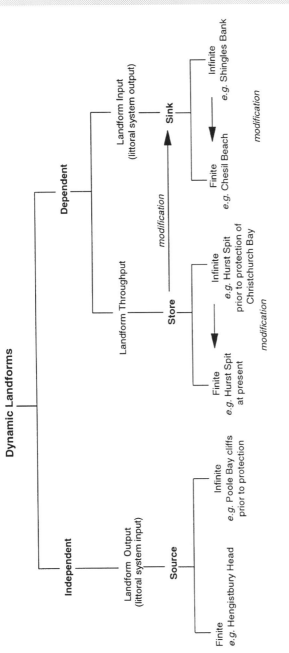

Fig. 10.1. Geomorphological classification scheme for dynamic landforms (based on Bray & Hooke 1995).

Landform stability and modification

Landforms *migrate* between classification categories as they and their parent transport systems slowly evolve, or suffer abrupt human modification (Fig. 10.1). Such modifications are usually followed at varying intervals by significant changes in landform behaviour and stability. Bray & Hooke (1995) found that linked sequences of modifications exacerbated by management reactions may intensify through positive feedback and eventually threaten the integrity of all dynamic landforms within a system (Fig. 10.2). Primary interventions interfere with or isolate sediment sources.

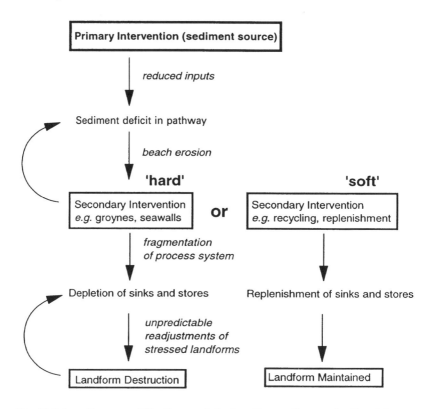

Fig. 10.2. Landform modification and destruction: self perpetuating interventions are generated by positive feedback. Note that impacts can be averted through adoption of 'soft' engineering approaches.

These lead to secondary interventions further downdrift as responses to the resulting beach depletion. Transport pathways become dislocated, landforms functioning as stores switch to finite open systems and sinks become sensitive closed systems. Ever increasing commitments towards additional measures can be engendered by initially modest, but poorly planned interventions. The stresses produced tend to increase the dynamism of landforms, thus prompting direct stabilization measures. Thus, by analysing landforms as functional components of littoral systems, their dynamic behaviour can be acknowledged fully alongside other coastal attributes.

Landform management within SMPs

Strategic management should aim to identify interdependencies and (i) avoid new damaging interventions (ii) break existing positive feedback sequences so as to restore or recreate process systems that can sustain dynamic landforms in the future. SMPs are eminently suitable for delivering such policies as they are deliberately formulated within process units and include specific objectives towards '*maintaining and enhancing the natural coastal environment*' (MAFF 1995). In spite of the diversity of approaches presently being applied, the problems posed by dynamic landforms can and should be tackled by a common method outlined as follows.

Each plan should develop a conceptual model of the behaviour of the coastal system and its component landforms according to the procedure outlined in Fig. 10.3. The first step is to explain the organization and natural evolution of the system based on an understanding of its geomorphological history. Secondly, the identification of system components (landforms), including their processes, forms, interlinkages and variability giving special attention to their position and function within the overall system (Fig. 10.1). Both 'natural' behaviour and the extent of modification need to be evaluated. It is proposed that analysis should result in identification of coherent 'landform units' including littoral and terrestrial elements. The potential effects of the strategic options of 'build forward', 'protect', 'retreat' and 'do nothing' should be evaluated for landform units alongside the existing land use

Identify Process Systems	→	Identify System Components (especially dynamic landforms)	→	Identify Typical Form, Processes and Extent of Modificartion	→	Ensure Freedom to Operate
• littoral cells • sub-cells • system boundaries		• sediment sources	→	• cliff erosion mechanisms • erosion rates • fluvial or marine sources • sediment yields	→	• avoid protection • control erosion rather than stabilise • mitigate impacts of protection with equivalent replenishment
• geomorphological history		• transport pathways	→	• littoral drift • offshore transport • effects of barriers	→	• remove key barriers • mitigate effects of key barriers e.g. bypassing
		• stores	→	• overall volume • historic stability • recent mass balance • sensitivity to depletion	→	• maintain or restore natural inputs • mitigate depletion using sustainable recycling or replenishment • prevent or delay outputs only as a last resort
		• sinks	→	• overall volume • historic stability • recent mass balance	→	• maintain or restore natural inputs • mitigate depletion using replenishment if sources available • control dynamism using 'soft' engineering methods to gain time for long term solutions

Fig.10.3. Conceptual model for evaluating dynamic landforms within SMPs (based on Bray & Hooke 1995).

oriented 'management units'. This would provide the stronger physical basis for decision making requested by some practitioners (Burgess & Frew 1996). In effect, a two-tier landform (long term) and management unit (short term) approach should be developed along broadly similar lines to that proposed by Townend *et al.* (1996). Long-term options should be developed that will permit free operation of key process components. Alternatives are feasible where it is possible to mitigate damaging modifications. This might involve compensatory replenishment, or removal of especially disruptive structures so as to permit natural systems to function. Finally, key landforms themselves, need to be monitored. Essential short term measures for addressing immediate hazards are best implemented within management units, but with regard to land-forms. Remedial measures in themselves might not offer permanent solutions, but they may gain valuable time for development of sustainable long term options.

Case studies

The principles of landform oriented management are illustrated by reference to sites within Poole and Christchurch Bays on the south coast of England (Table 10.1). In both cases, problems produced by site specific interventions are being tackled by strategic manage-ment coupled with innovative use of soft engineering methods.

System organization
A distinct sedimentary organization developed along the south coast of England during the relatively stable sea-levels of the late Holocene (past 5000 years) following the post-glacial marine transgression. Sediments were formerly abundant having been eroded and driven onshore by rapidly rising sea-levels of the mid-Holocene. Thereafter, new sediment sources became relatively scarce and extensive reworking by natural processes formed the present diverse arrangement of littoral cells, transport pathways and accretionary landforms (Bray *et al.* 1995). Within this latter phase, cliff erosion has become the major natural source of new sediments. Poole and Christchurch Bays themselves are products of

cliff erosion and long standing contributors of sediment to the littoral system.

Table 10.1. Case study sites: summary characteristics

	Hengistbury Head	Hurst Spit
Landform	eroding cliffs	drift-aligned shingle spit
Status	cliffs finite, beach dependent on updrift inputs	dependent store, supplies material to Shingles Bank
Dependent features	Tertiary geological exposures, archaeological features, saltmarsh habitats	lagoon and saltmarsh habitats, Hurst Castle ancient monument
Modifications	isolation from natural sediment source (updrift protection)	isolation from natural sediment source (updrift protection)
Recent behaviour	accelerating erosion	overwashing and rapid retreat
Future threats	erosion could eventually destroy dependent features	non-intervention likely to result in destruction

Hengistbury Head

Composed of an elevated (up to 36 m O.D.) outlier of predominantly sandy Lower Tertiary (Barton Group) materials, Hengistbury forms a prominent headland of steep eroding cliffs (Fig. 10.4) and is the only such site remaining unprotected within Poole Bay forming a distinctive 'landform unit' (Fig. 10.5). It affords valuable protection to Christchurch Harbour and its residential margins as well as being important for its environmental qualities and offering excellent exposures of the marginal sandy facies of the Barton Group (Bristow *et al.* 1991; Daley 1996). Stabilization by protection works (primary intervention) of the former eroding cliffs updrift has caused a sediment shortage and beach erosion within the bay, together with loss of most exposures (Fig. 10.6). Although problems at Bournemouth have been tackled successfully by several cycles of beach replenishment, erosion continues to accelerate at Hengistbury. Since its topography falls sharply inland, the headland is a finite resource threatened with destruction.

Fig. 10.4. Hengistbury Head: excellent exposures of Barton Group strata due to rapid erosion. Dark grey Boscombe sands are at the base. Overlying Barton Clay includes bands of ironstone nodules and is capped by pale Warren Hill Sands.

In appraising the options for protecting the headland (secondary intervention), Bournemouth Borough Council commissioned strategic studies that identified the need for controlled retreat rather than complete stabilization (Bray 1993; HR Wallingford 1993). It involves maintaining the beach at a critical width such that marine erosion of the cliff toe is controlled, at reduced rates that are nonetheless capable of providing cliff sediment inputs and maintaining geological exposures. A series of rock groynes, carefully designed and adjusted in terms of length and spacing are proposed by the local authority as the appropriate method of beach management (Fig. 10.7). The existing terminal Long Groyne provides a model, but has intercepted sediment too efficiently,

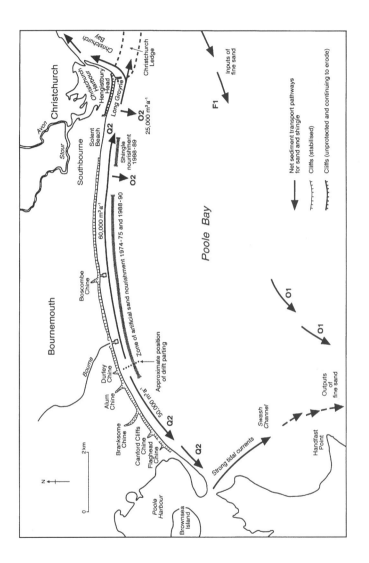

Fig. 10.5. Poole Bay: conceptual model of the process system. Note that Hengistbury Head is located downdrift of the extensive modifications to the west.

Fig. 10.6. Protected, partly stabilized cliffs in Poole Bay. Seawalls prevent sediment inputs to the beach and talus development rapidly conceals geological exposures. Artificial debris clearance is practised to maintain exposures at a few key sites.

promoting growth of sand dunes at the expense of geological exposures (Fig. 10.8). This suggests that contingencies for artificial clearance of exposures could also be necessary as practised elsewhere on the headland. Alternative methods of protection that incorporate maintenance of geological exposures are outlined by Powell (1993). The willingness of local authorities to consider such options is indicative of the changing attitudes to the management of shorelines. The proposed rock groynes would still have environmental and aesthetic impacts and there is still debate about the need for protection.

Hurst Spit
Situated at the eastern extremity of Christchurch Bay (Fig. 10.9), Hurst Spit forms part of a clockwise net sediment circulation that has historically been sustained by coast erosion and littoral drift (Q1 to Q6). Fines supplied from the eroding cliffs are progressively winnowed offshore (WO2 and WO3) so that supply to the spit (Q6)

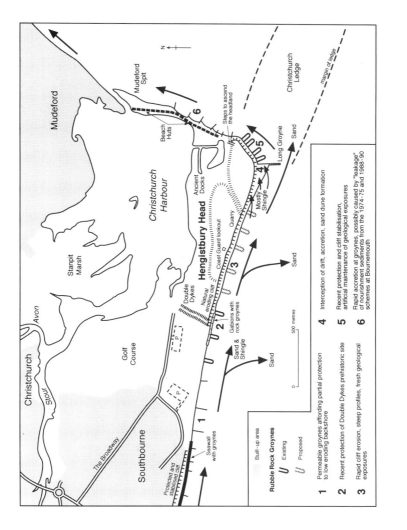

Fig. 10.7. Hengistbury Head site plan including locations of proposed rock groynes.

Fig. 10.8. Hengistbury Head: view east towards the Long Groyne. Note that sediment interception has caused beach and dune accretion so that adjoining cliffs are protected from wave action and geological exposures become covered by talus. Intercepted sediments are unavailable to downdrift coasts causing erosion problems and prompting extension of protection works eastward.

is almost entirely shingle (Nicholls & Webber 1987). Material drifting along Hurst Spit is lost offshore; entrained by strong tidal currents in Hurst Narrows and preferentially transported seaward (EO1) to the Shingles Bank that forms a sink for coarse material (Nicholls & Webber 1987; Dyer 1970; Velegrakis 1991). Wave dissipation occurs over the elevated crest of this bank and provides partial protection to the spit.

Major cliff segments at Highcliffe, Barton and Milford have been stabilised and protected with consequent loss of sediment supply (Lacey 1985). Associated shoreline structures and large rock groynes have intercepted beach drift and caused fragmentation of the natural littoral transport pathway. These practices have caused a downdrift sediment deficit that has depleted Hurst Spit, which

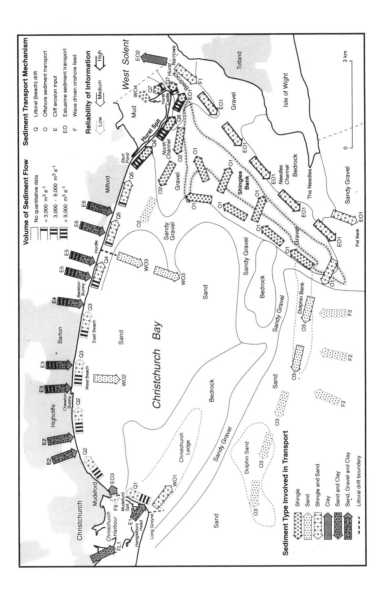

Fig. 10.9. Christchurch Bay: conceptual model of the process system (based on Bray et al. 1995).

Fig. 10. 10. Hurst Spit: recycling scheme in progress. Shingle is pumped on-shore and formed into a new free-standing barrier of similar configuration to the original prior to its depletion. The scheme is designed to maintain the stability of the spit by simulating the natural sediment supply process.

nevertheless continues to lose material offshore. The spit has become increasingly susceptible to overtopping and recent surveys have shown a major acceleration of recession compared with historical rates. Only continuous short term remedial works (Wright & Bradbury 1995), culminating in a major replenishment scheme in autumn 1996 (Fig. 10.10), have prevented its destruction. The replenishment is unusual in that it is intended to dredge the fill material from the Shingles Bank. Such actions are not normally permitted so close inshore, or in such shallow water due to fears of adverse shoreline impacts. In this case, the fill can be expected to return to its point of origin, so the scheme would constitute a recycling of material within a limited part of a single process system and wider impacts should be minimal. It is an example of a geomorphologically compatible solution based on systems under-standing. The alternative of permitting natural cliff inputs to resume updrift is not presently feasible due to the high concentra-tion of cliff top properties that would be put at risk.

Discussion

Within the examples presented, problematic modifications were so well established as to be considered irrevocable in the short to medium term. Thus, it was not feasible to tackle problems simply by removing interventions updrift so as to restore the original process systems. Instead, alternatives had to be developed by manipulating and simulating natural processes. Thus, at Hengist-bury, beach accretion will be carefully regulated and excess cliff talus removed mechanically, simulating toe erosion. At Hurst, replenishment sourced from the system sink should simulate natural inputs without producing additional adverse impacts. Perhaps the greatest problem is that these artificial systems will never operate as efficiently as their natural counterparts so that continuing material and technical inputs are likely to be necessary. For example, attempts to improve sediment retention may involve unacceptably large rock control structures. Consequently, long-term 'landform options' should be developed to ensure that: (i) new modifications are not produced, (ii) existing modifications are not reinforced and (iii) that opportunities to reinstate natural processes continue to be sought. Setback zones that regulate developments at the cliff-top to permit free retreat and maintain sediment yields are essential on the south coast of England.

To justify a landform oriented approach, conservationists must be able to demonstrate the value of the resource not only in terms of the landforms themselves, e.g. Goodman *et al.* (1996), but also the habitats, amenities and activities that they support (Leafe & Radley 1994; Brooke 1995).

Conclusion

Special approaches are needed for conserving dynamic coastal landforms and their valuable dependent features as integral parts of the landscape. It is important to recognize fully the status and positions of landforms within integrated process systems (littoral cells or sub-cells). A geomorphological classification of types based upon mutual interdependence is proposed for identification of landform units and aversion of damaging activities. Examples show

how this classification is applicable as the basis for conservation management even when there is very limited scope for complete restoration of natural processes due to established sequences of self-perpetuating, damaging past interventions. In these cases, careful simulation of natural processes appears to offer an alternative method of maintaining landforms, geological exposures and habitats. There are great opportunities for incorporating these considerations within the shoreline management plans being prepared by local authorities around England and Wales.

References

Bray, M. J. 1993. *Hengistbury Head Coast Protection Works: Impacts and Implications.* Report to the Borough Council of Bournemouth, Department of Geography, University of Portsmouth.

Bray, M. J. & Hooke, J. M. 1995. Strategies for conserving dynamic coastal landforms. In: Healy, M. G. & Doody, J. P. (eds) *Directions in European Coastal Management.* Samara, Cardigan, UK, 275–290.

Bray, M. J., Carter, D. J. & Hooke, J. M. 1995. Littoral cell definition and budgets for central southern England. *Journal of Coastal Research,* **11**, 391–400.

Bristow, C. R., Freshney, E. C. & Penn, I. E. 1991. Geology of the Country around Bournemouth. *Memoirs of the Geological Survey of the United Kingdom,* Sheet 329 (England and Wales), HMSO.

Brooke, J. 1995. Cost implications of dealing with environmental issues in river and coastal engineering schemes. *Journal of the Institution of Water and Environmental Managers* **9**, 1–6.

Burgess, K. & Frew, K. 1996. Shoreline management plans: thoughts for the future based upon practical experience. In: *Proceedings of the 31st MAFF Conference of River and Coastal Engineers, Keele.* MAFF publication No. PB 2666, 7.1.1.–7.1.8.

Daley, B. 1996. the Tertiary geological succession in Christchurch Bay. In: Bray M. *et al.* (eds) *Coastal Defence and Earth Science Conservation Field Excursion Guide,* University of Portsmouth, 5–21.

Dyer, K. R. 1970. Sediment distribution in Christchurch Bay, southern England, *Journal of the Marine Biological Association of the United Kingdom*, **50**, 673–682.

Lacey, S. 1985. *Coastal sediment Processes in Poole and Christchurch Bays, and the Effects of Coast Protection Works.* Unpublished PhD thesis, Department of Civil Engineering, University of Southampton.

Leafe, R. N. & Radley, G. 1994. Environmental benefits of soft cliff erosion. In: *Proceedings of the 29th MAFF Conference of River and Coastal Engineers.* MAFF, London, 3.1.1–3.1.13.

MAFF, 1995. *Shoreline Management Plans: A Guide for Coastal Defence Authorities.* Publication PB 2197, MAFF and the Welsh Office, London.

Nicholls, R. J. & Webber, N. B. 1987. The past, present and future evolution of Hurst Castle Spit, Hampshire. *Progress in Oceanography*, **18**, 119–137.

Powell, K. A. 1992. Engineering with conservation issues in mind. In: *Coastal Zone Planning and Management.* Thomas Telford, London, 237–249.

Townend, I. H. 1996. Defining shoreline management units for use in shoreline management planning. In: Fleming, C. A. (Ed.) *Coastal Management: Putting Policy into Practice.* Institution of Civil Engineers Conference Proceedings. Thomas Telford, London, 85–99.

Velegrakis, A. L. 1991. *Coarse-grained Sediment Deposits within Christchurch Bay: the Shingles Bank.* Report to New Forest District Council by the Department of Oceanography, University of Southampton.

Wright, D. & Bradbury, A. 1995. Hurst Spit and the Shingles Bank. In: *Inshore Dredging for Beach Replenishment? Papers and Proceedings of the SCOPAC Conference*, Lymington, 29 October 1994, 49–56.

11 Coastal erosion, coastal defences and the Earth Heritage in Scotland

R. G. Lees, J. E. Gordon & A. P. McKirdy

Summary

- Variations in rock type and structure, exposure, sediment supply and response to glacial loading have created a great diversity of landforms and active process environments along the coast of Scotland.

- Although coastal recession is not as widespread as in England, erosion in Scotland is prevalent within many beach–dune systems.

- Traditional responses to coastal erosion have involved sea-walls and rock-armour revetments, often resulting in loss of exposure and habitat, terminal scour and reductions in the natural dynamism and interest of the landforms.

- Current approaches being explored to address these problems include identification and description of the coastal cells of Scotland as a possible basis for the development of Shoreline Management Plans.

- Major reviews of the geomorphology of the Scottish firths and estuaries are also in progress, which will facilitate a more strategic approach to coastline management.

- Local initiatives include support for the assessment of specific problems and the development of solutions in partnership with local authorities and other interested parties.

Introduction

Scotland has a wonderfully diverse and dynamic coastline. At around 13 000 km in length, it encompasses over 60% of the British coastline. Extreme variation in exposure, rock type and structure, sediment supply and response to glacial loading have combined to create a distinctive and diverse range of landforms, active process environments and habitats. Thanks to its remoteness, much of the coastline remains undeveloped and undamaged by human interference.

In this paper we review briefly the nature of the Scottish coast and its geomorphological interest. We then examine the processes and patterns of coastal erosion, the resulting impacts and the traditional management responses. Finally, we discuss a range of alternative management approaches, including the application of Shoreline Management Plans based on the better understanding of physical processes achieved through the study of coastal cells.

Scotland's coastline: an Earth Heritage resource

The interest of the coastal geomorphology of Scotland comprises a range of landforms, sediments and processes and the interactions between them. Under the Geological Conservation Review 41 sites were identified to be of national importance under five distinct categories or networks.

Beaches of the Highlands and Islands (Fig. 11.1)
By far the largest group, these sites are characterized by extreme exposure, dynamism and change relative to the beaches of southern Scotland and England. Erosional landforms are widespread and many sites contain the distinctive machair landform and habitat. (Machair is defined as a wind built sand surface, stabilized by a sward of short grasses and herbs. It is synonymous in a landform sense with dune links or dune pasture, but is typically applied to coastal plains of north and west Scotland and characteristically composed of shell-rich sand.) Examples of sites within this network include Sandwood Bay and Dunnet Bay in Highland, Eoligarry on Barra, Ardivachar and Stoneybridge on South Uist, Machir Bay on Islay, Central Sanday in Orkney and St Ninian's Tombolo on Shetland. In a national (Great Britain) context, the beach complexes of the Highlands and Islands are important for:

- the machair landforms and habitats which are virtually unique in western Europe (some examples occur in NW Ireland);
- features associated with high-energy, exposed environments;

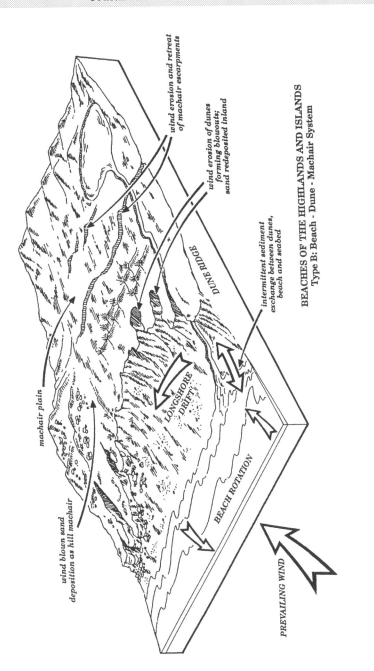

wind erosion and retreat
of machair escarpments

wind erosion of dunes
forming blowouts;
sand redeposited inland

DUNE RIDGE

intermittent sediment
exchange between dunes,
beach and seabed

BEACHES OF THE HIGHLANDS AND ISLANDS
Type B: Beach - Dune - Machair System

machair plain

LONGSHORE DRIFT

BEACH ROTATION

wind blown sand
deposition as hill machair

PREVAILING WIND

Fig. 11.1. Schematic diagram of the principal landforms and landforming processes of beach–dune coasts in the Highlands and Islands of Scotland. Drawing by C. Ellery.

- some of the largest and most impressive blown sand features; and
- features associated with glaciated coasts.

Beach and dune coasts of Lowland Scotland

These are typically large and comparatively stable beach–dune environments displaying less erosional landforms than their counterparts in the Highlands and Islands. Progradation of the coastline and of the beach and dune environments is a relatively common feature. Examples include Torrs Warren in Dumfries and Galloway, Strathbeg in Aberdeenshire, Tentsmuir in Fife and Morrich More in Highland. In a national (Great Britain) context, the beach complexes of Lowland Scotland are important for:

- some of the largest and most impressive blown sand features;
- some of the most extensive areas of sand coast progradation;
- features associated with glaciated coasts.

Shingle structures

Modern, active shingle structures occur relatively infrequently, although there are extensive suites of raised shingle ridges in many areas. This network comprises three sites only. Two of these, at Whiteness Head in Highland and Spey Bay in Moray, are among the most dynamic features on the Scottish coastline, the spits there being capable of advancing by up to 30 m per year downdrift. The third site, the Ayres of Swinister, is on Shetland a comparatively stable triple tombolo feature.

Salt marshes

Saltmarshes are relatively limited in distribution in Scotland and are generally confined to a number of estuary, back barrier and loch-head settings. These marshes are often founded on sandy, rather than muddy, substrates. Examples include the salt marshes of Morrich More, Culbin, the Cree and Solway estuaries and Loch Gruinart on Islay. In a national context, the saltmarshes of Scotland are important for:

- features associated with isostatic uplift;

- relatively young features that allow comparisons with more developed systems in England; and
- features associated with loch-head environments.

Rock and cliff coasts

The broad ranges in rock type and structure and extreme exposure to which many island coasts in particular are subject is reflected in the diverse nature of the sites within this network, from the highest vertical sea cliffs in the UK on St Kilda to the shore platforms at Tarbat Ness in Highland. Rock coast features are characteristic of many island coasts, such as those of Orkney and Shetland, as well as extensive parts of the mainland in northern and eastern Scotland, as at Duncansby Head in Highland and the Bullars of Buchan in Aberdeenshire. They include large glaciated sea lochs, low ice scoured coasts, low cliffs with shore platforms of variable width and extent, and high cliffs, varying according to patterns of rock type, glacial erosion and isostatic uplift. In the south and west of mainland Scotland, rock coasts are more intermittent or buried in drift or sand overlying shore platforms. In a national context, the rock coast features of Scotland are important for:

- features associated with resistant igneous and metamorphic rocks;
- features associated with high-energy, exposed environments;
- some of the highest and most impressive cliff coast features; and
- features associated with glaciated coasts.

Wider conservation interest

Although the theme of this volume is on Earth Heritage the conservation importance of the Scottish coastline is not restricted to its Earth Science interest alone. Many landform systems also play a vital role in supporting coastal habitats. Examples of such sites include Invernaver in Highland, where montane plant species occur close to sea-level due to the extreme exposure and climatic conditions, Morrich More, also in Highland, with its rich and diverse assemblage of saltmarsh, dune and dune slack plant species, and Yesnaby in Orkney with its distinctive cliff top vegetation, including the rare Scottish Primrose (*Primula scotica*). Moreover, many of the coastal landscapes which these landforms and habitats combine to create, in designated and undesignated areas alike, are internationally renowned for their beauty and, largely, unspoilt character. For instance, the beach at Cammusdaroch in Highland with the mountains of Rum in the distance provided a stunning backdrop for the film *Local Hero*, yet this site has no special conservation significance.

Scotland's coastline: erosion and defence

Because of the relative hardness of the rock strata and the isostatic uplift of much of the Scottish land mass throughout the Holocene, coastal recession is not as widespread in Scotland as in England. Evidence of erosion is, however, manifest within many beach-dune (Fig. 11.2) or beach–machair systems and, although this may, in places, reflect no more than the seasonal fluctuations of the coastal edge, there is often a perception among local residents and land owners that this represents a long-term trend. Unfortunately, long-term coastal evolution is rarely monitored in Scotland so the validity of such beliefs is uncertain.

Following a survey of all 647 sandy beaches in Scotland in the 1970s, Ritchie & Mather (1984) concluded that approximately 40% showed evidence of retreat, whereas only 10% appeared to be prograding. A further 20% appeared stable and the remaining 30% showed both erosive and progradational features locally or were backed by shingle ridges or man-made structures. Evidence of erosion is also common along other 'soft' shorelines such as shingle beaches and those backed by glacial deposits, such as till. Erosion appears particularly prevalent in the Western Isles and Northern Isles, away from the centres of glacial rebound but is by no means confined to these regions.

Extensive residential and industrial development is rare on soft coasts, but dunes and links especially are often used for golf courses, caravan parks and MOD facilities. In the more remote island groups, cemeteries and archaeological monuments are also often located in such environments. Consequently, proposals for coastal protection are common-place. The layout of golf courses, in

Fig. 11.2. Frontal erosion of forested dune on the flank of the Morrich More, near Tain, Highland.

particular, is jealously guarded at many sites, to the extent that emplacement of coastal protection is considered more viable, desirable or cost effective than relocation of tees and greens. Existing development landward of such courses may, moreover, constrain relocation in that direction. Tees and greens at many of Scotland's most famous links courses have therefore been protected from erosion, as at St Andrews, Dornoch, Troon and Carnoustie.

Elsewhere, as in England and Wales, seafront roads and property in towns and villages are often protected by sea walls and revetments (Fig. 11.3) though, because of the built-up character of many such sites, the impact upon the natural heritage in these areas is generally low.

Traditional methods for coastal protection in Scotland have, as elsewhere, favoured the construction of sea walls and concrete or rock armour revetments. Because of the hardness of the rock strata, it is generally rare for sites of *geological* interest to be subject to severe erosion and hence for exposures to be obscured behind sea defences. Instead, it is the softer, Quaternary exposures and in particular those landforms which are most dynamic which are most

Fig. 11.3. Concrete seawall, sheet piling and rock armour revetment protecting the promenade and pavilion at Montrose, Angus. The dune ridge directly behind the defences is gradually being eroded now by wind activity. Adjacent unprotected dunes (out of the picture) are retreating by up to 4 m per year at present, possibly as a consequence of a shift in the direction of net littoral drift, which previously fed sand to this area.

severely impacted by such defences. Indeed, it is the very dynamism of beach–dune systems which, in the Highlands and Islands especially, is both their most distinctive feature and, if developed, the characteristic which most predisposes them to calls for protection.

The problems of such defences which occur in dynamic environments elsewhere are equally manifest in Scotland: terminal scour, beach lowering and sterilization of previously active beach–dune systems. The remoteness of much of the coastline creates a further problem in the prevalence of *ad hoc* and non-consented protection measures such as tipping of rubble (Fig. 11.4) or even dumping of cars. The consequences of such initiatives upon retreating coastlines is obvious, affecting landscape, conservation interest and amenity alike with negligible protective benefit.

In summary, coastal erosion in Scotland is widely distributed but

Fig. 11.4. Tipping of hard core from a demolished building on S. Uist, Western Isles, purportedly as a means of infilling an incipient blow-out and preventing coastal erosion. *Ad hoc* 'defence' initiatives such as this are not uncommon in remoter areas of Scotland, and can be particularly damaging to the natural environment as the rubble used may spread along adjacent beaches when the dune toe is eroded by storm wave activity. In this particular instance, the debris shown was removed mechanically by the landowner after the above photograph was taken.

is generally confined to beach-dune systems, shingle beaches and sites where glacial deposits crop out near the shore. The principal impacts of coastal defence methods traditionally employed in such situations are interference with natural beach building processes (with consequent sediment starvation downdrift), terminal scour, sterilization of previously active coastal landforms and loss of habitats or, occasionally, exposure.

Scotland's coastline: management approaches

No strategic approaches to coastal defence in Scotland, nationally or regionally, have been adopted or promoted to date and consequently protective work has proliferated in an *ad hoc* and unregulated fashion, each scheme being considered on its own merits. Moreover, no nation-wide records or maps of coastal defences exist.

In March 1996 the Scottish Office issued a discussion paper on the coastline (Scottish Office 1996) which included proposals for the establishment of local coastal fora and a national Coastal Forum to assist coastal management in Scotland, as well as the provision of further guidance on key issues relating to the coast. No recommendations relating specifically to coastal erosion or defence were made.

To date there has been no central Government encouragement or financial support for the preparation of Shoreline Management Plans in Scotland, such as have been promoted in England and Wales by MAFF. This is possibly due to the more restricted nature of coastal erosion in Scotland compared to England, the relative infrequency of threats from erosion to infrastructure and property and because of the rural, undeveloped character of much of the coastline. However, there are many areas such as on Tayside and along the shores of the Firth of Forth, the Firth of Clyde and the Moray Firth where these conditions do apply and which would benefit from a more structured approach to management of coastal erosion. For these coasts, in particular, the main aim of a Shoreline Management Plan, to provide the basis for sustainable coastal defence policy, is just as relevant in Scotland as south of the Border. Indeed, even along less developed and more indented coastlines, the basic objectives in developing a plan, such as 'predicting the likely future evolution of the coast' and 'identifying all the assets within the plan area which are likely to be affected by coastal change' (MAFF 1995), are just as appropriate given the dynamic nature of the beach–dune systems within such settings and their frequently high nature conservation value*.

Consequently, Scottish Natural Heritage (SNH) is developing a number of approaches aimed at safeguarding coastal landforms and habitats threatened by construction of defences. These focus on

---

* Since preparation of this paper, the concept of Shoreline Management Planning has been commended by the Scottish Office Development Department in the recently published National Planning Policy Guideline (NPPG) 13: *Coastal Planning* (Scottish Office 1997).

improving understanding of natural process operating around the coast and promoting the need for structured, strategic management of coastal erosion and protection.

Coastal cells in Scotland

SNH, the Scottish Office Agriculture, Environment and Fisheries Department and Historic Scotland are part-way through a major three-year research initiative to define the coastal cells around mainland Scotland. This work, conducted by HR Wallingford Ltd, follows the same basic approach as developed for England and Wales, although there are some significant differences. For instance, major sediment sinks within firths or estuaries are not used as cell boundaries in order that opposite banks are not covered by separate management plans. Also, on deeply indented coasts, such as along much of western Scotland, each major bay or sea loch constitutes a distinct cell. For practical reasons these are not all distinguished but have been grouped together according to other factors pertinent to shoreline management such as exposure and physical character. The island coasts of the Outer Hebrides, Orkney and Shetland are also being studied.

For the mainland, seven major cells have been identified, divided into 24 sub-cells (Fig. 11.5). An overview of these, and the four cells and 16 sub-cells identified in the Northern and Western Isles, is to be published imminently and copies forwarded to planners in the new unitary councils.

Further research is now adding detail to these cells, including identification and description of patterns of longshore drift, areas of erosion and accretion, existing coastal protection and management measures and assessment of the potential effects of climate change on the coastline.

In the short term, this research should allow SNH and others to identify coastal landforms and habitats threatened directly or indirectly by proposed coastal protection works, enabling modifications to be made at the planning stage if necessary. In addition, it should allow those sites where erosion is crucial to the health of adjacent beaches to be distinguished and, if appropriate, for that erosion to continue. In the long term, however, it is hoped that the

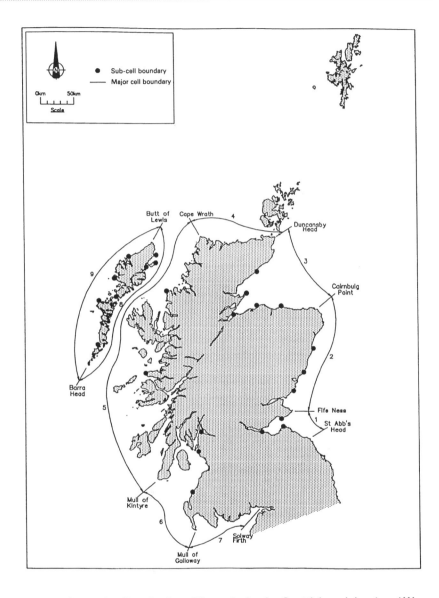

Fig. 11.5. Coastal cell and sub-cell boundaries for Scottish mainland and Western Isles. Cell boundaries for the coastlines of Orkney and Shetland are not shown due to scale. Cells have not been defined for the remaining Scottish islands. See text for details of cell definition. (Source: HR Wallingford 1995a.)

information generated will provide the impetus for the preparation of Shoreline Management Plans.

One approach may, for instance, involve SNH co-ordinating preparation of a pilot Shoreline Management Plan for one of the cells or sub-cells identified in the overview report in partnership with the relevant unitary councils and other appropriate organizations and landowners. Two such Plans covering parts of the Scottish coastline are being developed at present. The first is that being prepared under direction from MAFF for the Northumberland coastline as the cell concerned extends across the national border to St Abbs Head in Berwickshire. The second covers an area of the inner Moray Firth from Burghead to the Sutors and has been promoted by the former Highland Regional Council. SNH is supporting both initiatives and has contributed financially to the latter. Once the efficacy of the Shoreline Management Planning process has been demonstrated, it is hoped that this strategic approach will be adopted wherever potentially conflicting pressures are identified.

Focus on Firths: landforms and processes
Reviews of coastal landforms, processes and management options within the major Scottish firths or estuaries are also in progress as part of SNH's 'Focus on Firths' initiative which seeks to promote the integrated management of the natural resources of the country's firths. Its principal aims are to increase understanding and awareness of the natural heritage and to bring about the wise and sustainable use of the Scottish firths. These aims are being realised primarily through the establishment of firth-based fora and the development and implementation of firth-wide management strategies. Because of the profound influence which landforms, sediments and geomorphological processes exert upon the distribution and character of many of the habitats and biological communities which exist within the estuarine environment, as well as upon the location of the areas subject to coastal erosion and flooding, their mapping and description is considered vital to the development of sound, integrated management strategies.

The reviews conducted so far cover the Dornoch, Cromarty and Inverness–Beauly Firths, the estuaries of the Outer Moray Firth,

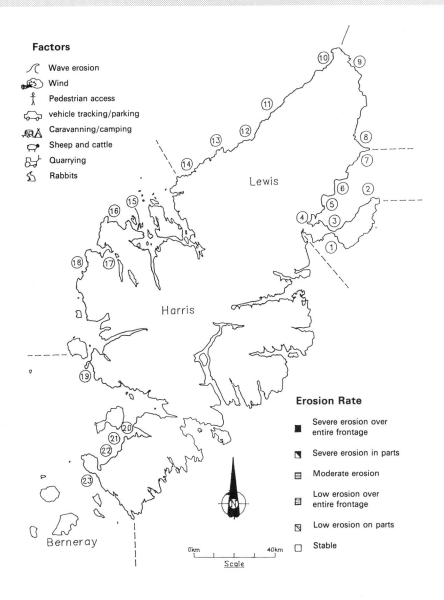

Factors

- ⌒(Wave erosion
- 🌬 Wind
- 🚶 Pedestrian access
- 🚗 vehicle tracking/parking
- 🚙⛺ Caravanning/camping
- 🐑 Sheep and cattle
- ⛏ Quarrying
- 🐇 Rabbits

Lewis

Harris

Berneray

Erosion Rate

- ■ Severe erosion over entire frontage
- ◥ Severe erosion in parts
- ▤ Moderate erosion
- ▦ Low erosion over entire frontage
- ◹ Low erosion on parts
- □ Stable

0km ⊢——⊣——⊣ 40km
Scale

Beach Unit	Beach	Erosion Dune	Machair	Cliffs	Factors
1 Gob na Creige to Gob Shilldinish		–	–	■	
2 Port nan Giuran		–	–	–	
3 Aiginis to Melbost Point				■	
4 Melbost Point to Aird Thunga				■	
5 Traigh Chuil				–	
6 Traigh Rabac and Traigh Ghriais				■	
7 Giordale Sands		–	–		
8 Traigh Mhor and Traigh Geiraha					
9 Port of Ness		–	–	■	
10 Traigh Sands to Dell Sands				■	
11 Borve to Shader		–	–	■	
12 Barvas to Loch Ereray				–	
13 Arnol to Shawbost		–	–	–	
14 Dalbeg and Dalmore Bays		–			
15 Valtos and Traigh na Berie				–	
16 Traigh na Clibhe		–			
17 Uig Sands				–	
18 Mangeresta					
19 Hushinish		–		–	
20 Traigh Rosamol to Traigh Nisabost				–	
21 Traigh Iar to Borve				–	
22 Traigh Scarasta				–	
23 Northton and Traigh na Cleavag				–	

Fig. 11.6. Assessment of relative severity of erosion and principal factors involved on beaches of Harris and Lewis, Western Isles. See text for discussion. (Source: HR Wallingford 1995b).

the Dee, Don and Ythan estuaries and the Firth of Forth. These studies have, in addition, identified the principal coastal defence schemes present within each area and assessed briefly their impact upon the landforms and processes. Ultimately, it is intended that the landform and process information generated will form the basis of a GIS for each estuary, thereby facilitating a more strategic approach to coastline management.

Practical initiatives

SNH has also funded research on more site-specific problems. For example, in the Western Isles grazing clerks questioned by the former Western Isles Island Council (WIIC) in 1993 reported that coastal erosion was prevalent on virtually every dune and machair coastline in the islands (WIIC 1993). Not only had this erosion led to various *ad hoc* defence initiatives by various bodies, which in

Fig.11.7. May 1993. Frontal erosion of dune ridge at Gairloch, Highland, caused by the 'Braer' storm four months before picture was taken. Slumping of the face and winnowing of sand below the dune crest by wind action reduced the slope profile in the interim period but further reprofiling was recommended as a means of encouraging slope stability and growth of dune grasses.

places were both damaging to the natural environment and of dubious value in terms of coastal protection (Fig. 11.4), but there was also a concern that other activities, such as grazing practices or sand extraction, might be exacerbating the situation.

In partnership with WIIC, SNH subsequently funded a study, via the Minch Project, of the extent and causes of coastal erosion in nine of the permanently inhabited islands. This concluded that coastal erosion was predominantly due to natural factors but that sand extraction from the foreshore and trampling and over-grazing by sheep and cattle were contributing to sand loss locally (Fig. 11.6). On the other hand, adverse effects caused by coastal defences, such as interruption of longshore drift or sterilization of eroding sand supplies behind sea walls, were very rare. Appropriate management recommendations were made, including the prepara-

Fig. 11.8. August 1993. Dune ridge at Gairloch, Highland, after dune reprofiling. Following reprofiling, this slope was planted with dune grasses to increase stability and encourage further sand accretion. Bi-annual monitoring since then indicates that the slope has remained largely intact, further sand having been deposited on its surface though some has been lost from the toe.

tion of a Shoreline Management Plan, and it is hoped to produce a summary of the findings in leaflet form to distribute to residents of coastal areas in these islands.

SNH may also support local coast protection measures where these are of benefit to the natural heritage and amenity. For example, at Gairloch in Highland, following rapid erosion in the winter of 1992/93 of the dune ridge behind the beach (Fig. 11.7), SNH, in partnership with local interests, has supported a scheme involving the recycling of sand from the foreshore at the southern end of the beach back on to the eroded dune face at its northern end (Fig. 11.8), accompanied by a programme of sand fencing and dune grass planting. This should maintain the natural landforms and habitat as well as the ability of the dune system to trap blown sand, features which would be lost if more traditional hard engineering options were pursued.

Conclusion

Although coastal erosion and resulting coast protection measures are not as widespread a threat to the earth heritage of Scotland as in other parts of Britain, there are growing pressures on many areas of soft coast. The traditional response, in the form of *ad hoc* coast defences, typically consisting of rock armouring or revetments is beginning to give rise to predictable problems of downdrift erosion and deactivation of beach–dune systems. Through mapping of coastal cells and preparation of inventories of landforms, sediments and process systems, it should be possible to provide more robust advice and a more secure physical basis for coastline management, for example through Shoreline Management Plans, to help safeguard a coastline which is still one of the country's most valuable and unspoiled natural resources.

References

HR Wallingford 1995a. *Coastal Cells in Scotland.* Unpublished report to Scottish Natural Heritage, the Scottish Office (Agriculture, Environment and Fisheries Department) and Historic Scotland. HR Wallingford Ltd, Report EX 3176.

HR Wallingford 1995b. *Survey of Coastal Erosion in the Western Isles.* Unpublished report to the Minch Project. HR Wallingford Ltd, Report EX 3155.

MAFF 1995. *Shoreline Management Plans. A Guide for Coastal Defence Authorities.* Ministry of Agriculture, Fisheries and Food, May 1995, PB 2197, London.

Ritchie, W. & Mather, A. S. 1984. *The Beaches of Scotland.* Countryside Commission for Scotland, Perth.

Scottish Office 1996. *Scotland's Coasts. A Discussion Paper.* HMSO, Edinburgh.

Scottish Office 1997. *Coastal Planning.* National Planning Policy Guideline (NPPG) 13. The Scottish Office (Development Department).

WIIC 1993. *Coast Protection in the Western Isles.* Unpublished report to Environmental Services Committee, April 1993, Comhairle nan Eilean, Stornoway.

Part Four

Resources and evaluation

Various aspects of resource exploitation and of conservation as a resource in relation to coastal management are explored in this part. The sediment itself is a resource as beach material providing natural or artificially enhanced protection. Sources and policies of exploitation for additional mineral resources are discussed. Such resources need to be used efficiently and a case study of beach replenishment demonstrates how understanding of behaviour of replenished beaches may help in their future management. The geology and geomorphology of the coast may itself be regarded as an economic asset and data on visitor characteristics are analysed. Finally, the arguments for earth science conservation in the public interest are summarized.

12 Resource, evaluation and net benefit

Russell Arthurton

Summary

- Various natural sources of sedimentary materials, as beach deposits, contribute to the defence of vulnerable shorelines.

- This paper considers the resource options for additional materials for use in artificial beach recharge schemes, both capital works and maintenance over the long term.

- In examining the options for the provision of suitable materials, the paper questions some of our existing priorities for conservation in the coastal zone.

- The favoured resource options should not only form part of a regional shoreline management strategy but also be viewed in the context of the wider use of coastal and sea bed sand and gravel resources.

- The aim is to achieve effective local defence solutions that are sustainable in terms of financial and material resources, while beneficial in respect of wider environmental criteria.

Protecting our coastal assets

The physical action of marine and atmospheric processes on geological materials gives the coastal zone its fundamental character. The resulting dynamic environment provides the basis for opportunistic and diverse colonization and ecosystem development. Our own contribution to such development has had its impact on coastal zones worldwide and dominates many of them. We have sought to preserve and enhance what we regard as our coastal assets by protective engineering and reclamation. Through our manipulation of the natural physical environment, we have aimed, by various defensive or protective measures, to minimize what we have perceived as the negative impacts of coastal interaction – in particular the marine flooding of low-lying coastal land and the erosion, and consequent recession, of soft, or otherwise unstable, cliffs.

A major challenge in shoreline management is to protect, or otherwise manage, specific coastal assets without jeopardizing the wider coastal environment, not just in the present but over the long term as well. The recharge of beach sediments by artificial means where natural supplies are inadequate to provide the required standard of defence is now practised in many parts of the world (Davison *et al.* 1992), part of a trend towards the use of soft engineering methods in coastal defence rather than the construction of hard structures such as rock groynes or concrete sea walls. In England the practice applies to shingle as well as sand beaches (Humphreys *et al.* 1996; Simm *et al.* 1996). This paper reviews the resource options for suitable recharge materials, and their sustainability.

Natural sediment supplies

Beaches, sand dunes and saltmarsh are natural providers of coastal defence, though the level of defence varies from place to place and time to time. The sediments that form beaches and contribute to dune fields and saltmarsh on temperate shores that have not been the subject of artificial recharge have come mainly from two contrasting sources.

The discharge from rivers along much of the European Atlantic seaboard adds mainly fines (mud) to the marine budget, carried largely under conditions of landwater flood. Much of this discharge, however, may not escape the estuarine environment, instead becoming fixed on estuarine tidal mudflats and saltmarsh.

Marine erosion of coastal cliffs and the sea bed is the other important natural source of new material, coarse (sand, gravel and boulders) as well as fine. This is the dominant source where the coastal geology comprises soft or otherwise readily erodible materials (Fig. 12.1). During the Holocene period, huge quantities

Fig. 12.1. Sand is delivered to a North Norfolk beach from the erosion of soft cliffs.

of such material have been introduced to the marine budget, derived, for example, from the cliffs of soft Quaternary formations on the English North Sea coast. Latterly, the input from coastal erosion has been substantially curbed by various protective structures as, for example, in North Norfolk (Clayton 1989).

The supply of sediment from the sea bed, particularly the foreshore and nearshore, results from wave action and tidally generated currents remobilizing penecontemporaneous or earlier Holocene sediment accumulations and introducing new material to the budget by abrasion of the bedrock. Such remobilization may recycle sediments that form cohesive and non-cohesive estuarine and littoral deposits, accreted earlier in the Holocene under sea level conditions that may have differed little from those of the present day. The release of fines from eroding marsh and tidal flat deposits and the remobilization of sand and gravel from earlier-formed beach deposits that have been temporarily banked on ness shores are examples of such sources.

Beach recharge from offshore sources

The resource options for obtaining suitable material for artificial beach recharge schemes carried out in England and Wales tend to have been considered on a site-specific basis. Now, through the agency of regional groups of coastal authorities, shoreline management in England and Wales is being viewed in a wider perspective, both spatially and temporally (MAFF 1995). Questions are being raised at the regional and national levels concerning the strategic use of artificial beach recharge and, in particular, whether the supply of suitable marine-dredged materials can be maintained where required over the long term (Humphreys et al. 1996).

If the enhancement of the standard of coastal defence through beach recharge is a long term goal, the management strategies that are adopted must take account of all resource options on the regional scale. There is a need to consider the scope for the supply of material from offshore sources as part of a regional strategy. Such a strategy should consider the physical and ecological impacts of material extraction (Campbell 1993), and the implications of enhanced protection on the natural delivery of beach-forming materials from eroding soft cliffs. The chosen defence works should aim to make the best use of the available material resources, bearing in mind the interests of other stakeholders in those resources, including landowners, the fishing industry and those concerned with conservation.

Estimates of the likely workable resources of sand and shingle around England and Wales suitable for beach recharge (Humphreys et al. 1996) have indicated that the total demand for sand – from the construction industry as well as for beach recharge – could easily be met for the foreseeable future without excessive shipping costs. Estimates of sand resource volumes off the east coast of England were 90 times greater than the anticipated total 20-year demand of sand from that region. Off the south coast, sand was shown to be less plentiful, but resource volumes were nonetheless some 30 times in excess of the expected total demand for the 20-year period.

The capacity of sea bed resources for meeting the likely combined demands for shingle (with a grain-size greater than 5 mm) for beach recharge and construction aggregates is, however, less assured. Taking a regional view, marine resources of shingle were seen by Humphreys *et al.* (1996) as being adequate to meet the likely combined demands of beach recharge and the aggregate industry. However, in some sub-regions the demand over the 20-year period was anticipated to exceed the available workable resources. The southeast of England was seen as most critical, in particular the Thames Estuary dredging area. The demand for recharge shingle there might necessitate supply from farther afield. For shingle, there is the additional problem of ensuring the cosmetic compatibility between indigenous beach materials and recharge materials derived from distant sources.

Greater use of offshore sand resources

Marine sand has been dredged for placing as recharge for many schemes in England and Wales, particularly on the east coast of England. The largest placement to date is that on the Mablethorpe–Skegness shoreline in Lincolnshire, for which an estimated 10.8 million cubic metres are quoted as being required for completion of the capital works (Humphreys *et al.* 1996).

The capacity of the sea bed resources of sand off eastern England to yield adequate recharge material for the foreseeable future is huge. While tight grading specifications may be difficult to achieve, there are likely to be many locations where suitable materials can be dredged without significant detriment to fisheries or to the stability of the shoreline. In an area of sea bed off Happisburgh in North Norfolk, for example, there are an estimated 4.6 billion cubic metres of such sand that may be accessible over the long term (Humphreys *et al.* 1996). The area covers part of the Norfolk Banks, and includes both active and moribund tidal sand ridges which rise some 30 m above the general sea floor and are elongated in some cases over tens of kilometres.

The proximity of abundant resources offshore to wasting beaches on the Lincolnshire and East Anglian coasts, such as that illustrated in Figure 12.2 makes the prospect of a sustained supply of marine

Fig.12.2. Sparse beach deposits provide little protection to eroding soft cliffs on the Suffolk coast.

sand for strategic recharge realistic, in terms of supply at least. The possibility of extending the lengths of shoreline for which recharge might economically improve the standard of protection deserves consideration.

Improved management of shingle resources
Compared with sand, shingle resources are much more limited
(Humphreys *et al.* 1996). While large areas of the sea bed have
gravel at the surface, this material is commonly only of veneer
thickness – a layer in some places only one pebble thick and resting,
for example, on bedrock or till (Harrison *et al.* 1998). Deposits of
gravel which can be expected to yield significant supplies of shingle
are generally of a relict nature, having formed under environmental
conditions very different from those of the sea bed at present.
Except in a few locations subject to exceptional tidal streams,
deposits of gravel at the sea bed are finite and have no prospect of
replenishment in the present hydrodynamic regime. Thus there is a
need to use the marine resources of gravel with prudence and
economy. In particular, consideration should be given to reserving
certain resources specifically for the local recharge market. While
the coarse aggregate market may accept the use of crushed rock as
reserves of sea bed gravel become exhausted, it is unlikely that the
use of materials other than gravel would be acceptable, or indeed
feasible, for the recharge of shingle beaches.

Role of soft cliffs as material suppliers

Soft cliffs, such as those composed of glacial sediments in eastern
England, provide conflicts of interest to coastal management
authorities. On the one hand there may be pressure on authorities
to prevent or minimize erosion in order to safeguard property or
other investments in the vicinity of the cliff top. On the other, there
may be demands from neighbouring shoreline managers, as well as
conservation and environmental interests, to allow natural erosional processes to operate without hindrance. The challenge is to
establish an appropriate response that will arbitrate between the
various interests and produce an overall benefit.
  Soft cliffs are potentially major sediment suppliers to the marine
system. During the Holocene transgression of the southern North
Sea basin, they have fulfilled this role on the grand scale, feeding
several cubic kilometres of sedimentary material to the marine
budget. One of the most important impacts of any scheme aimed at
the protection of soft cliffs is the effect on the input of sediment to

Fig. 12.3. Gravel forms a substantial component of these cliffs on the Suffolk shore at Dunwich.

the marine environment. While a completed scheme may scarcely affect the beach environment at the site itself, its real impact is likely to be on downdrift shores whose beaches may become starved of incoming sediment. In such circumstances erosion, and thus coastal recession, may be aggravated. A decision to protect eroding cliffs is likely to have long-term implications on the stability of shores well outside the limits of the scheme site.

Any reduction in sand input resulting from the protection (by any means) of sand-dominated cliffs may sensibly be compensated by sand recharge where the accessible sea bed resources are abundant. The reduction of shingle input through the protection of gravelly cliffs may be more difficult to justify in view of the relative scarcity of sea bed shingle resources. Gravelly cliffs, such as that shown in Fig. 12.3, are a prime resource for natural beach feeding.

Recycling of beach deposits

The recycling of beach shingle may become increasingly important as resources of sea bed gravel become scarcer and the input of shingle material from soft cliff erosion becomes reduced through the implementation of coastal protection schemes. Recycling is an established practice in the USA, though generally involving sand (Davison *et al.* 1992).

Recycling is appropriate to shorelines where there is a clear net alongshore drift. In essence the technique aims to transport material artificially from parts of a beach with net accretion and to place it updrift, directly or indirectly feeding those parts of the beach with net erosion (Simm *et al.* 1996). The practice makes sensible use of what is an increasingly precious resource. It deserves serious consideration as an option in the management of shingle shores.

On shorelines where beaches have had a tendency to net accretion over a long period, a substantial resource of beach deposits may have accumulated as ness landforms. The ness deposits at Winterton in Norfolk, for instance, extend for some 3 km along the coast to a maximum width of some 500 m and comprise an estimated 10 million cubic metres of beach sand and shingle, with a capping of wind blown sand. On the south coast of England at Dungeness, recycling of ness deposits has been in operation on a maintenance basis for some years, material being transferred from an accretionary east-facing beach to an erosional south-facing beach. While there are certainly important conservation assets associated with these coastal landforms, consideration could be given to a more widespread use of some of these beach materials in recycling schemes.

Conclusions

This paper seeks to promote rational strategic management of the sand and gravel resources available for, or otherwise relevant to, the defence of vulnerable shorelines. Where accessible marine resources of sand are abundant, as off parts of the east coast of England, their enhanced use for recharge may be the preferred option on environmental and economic grounds. For some areas, marine resources of shingle may need to be earmarked for recharge use as a precaution against the depletion of suitable materials over the next 20 years or so. In addition, special consideration should be given to the resource value of vulnerable gravel-bearing cliffs as shingle feedstock for natural beach recharge. Finally, the potential for the greater use of recycling of beach deposits needs investigation as part of a wider aim to achieve a net benefit in coastal defence works and in the strategic management of the wider coastal resource.

Acknowledgements

The author is grateful to colleagues at BGS for their stimulation and encouragement in preparing this paper, which is published with the approval of the Director, British Geological Survey, NERC.

References

Clayton, K. M. 1989. Sediment input from the Norfolk cliffs, eastern England – a century of coast protection and its effect. *Journal of Coastal Research*, **3**, 433–442.

Campbell, J. A. 1993. *Guidelines for Assessing Marine Aggregate Extraction*. Laboratory Leaflet, MAFF Directorate of Fisheries Research, 73. Lowestoft.

Davison, A. T., Nicholls, R. J. & Leatherman, S. P. 1992. Beach nourishment as a coastal management tool: an annotated bibliography on developments associated with the artificial nourishment of beaches. *Journal of Coastal Research*, **8**, 984–1022.

Harrison, D. J., Laban, C., Leth, J. O. & Larsen, B. 1988. Sources of sand and gravel on the northern European continental shelf. The Geological Society, London. In: Latham, J.-P. (ed.) *Advances in Aggregates and Armourshore Evaluation*. Engineering Geology Special Publication, **13**, 3–13.

Humphreys, B., Coates, T. T., Watkiss, M. J. & Harrison, D. J. 1996. *Beach Recharge Material-Demand and Resources*. Research Report 154, Construction Industry Research and Information

Association, London.

MAFF. 1995. *Shoreline Management Plans. A Guide for Coastal Defence Authorities.* MAFF, London.

Simm, J. D., Brampton, A. H., Beech, N. & Brooke, J. 1996. *Beach Management Manual.* Research Report 153, Construction Industry Research and Information Association, London.

13 Beach replenishment: implications for sources and longevity from results of the Bournemouth schemes

N. J. Cooper & D. A. Harlow

Summary

- Beach replenishment is an effective shoreline management tool which can restore immediately coast protection and
amenity functions of a beach.

- Issues concerning material sources and replenishment
scheme longevity need to be addressed as future scheme
use proliferates.

- From analysis of a long-term beach monitoring record in
Poole Bay, southern England, it is suggested that a viable
trade-off can be made between tight particle size grading
control and the presence of retention structures in the
design of effective replenishment schemes.

- The conservation of sediment resources is essential if
replenishment is to be a sustainable option in the longer
term.

Introduction

Coastal landforms are dynamic systems which require a balanced
management approach in attempt to resolve all of the conflicts
arising from their use. Coastal managers have long recognized four
realistic shoreline management options, namely protection, accom-
modation, retreat and 'monitor'. However, society's desire to build
infrastructure close to the coast and to utilize the coast and its
resources has commonly led to the protection option being
implemented preferentially. Historically, such protection was based
on the philosophy of maintaining a fixed line of defence against the
sea, but relatively recent fundamental changes in attitudes towards
coastal management have seen greater appreciation of the coastal
processes operative, and the increasingly frequent use of 'soft'
engineering techniques which work with the forces of nature rather

than against them. From such understandings, it has been recognized that a substantial beach is the best form of shoreline defence (Brampton 1992; Fleming 1992; Riddell & Young 1992), primarily because it can accommodate the dynamic changes resulting from the daily wave and tidal regime and also longer-term climatic changes.

Beach replenishment is one such 'soft' engineering shoreline management technique which attempts to resolve the combined problems of reduced input to the littoral sediment budget and continued throughput of material by the artificial addition of a suitable quality sediment to the coastal system. This involves the rebuilding of a beach to a width that provides some degree of storm protection, and often additional recreational and amenity benefits. Due to these benefits, and also because of its effectiveness as a shoreline management tool, the future use of beach replenishment is likely to proliferate. Consequently, the demand for, and cost of finite fill material sources is set to increase. Therefore, issues concerning the suitability of source material and the optimization of scheme longevity by conserving the imported fill need to be addressed.

However, despite increasingly widespread use from the 1970s onwards, the understanding of the performance and impacts of replenishment schemes remains relatively poor (Davison *et al.* 1992). This is largely due to insufficient pre- and post-placement monitoring to allow for objective project appraisal. These deficiencies hinder the efficient design of new schemes and make it difficult to 'fine-tune' existing schemes. However, one of the highest quality and longest duration beach monitoring records concerning beach replenishment exists for the Bournemouth frontage. Bournemouth is centrally located within Poole Bay on the south coast of England, and two major sand replenishment schemes have been undertaken at this site. Consequently, analysis of the data obtained from this beach monitoring programme can provide important information concerning the use and performance of beach replenishment as a shoreline management tool.

This paper describes the use of replenishment as a beach management tool, presents an assessment of the effectiveness of the two major sand replenishment schemes undertaken along the

Poole Bay frontage, and demonstrates the managerial benefits which can be derived from a long term beach monitoring record.

Beach replenishment as a shoreline management tool

Beach replenishment has gained in popularity since the first recorded case in the USA in 1922. This scheme involved the deposition of 1.3 million m^3 of material dredged from New York Harbour along a 1 km frontage at Coney Island (Hall 1952; Davison et al. 1992). Many US projects undertaken between the 1950s and 1970s performed poorly due to the use of too fine-grained fill material (Dean 1983), but from the 1970s the more common use of material from offshore borrow sites improved scheme performance. It was in the 1970s that replenishment gained more worldwide acceptance and employment, with the most active nations being the Netherlands (Roelvink 1989), Denmark (Thyme 1989), Germany (Kelletat 1992), Australia (Bird 1990) and the UK (May 1990). The technique is currently becoming increasingly utilized in Africa and Latin America, especially in countries such as South Africa, Cuba and Brazil (Davison et al. 1992).

When considering the advantages of beach replenishment as a shoreline management tool, its increasing use is understandable. The prime benefit is, due to the artificial addition of sediment, a reduction in erosion and flooding at coastal localities, without the negative downdrift effects commonly associated with engineered structures. Beaches which have been artificially nourished with material have a greater degree of flexibility to adjust their profiles to differing hydrodynamic conditions than traditional 'hard' defences (such as seawalls) (Madalon et al. 1991). This advantage is likely to manifest itself even more as the impending problems of global sea-level rise and increased storminess take effect (Bray et al. 1992). Replenished beaches are often also major recreational and amenity assets. However, it must be recognized that beach replenishment is a form of 'dynamic' management which requires a long term commitment in terms of maintenance of the initial scheme. Generally, smaller periodic 'top-ups', or recycling of beach material is required. In the absence of such measures, scheme performance is liable to diminish over time.

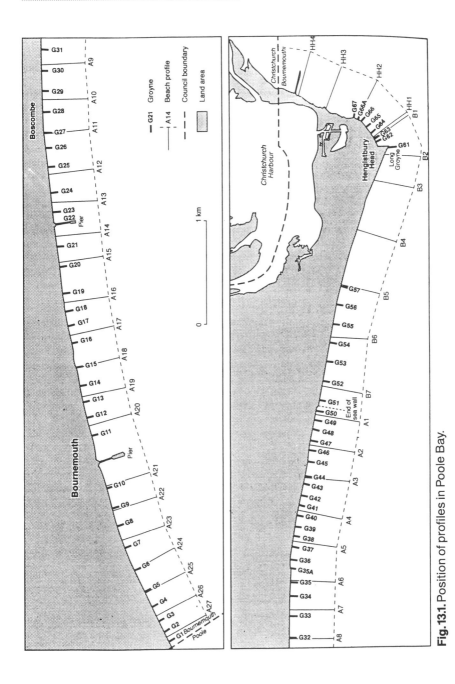

Fig. 13.1. Position of profiles in Poole Bay.

Bournemouth sand replenishment schemes

Bournemouth is located in Poole Bay on the south coast of England (Fig. 13.1), and is critically dependent upon the tourist economy generated largely due to the presence of golden sandy beaches. The frontage has experienced a progression of protection measures to control erosion. The historical protection measures of seawalls and groynes had limited success in retaining beach material and this philosophy of 'hard' protection altered following a period of damage in the 1960s (Lelliot 1989) to establish one of the largest and longest running programmes of beach replenishment in the UK (May 1990; Bray & Carter 1996).

In 1970, a pilot replenishment scheme (Beach Improvement Scheme 1 – or BIS1) was carried out, involving the emplacement of $84\,500\,m^3$ of dredged sand at MLW along a 1.8 km frontage (Lelliott 1989). The experience gained from this pilot study gave the Local Authority the confidence to undertake a full scale scheme in 1974/5 (BIS2). This involved pumping directly onto the beaches, over a 8.5 km frontage, some $654\,020\,m^3$ of marine dredged sand specified to replicate the indigenous material. This was the largest scheme of its kind at this time in the UK (May 1990). A further $749\,300\,m^3$ of material escaped into the nearshore zone during the two stage placement process, but ultimately a large proportion of this material moved onshore to further nourish the beaches (Hodder 1986). After remaining effective for about 13 years, critically low beach levels were again observed in 1987. At this time damage to seawalls occurred, and MHW migrated landward, often intercepting the seawall itself. Subsequently a third sand replenishment scheme was undertaken in three phases from 1988–1990, involving the deposition of $998\,730\,m^3$ of dredged fill directly onto the beach. The coincidental dredging of the Poole Harbour entrance at the same time as the need for beach replenishment material substantially reduced the costs of BIS3 (Turner 1994), although there was no control over the size specification of the fill material.

Beach monitoring data

BIS2 was of sufficient national importance to encourage the Department of the Environment to fund a research project into coastal processes in Poole and Christchurch Bays (Halcrow 1980). A bi-annual beach profiling survey was instigated in July 1974 and has been maintained by Bournemouth Borough Council following the conclusion of BIS2. MAFF again funded research during and

Table 13.1. Dates of Beach Profile Surveys

Survey date	Survey no.	Remarks	Survey date	Survey no.	Remarks
01/07/74	1		27/03/82	26	
01/08/74	2	incomplete data	03/11/82	27	
26/11/74	3	topographic	15/04/83	28	
14/12/74	4	incomplete data	12/11/83	29	
26/01/75	5	topographic	19/03/84	30	
13/02/75	6	incomplete data	12/10/84	31	
25/02/75	7		08/05/85	32	
13/03/75	8	incomplete data	15/10/85	33	
28/03/75	9		23/06/86	34	
12/07/75	10		01/03/87	35	
05/09/75	11		01/10/87	36	incomplete data
18/11/75	12	partial survey	01/05/88	37	
30/03/76	13	incomplete data	13/09/88	38	
23/09/76	14		19/04/89	39	
05/04/77	15	B6&7 data lost	30/09/89	40	
13/09/77	16		07/12/89	41	
01/04/78	17		27/03/90	42	partial survey
17/10/78	18		01/05/90	43	
27/04/79	19		29/11/90	44	partial survey
11/09/79	20		17/04/91	45	
29/04/80	21		11/09/91	46	
30/10/80	22	topographic	05/05/92	47	
13/11/80	23		10/10/92	48	
06/04/81	24		26/03/93	49	
16/10/81	25		04/11/93	50	

after BIS3. Suitable sites for profile lines were chosen at regular intervals along the coast (Fig. 13.1) and surveys on 50 dates have so far been processed and analysed (Table 13.1). Profile lines were originally located centrally within groyne compartments, but with the rebuilding of 40 groynes since 1970, some sites are now much closer to the edge of the groyne compartments. However, a review has shown that this has no effect on the variability of the record (Harlow & Cooper 1995a). The beach profiles are in two parts, a topographic survey above MLW and a hydrographic survey that extends from MHW to 450 m seaward of the origin. This chainage point of 450 m is approximately the point at which the 1 : 400 offshore gradient changes to 1 : 40 and represents the 'closure point' for erosion (i.e. no significant changes occur beyond this point). The surveying methods adopted were the best available technology and have been steadily updated with technological advances. Recent hydrographic surveys have been undertaken using a Global Positioning System. As the origin (a pin in the seawall) and orientation of each profile line has been fixed and consistent measurement procedures have been maintained throughout, the data sets are of extremely high quality (Gao & Collins 1994). The availability of such a long-term monitoring record is very rare and must be considered a valuable asset.

Beach profile analysis

Net volume

Total net beach volume over time has been plotted for all of the profiles in Poole Bay (Fig. 13.2). This shows the major volumetric improvements produced by BIS2 & 3, followed by a two-phase decay. BIS2 increased the total net beach volume from a low of about 6 million m^3 in early 1975 to a peak of 7.7 million m^3 in 1979, after which the volume decreased to 6.9 million m^3 in 1988. The post-peak volumetric decay comprised two phases, an early rapid loss rate of 286 700 m^{3}a^{-1} for two years, followed by a slower rate of 26 100 m^{3}a^{-1} for the following seven years until BIS3 was commenced in 1988. BIS3 increased the volume to a peak of 8 million m^3 in 1990, and thereafter it decreased to 7.89 million m^3 in late 1993, following a similar trend to the BIS2 post-peak decay.

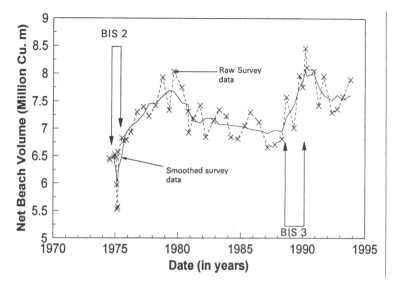

Fig. 13.2. Net beach volume in Poole Bay.

There are two reasons for this observed decay pattern after replenishment. Firstly, the PSD of the imported fill initially adjusts to the beach environment and physical processes operative, and some loss is attributed to this. Secondly, the groynes are, at first, over-filled (often buried) immediately after replenishment and losses are rapid until beach levels fall to those at which the optimum groyne effectiveness is restored. In view of this, it may be more effective to replenish the beaches with smaller material volumes at more frequent intervals so that the groynes are never completely buried. This approach is likely to have the added benefit of reducing the average annual material requirement for replenishment schemes (Dette *et al.* 1994), however, the economics of dredger operations and source availability constraints make the adoption of this technique unlikely. The second phase of the decay pattern exhibits slower rates of material loss and is attributable to linear background erosion of the coastline.

Future replenishment
Due to the consistency in beach volume changes after both

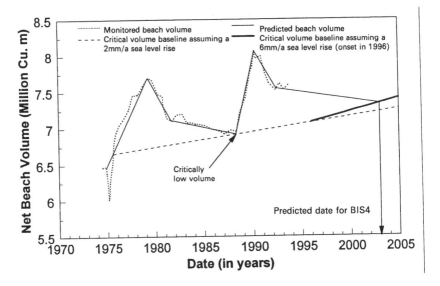

Fig. 13.3. Net beach volume predicted.

replenishment schemes, the date for a future beach replenishment scheme (BIS4) can be anticipated using a predicted rate of volumetric decline from the present day (Harlow & Cooper 1995b). After BIS2 in 1974–5, unacceptable damage to the seawall began to re-occur in 1987, when the total net beach volume was 6.9 million m^3. Assuming this volume to be critically low at this particular time, and assuming a maximum rate of sea-level rise of 6 mm a^{-1} (Bray *et al.* 1992, 1994), it can be anticipated that BIS4 will be required before the year 2003 (Fig. 13.3). Continued monitoring of beach volume should identify whether the predicted rate of volumetric decline is reliable, or whether it might be sensitive to changes in external regulators (e.g. wave climates, storm frequency and sea-level rise). The advantage of replenishment is that it can be adjusted to cope with unforseen situations provided that adequate monitoring is undertaken (Stive *et al.* 1991).

Groynes
Groyne construction has been observed to immediately increase beach areas along 12 of the 19 profile lines considered. (Groynes

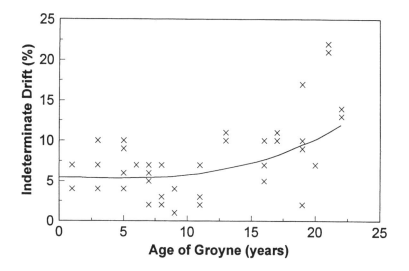

Fig. 13.4. Indeterminate drift with respect to age, 1994.

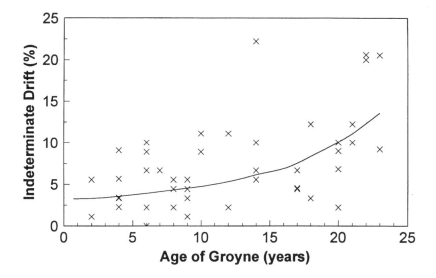

Fig. 13.5. Indeterminate drift with respect to age, 1995.

adjacent to remaining profiles were either constructed at a date too close to direct replenishment dates for effects to be discernible, or prior to the monitoring programme, and hence have not been considered.) The removal of groynes for reconstruction has always led to a dramatic localized loss in beach volume.

Throughout 1994 and 1995, littoral drift observations were regularly recorded at each of the groynes along the frontage (Harlow 1995). Using the assumption that an ineffective groyne does not interrupt the littoral drift, and hence indeterminate observations were recorded, it was found that groyne effectiveness deteriorates with age (Figs 13.4 and 13.5). This demonstrates the importance of long-term maintenance of the groyne field for fill retention and hence replenishment scheme longevity.

The majority of the most ineffective groynes in Poole Bay (i.e. those with highest percentage occurrence of indeterminate drift on Figs 13.3 and 13.4) are located between Boscombe Pier and the end of the seawall (Fig. 13.1). Over this segment of the frontage the groyne spacing : length ratios are generally relatively large, and the

Fig. 13.6. Bournemouth beach replenishment operations.

Fig. 13.7. Pumping sand onto the beach during replenishment at Bournemouth.

age of 28% of these groynes ranges between 18 and 22 years. Post replenishment rates of volumetric decline over this segment are markedly greater than other sections of the beach (Cooper 1997). From this it can be concluded that the performance of the replenishment scheme could be further improved by the reconstruction and additional construction of groynes in this segment (as is currently being undertaken by Bournemouth Borough Council).

Conclusions

The existence of a high quality long-term beach monitoring record in Poole Bay has beneficial implications for the wider aspects of coastal management. Historically, protection measures have been undertaken in response to damage to coastal defences and infrastructure, as in the cases of BIS2 and BIS3 which were commenced after critically low beach levels at certain locations resulted in costly damage to the seawall. However, the need for future replenishment schemes can now be predicted using the long-term monitoring data that are available, thus changing the management philosophy from a reactive to a pro-active one. This will, in the long run, have the economic benefits of saving on seawall damage and allowing funding for future replenishment schemes to be sought in advance. It should also help to ensure that consistent beach volumes can be maintained for amenity purposes, and aid in the more rational planning of resources. This, of course, assumes that, given the high economic assets of Bournemouth, protection must continue.

The detailed analyses undertaken demonstrate the importance of a well maintained groyne field in the retention of fill from replenishment schemes. Future scheme longevity in Bournemouth will undoubtedly suffer without such measures.

The successful effect of sand replenishment is such that residents and tourists now take Bournemouth's excellent sandy beaches for granted. Future replenishment schemes could potentially be more effective as a protection measure if a coarser fill were used, but this is undesirable from the amenity point of view and is therefore not a realistic option.

A reduction in the average annual sand requirement for beach replenishment schemes (or subsequent maintenance) could be achieved by using smaller fill volumes at shorter intervals (Dette et al. 1994). This would also reduce the large volumetric losses associated with the early years of replenishment schemes, and should also ensure that beach volumes never again approach the critically low levels recorded in 1974 and 1988.

The next replenishment is unlikely to coincide with dredging of Poole Harbour, so an alternative 'borrow' source must be found. If the cost of, and demand for, beach fill increases in the future, emphasis will move towards more efficient conservation of sediments, with beach monitoring as a critical component of this strategy.

References

Bird, E. C. F. 1990. Artificial beach nourishment on the shores of Port Phillip Bay, Australia. *Journal of Coastal Research,* **SI(6),**

55–68.

Brampton, A. H. 1992. Beaches – the natural way to coastal defence. In: *Coastal Zone Planning and Management.* Thomas Telford, London, 221–229.

Bray, M. J. & Carter, D. J. 1996. Poole Bay and Hengistbury Head. *In*: Allison, R (ed.) *Landforms of East Dorset.* Geologists Association Guide, Geologists Association, London (in press).

Bray, M. J., Carter, D. J. & Hooke, J. M. 1992. *Sea-Level Rise and Global Warming: Scenarios, Physical Impacts and Policies.* Department of Geography, Portsmouth Polytechnic, Report to SCOPAC.

Bray, M. J., Hooke, J. M. & Carter, D. J. 1994. *Tidal Information: Improving the Understanding of Relative Sea-Level Rise on the South Coast of England.* Department of Geography, University of Portsmouth, Report to SCOPAC.

Cooper, N. J., 1997. *Engineering Performance and Geomorphic Impacts of Shoreline Management at Contrasting Sites in Southern England.* PhD Thesis, University of Portsmouth.

Davison, A. T., Nicholls, R. J. & Leatherman, S. P. 1992. Beach nourishment as a coastal management tool: an annotated bibliography on developments associated with the artificial nourishment of beaches. *Journal of Coastal Research,* **8**, 984–1022.

Dean, R. G. 1983. Principles of beach nourishment. In: Komar, P. D. (ed.) *CRC Handbook of Coastal Processes and Erosion.* CRC Press Boca Raton, Florida.

Dette, H. H., Fuehrboeter, A. & Raudkivi, A. J. 1994. Inter-dependence of beach fill volumes and repetition intervals. *Journal of Waterway, Port, Coastal and Ocean Engineering,* **120**, 580–593.

Fleming, C. A. 1992. The development of coastal engineering. *In*: *Coastal Zone Planning and Management.* Thomas Telford, London, 5–20.

Gao, S. & Collins, M. B. 1994. *Beach Profile Changes and Offshore Sediment Transport Patterns Along the SCOPAC Coast: Phase I Technical Report.* Report No. SUDO/TEC/94/95/C. Department of Oceanography, University of Southampton.

Halcrow, Sir William & Partners, 1980. *Poole and Christchurch Bays Research Project, Phase One Report, 2 Volumes.* Report to the Department of the Environment.

Hall, J. V. 1952. *Artificially Constructed and Nourished Beaches in Coastal Engineering.* Proceedings of the 3rd Coastal Engineering Conference, ASCE, New York, 119–133.

Harlow, D. A. 1995. *The Direction of Littoral Drift in Poole Bay and The Effectiveness of the Groynes.* The 30th Conference of River and Coastal Engineers, Keele University, 1995.

Harlow, D. A. & Cooper, N. J. 1995a. *Poole Bay Beach Monitoring, 1974–1994.* Internal Report, Bournemouth Borough Council, Development Services Directorate, Drainage and Coast Protection Section.

Harlow, D. A. & Cooper, N. J. 1995b. *Bournemouth Beach Monitoring: The First Twenty Years.* Institution of Civil Engineers Coastal Management '95 Conference, Bournemouth, 1995.

Hodder, J. P. 1986. *Coastal Sediment Processes in Poole Bay, with Particular Reference to the Bournemouth Beach Replenishment of 1974/75.* unpublished M.Phil. thesis, Department of Civil Engineering, University of Southampton.

Kelletat, D. 1992. Coastal erosion and protection measures at the German North Sea Coast. *Journal of Coastal Research,* **8**, 699–711.

Lelliott, R. E. L. 1989. Evolution of the Bournemouth defences. *In*: *Coastal Management.* Thomas Telford, London, 263–277.

Madalon, L. J. Jr, Wood, W. L. & Stockberger, M. T. 1991. Influence of water-level variation on the performance of Great Lakes beach nourishment. *Proceedings Coastal Sediments '91.* ASCE, New York, 2052–2066.

May, V. J. 1990. Replenishment of the resort beaches at Bournemouth and Christchurch, England. *Journal of Coastal Research,* **SI (6)**, 11–15.

Riddell, K. J. & Young, S. W. 1992. The management and creation of beaches for coastal defence. *Journal IWEM,* **6**, 588–597.

Roelvink, J. A. 1989. *Feasibility of offshore nourishment of the Dutch sandy coast.* International Conference Hydraulic and Environmental Modelling of Coastal, Estuarine and River Waters, Bradford, England.

Stive, M. J. F., Nicholls, R. J. & de Vriend, H. J. 1991. Sea-level rise and shore nourishment: a discussion. *In*: van de Graaff, J., Niemeyer, H. D. and van Overeem, J. (eds) *Artificial Beach Nourishments*. Coastal Engineering, **16**, 147–163.

Thyme, F. 1989. Beach nourishment on the west coast of Jutland. *Journal of Coastal Research*, **6**, 201–209.

Turner, N. 1994. Recycling of capital dredging arisings – the Bournemouth Experience. In: *Papers and Proceedings, SCOPAC Conference. Inshore Dredging for Beach Replenishment?* Held on 28 October 1994, Elmer Court Country Club, Lymington, Hampshire.

14 Selling coastal geology to visitors

Thomas A. Hose

Summary

- From the 1970s onwards several geological sites have been interpreted for general visitors.
- An appreciation of the perceptions, knowledge and understanding of geology that such visitors have is crucial to effective future geological interpretive and conservation management strategies.
- Geotourism, examined within the broader heritage and interpretation context, is considered as a model for such provision.
- The analyses of some of the data from four visitor study surveys undertaken in England are presented and contextualised within the broader interpretation framework.

Coastal geotourism

Geological conservation – addressing the seaside audience

Fossil hunting and pebble collecting are popular activities, especially during the holiday season, at tourist sites around England's actively eroding coast. The inclement out-of-season sea conditions create a ready supply, at the obvious and sometimes dramatic expense of subaerial hectarage, of new collectible material; such events reinforce the perceived need of civil engineers, planners, local populations and their politicians for coastal defences:

> Britain's rich heritage of internationally important geological sites is well known to engineers and geologists alike, but ... the undertaking of protective works on unstable slopes or cliffs designated as Sites of Special Scientific Interest bring conservationists and engineers into conflict. (McKirdy 1987).

Unfortunately, despite their potential to resolve such conflict, few geology interpretive schemes (Page & Wray 1995) which could enable the various constituencies to recognise and appreciate the commercial and academic value of such sites, have been developed.

Geological interpretation and the Public

Geology's interest and perceived value to visitors can be masked by complex terminology and a concentration on obscure detail. Ham (1992) has said:

> Environmental interpretation involves translating the technical language of a natural science or a related field into terms and ideas that people who aren't scientists can readily understand. And it involves doing it in a way that's entertaining and interesting to these people.

It is somewhat unfortunate that many interpretive schemes focus on Sites of Special Scientific Interest. Chosen for scientific, rather than interpretive, value, most have seemingly little to interest general visitors. The somewhat difficult task of interpreting such sites is hindered when basic interpretive principles on the informational, graphical and linguistic style and content of interpretive publications and (including their siting) panels, are neglected; for example, from an interpretive plaque at a disused Carboniferous Limestone quarry on the western edge of the Peak District:

> Limestones are sedimentary rocks composed of calcium carbonate ($CaCO_3$). They contain ancient shells and skeletons belonging to organisms ... CARBONATE MUDMOUNDS seen here high on the cliff face. The origin of these structures is complex although ancient algae are believed to have influenced their development. The more noticeable of the mudmounds has been shown to be inverted. It must therefore have been detached and transported from the original position before being incorporated into the bedded sediments here.

Site-focused interpretation programmes use either on-site display panels or trail guides; museum exhibitions and heritage centre displays are also commonly employed. Visitors to such sites can be categorized (Miller 1991) as at:

• Level One: generally curious, somewhat unknowledgable, casual visitors;

- Level Two: interested, having made a conscious decision to visit, visitors;
- Level Three: the, having made a conscious decision to visit, knowledgeable minority of visitors.

Most visitors to coastal recreational sites, including those with some evident geological interest, are at Level One.

Geotourism – the way forward?
The author's research on geological interpretation for such visitors, examines their nature, and on-site behaviour and develops the theme of geotourism which is:

The provision of interpretive and service facilities to enable tourists to acquire knowledge and understanding of the geology and geomorphology of a site (including its contribution to the development of the Earth sciences) beyond the level of mere aesthetic appreciation. (Hose 1996).

It is an interpretive strategy that promotes visitor awareness of the importance of, and need to conserve, geological sites with some general visitor interest. Interpretive provision to be effective must be widespread for, in the USA (Miller 1991), 'Studies consistently indicate that a single exposure in a zoo, museum or park program will have little lasting effect on a visitor. However, repeated exposure ... can have a significant and profound effect.' Geological conservation is an essential geotourism component; geotourists must be encouraged to collect only loose material, to notify professional geologists of important finds and to develop their photographic and artistic skills.

Past experiences and expectations
General interpretive considerations have emerged from the author's geology-centred and other workers' environmental-centred research:
1. visitors have past experiences that they bring to a site;
2. first impressions count – they influence future usage;
3. visitors learn best when involved in the learning process.

Their past experiences, and natural curiosity, must be taken into account when developing interpretive materials. The attracting and holding power of graphics which save on, and are more memorable than text, cannot be overemphasized. Effective communication reveals a site's story, preferably as part of an overall theme, through a unique ending or point of view.

Visitor behaviour and geological conservation

Interpretation seeks to present meaningful information and to elicit an appropriate response; a possible underpinning theoretical model is that of Ajzen & Fishbein (1980), relevantly employed (Taylor 1994) to analyse visitors to a botanical conservation exhibit. Essentially, visitors' actions can be explained, and the success of the communicated message assessed, by their:

- intention to perform the desired behaviour;
- attitude towards the desired behaviour;
- perception of the 'subjective norm' (pressure put on them to perform the desired behaviour);
- beliefs underlying the 'subjective norm' and their attitudes (behaviour leads to evaluated outcomes).

Behaviour indicative of a positive response to geological interpretation might include visitors' expressed support for and/or membership of conservation/geological bodies; equally it might stop the indiscriminate hammering of hard rock exposures and over collecting of specimens, so commonly reported by earth science conservationists, by geological field parties (Toghill 1972), and casual rockhounds:

> Beliefs underly a person's attitudes and subjective norms and ultimately determine intentions and behaviors. Behavioral change is ultimately the result of changes in beliefs. In order to influence behavior, people have to be exposed to information which will produces changes in their beliefs. (Taylor 1993).

Consequently, effective geological interpretive provision must present *information* at an appropriate visitor level; it must fire their imagination, involve them, impart something of the fascination of the subject and indicate why *some* conservation is necessary. Purely descriptive provision, coupled with some prohibition notice, is probably highly ineffective. Several guidelines and reviews (Badman 1994; Page 1992; Page *et al.* 1996; Wray 1991) covering the selection of geological sites for conservation and the management of geology interpretive provision have been issued.

The visitor understood and understanding?

The surveys outlined
Noting that:

> Interpretation is a fascinating field. It involves a variety of media, a knowledge of the site resources and your visitors. One of the most challenging tasks is the analysis of visitors and applying visitor patterns and learning strategies to a specific site. (Miller 1990),

visitors to both coastal and inland interpreted geology sites have been surveyed by the author; the research has particularly focused on psychographic profiling of visitors and an assessment of their interaction with geology interpretive provision. Data from four sites with relevance to the theme of coastal protection and geological conservation are presented below. The sites typify both popular coastal and inland holiday locations, together with some evaluation of the resident populations of the source areas from which the visitors to the former are drawn. Also, the sites literally display a broad cross-section of current geology interpretive media styles and practices, together with a range of geological conservation issues. Hence, the analysis of the data from the various visitor surveys provides a basis for assessing the likely knowledge and understanding of, and attitudes to, geology and site conservation of visitors to coastal sites of geological significance.

Various methodologies were employed to gather the summative evaluation data presented in the appended figures and discussed within the text:

1. respondent-completed questionnaires;
2. structured interviews;

3. observation studies;
4. tracking studies;
5. photographic recording of interpretive materials and visitor behaviour.

The principal survey vehicles were questionnaires and interviews focused on adults and party leaders visiting the sites, since their knowledge, opinions and attitudes to geology are crucial to evaluating the success of the various geology interpretive schemes.

The sites
Hunstanton and Charmouth, as well as being popular with geologists, are much visited coastal recreational tourist sites. The low red and white Chalk cliffs of Hunstanton, Norfolk are interpreted by a single geology panel erected by English Nature in 1993 (Hose 1994b, Page 1994); additionally a photocopied information leaflet (Stevenson 1992) is available from the town's Tourist Information Centre. At Charmouth, Dorset the geology of the adjacent tall, highly unstable cliffs of fossil-packed Liassic dark shales, limestones and sandstones is explained by a geology interpretive panel and displays (including a 'hands on' centrepiece and a small audio-visual theatre) at the Heritage Coast Centre (Edmonds 1996); the area is very popular with both amateur and professional fossil collectors. Dudley and Ludlow are inland market centres. Dudley, West Midlands dominated by its Mediaeval castle perched upon an outcrop of Wenlock Limestone is distinctly industrial and urban in character; it has a number of tourist attractions, such as Dudley Zoo and The Black Country Museum, which are principally of interest to visitors from within the Birmingham conurbation. The Dudley Museum 'Time Trail' exhibition (Reid 1994) opened in November 1992; its main theme, explored through dioramas juxtaposed with large fossil-rich rock slabs, is the changing environments of the area (especially the internationally geologically significant Wren's Nest National Nature Reserve) over the past 400 million years. Ludlow, Shropshire with its Medieval castle and historic building core, is also built upon Wenlock Limestone, and is one of England's most perfect country towns (Cormack 1976); it is a popular venue for tourist

excursions from the English Midlands. Accessed, for an admission charge, via the tourist information centre, is the 'Reading the Rocks' exhibition; opened in 1995, this outlines the outstanding contribution of the nearby rocks and local/national geologists to the development of scientific geology in the nineteenth century. The area, with a sometimes detrimental impact upon sites (Toghill 1972), continues to be popular with geological field parties. Particularly noteworthy exhibits within 'Reading the Rocks' are a video microscope, a cartoon biography of the geologist Murchison, a diorama of early bony fishes and a display on the world's oldest known land animal – a predatory mite smaller than a pinhead!

The site surveys

At Hunstanton, on three successive Sundays in May 1994, over 10 hours, visitors who had viewed the panel for more than 30 seconds were interviewed. A log was kept over some 12 hours of visitors' response to the panel. Thirty-two visitors (80% response rate) were interviewed. At Charmouth, for six hours over three days in June 1994, visitors' response to the interpretive panels was logged. Additionally, over seven consecutive days in August 1994, 58 visitors were interviewed (90% response rate) as they exited the Centre. During August 1994 respondent-completed questionnaires were also issued from the Centre; 143 were returned. At Dudley, over four Saturdays in June/July 1995 52 (83% response rate) visitors exiting the 'Time Trail' exhibition were interviewed. At Ludlow, respondent-completed questionnaires were distributed within the exhibition space; 64 were returned during the period May to August 1995.

Outdoor interpretive panel usage

The Hunstanton panel's seemingly low (24%) response rate (Fig. 14.1) is actually, when compared with data from other sites (Bitgood et al. 1986), quite encouraging; its attracting and holding power rose as high tide approached, forcing people off the main sandy beach and onto either the promenade or the beach beneath the cliffs. The maximum recorded viewing time was 2.51 min and the mean was 1.02 min; one minute was judged to be the minimum viewing time required to assimilate the panel's data. The unseasonal

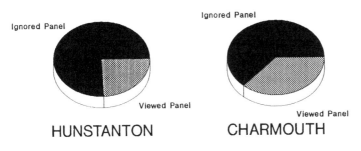

HUNSTANTON   CHARMOUTH

Fig. 14.1. Visitors response to information panels (coastal surveys).

inclement weather undoubtedly affected visitor behaviour towards the panel! At Charmouth, the interpretive panels' attracting (Fig. 14.1) and holding power *appeared* to be high. The maximum viewing time logged was 4.36 min and the mean was 1.04 min; it was greatest in the afternoon, when it was cooler, and at high tide. However, very few visitors actually read the geology interpretive panel; most were more interested in the adjacent panels on local wildlife and topography; consequently, interviews to assess its interpretive success were suspended. The interpretive success of the Hunstanton panel can be noted; 42% of respondents recalled the area was 'like the Bahamas' and 27% 'a warm, clear tropical sea' when the cliff's rocks were made. Some 53% of interviewees gave an accurate indication of the age of the rocks forming the cliffs. Clearly, the use of common terms and colourful word pictures was helpful to visitors. The clear warnings on cliff safety and geological conservation were ignored by many visitors at Charmouth.

General site survey findings
The generally similar visitor age profiles (Fig. 14.2) of Hunstanton/ Ludlow and Dudley/Charmouth reflect the former's retiree base and the latter's attractiveness to those in mid life-cycle (with children). Consideration of the party size (Fig. 14.3) and visitation patterns (Fig. 14.4) of respondents and interviewees reinforces this conclusion – note the high proportion of couples at Hunstanton. The concentration of party sizes of three and four persons at Charmouth and Dudley is indicative of the attractiveness of these

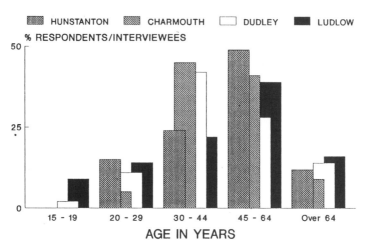

Fig. 14.2. Age profile of interviewees (inland and coastal surveys).

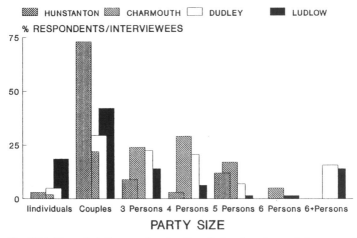

Fig. 14.3. Size of visitor parties to sites (inland and coastal surveys).

sites to families. At all of the sites, national newspaper readership (Fig. 14.5) was restricted to some 60% of respondents and interviewees. Interestingly, whilst Dudley and Hunstanton interviewees were tabloid inclined, Charmouth and Ludlow respondents had a comparatively high readership of broadsheets. Comparison with initial educational attainment levels (Fig. 14.6) suggests a clear

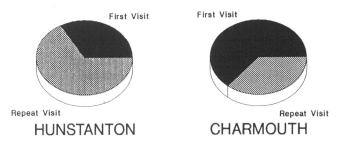

HUNSTANTON   CHARMOUTH

Fig. 14.4. Pattern of site visitation in the past 12 months (coastal surveys).

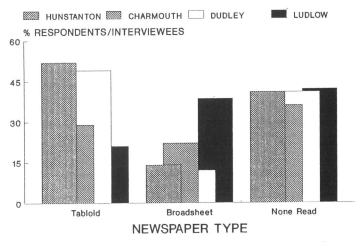

Fig. 14.5. National press readership of visitors (inland and coastal surveys)

correlation of high broadsheet readership (Fig. 14.5) with those who have completed higher education. The unexpectedly high reported 'A' Level initial study level at Dudley appears to be a recording error. The generally low level of initial educational attainment at Hunstanton probably reflects past regional employment trends, coupled with the mature age of many interviewees. The high level of tertiary education of Charmouth's respondents is noteworthy and is also reflected in the level of geological study.

The level of geological education (Fig. 14.7) is very low at all of the sites; however, at Charmouth, hobby geologists (at Miller's

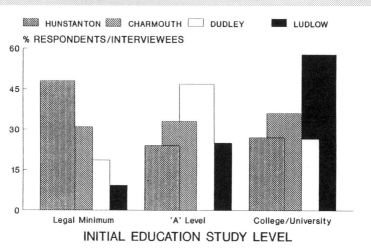

Fig. 14.6. Initial education study level of interviewees (inland and coastal surveys).

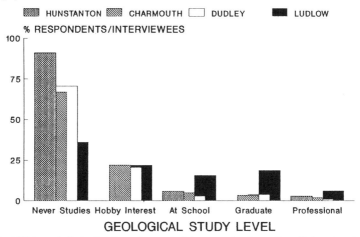

Fig. 14.7. Level of study of geology of visitors to the four sites (inland and coastal surveys).

Level Two) are clearly represented. Media hype, as much as genuine geological knowledge, clearly influenced interviewees' ability to name geological systems (Fig. 14.8); the release of the major film 'Jurassic Park' was contemporaneous with the surveys.

A third of Charmouth interviewees could name the Cretaceous system; very few of the Hunstanton interviewees could recall the

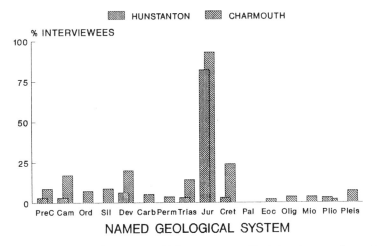

Fig. 14.8. Geological systems which were named by interviewees (coastal surveys).

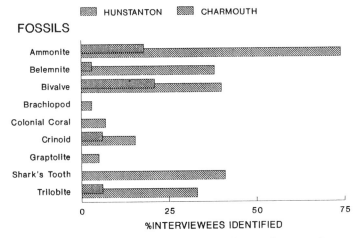

Fig. 14.9. Fossils recognized by interviewees (coastal surveys).

same system from the panel. Overall, interviewees had a very poor knowledge of basic stratigraphy. By comparison, recall and identification rates for fossils (Fig. 14.9), especially at Charmouth, were quite good. Ammonites, and bivalves were the most readily

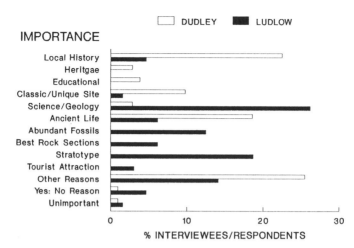

Fig. 14.10. Perceived importance of sites at exact locations (inland surveys).

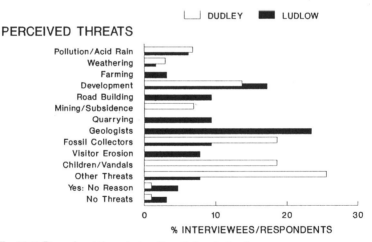

Fig. 14.11. Perceived threats to sites (inland sites).

recognized fossils. At Charmouth these, and belemnites, are the commonest fossils; over a third of its interviewees could identify most of the common fossil types. Hunstanton interviewees were probably disadvantaged by the general lack of local fossil-rich exposures; the ability of Hunstanton interviewees to identify the fossil bivalve, similar to forms found living on the beach today, suggests that access to fossil displays might improve their recognition ability.

The museum surveys at the inland sites were especially designed to examine the knowledge and perceptions of the local geology of interviewees and respondents; only around a third had any real knowledge of the local important geology sites and their populist publications. Again, at both museums, one quarter or less acknowledged the important local fossils; a significant proportion expressed no real interest in them! Perceived site importance (Fig. 14.10) generally centred upon the concepts of heritage, local history and civic pride. Additionally, at Dudley 'ancient life' and at Ludlow 'importance to science/geology' and 'stratotype' were significant categories. Common perceived threats (Fig. 14.11) to the local geology were 'development' and the activities of fossil collectors and geology parties. 'Vandals and unruly children' were significant perceived threats for Dudley's urban interviewees. Ludlow respondents were also most concerned about 'road building' and 'quarrying'. The perceived threats of 'pollution and acid rain' at both sites is indicative that general environmental concerns are widespread if somewhat misunderstood!

Rockhounds considered

Geotourism retailing and marketing

Observation studies and responses to interview questions on the nature and pricing of geology retail goods indicate that inexpensive souvenirs, moderately-priced giftware, prepared fossils, mineral specimens and postcards are prime retail items; the latter's interpretive value is considerably underexploited. Geology leaflets, maps and books, whilst frequently examined by visitors, are marginal retail items. Clearly, populist geological literature could benefit from improvements in design and informational style and content; the tabloid readership levels (and consequently under 15 years of age reading ability) set clear limits to the vocabulary and style of such interpretive materials. Interestingly, many visitors expressed the view that leaflets should be free.

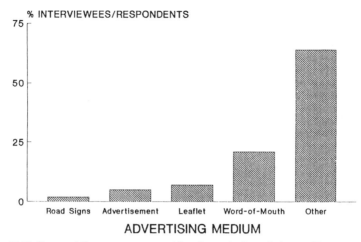

% INTERVIEWEES/RESPONDENTS

ADVERTISING MEDIUM

Fig. 14.12. Coastal Survey: source of first knowledge of site at Charmouth.

Conclusions

Despite some regional visitor base variation, general trends are evident. Overall, education levels were higher at specifically geological, compared with more general recreational, sites. Most visitors arrived in couples and small family groups; interviewees from the latter frequently expressed the view that the decision to visit had been prompted by the site's entertainment and educational potential for children. The sites held little attraction for those aged 15–29 years. 'Hands on' and 'live interpretation' (especially guided walks) are the most popular and enjoyable interpretive vehicles for visitors; the chance to converse with an 'expert', especially for those visitors with children, is much appreciated. Traditional displays and panels best attracted, held and informed visitors when bold graphics and simple, focused storylines were employed (Hose 1994a,b); some keen awareness of general and geologically specific conservation issues was apparent. Evidently, geological interpretive schemes can be visitor attractions in their own right, capable of providing enjoyable memorable experiences for visitors (Hose 1994b). However, as the Charmouth data (Fig. 14.12) indicate, their promotion and marketing could be considerably improved. Formal promotional items (advertisements and leaflets) were much less important than personal recommendation; most were only aware of the centre as they entered the car park! Given the international significance of the area's geology it is a sad reflection of both the site-specific and more general promotion of the UK's rich geological heritage. In closing, remembering the intent of geology interpretive schemes to both inform and influence visitors, Nicholas Steno, arguably the founder of scientific geology, writing in Renaissance Italy aptly concluded: 'What we see is beautiful, what we know is more beautiful, what we cannot grasp, most beautiful'.

Acknowledgements

The receipt of a research grant from the Buckinghamshire College enabled the initial fieldwork to be undertaken. The co-operation of the staff of the various survey sites is gratefully recorded.

References

Ajzen, I. & Fishbein, M. 1980. *Understanding Attitudes and Predicting Social Behaviour*. Prentice Hall, Englewood Cliffs, USA.

Badman, T. 1994. Interpreting earth science sites for the public. *In*: O'Halloran, D. Green, C., Harley, M., Stanley, M. & Knill, J. (eds) *Geological and Landscape Conservation*. Geological Society, London, 429–432.

Bitgood, S. C., Patterson, D., Benefield, A. & Roper, J. T. 1986. *Technical Report No. 87\640 – Post-Occupancy Evaluation of the Predator House at The Birmingham Zoo*, Center for Social Design, Jacksonville, USA.

Burek, C. V. & Davies, H. 1994. Communication of Earth Science to the public – how successful has it been? *In*: O'Halloran, D. Green, C., Harley, M., Stanley, M. & Knill, J. (eds) *Geological and Landscape Conservation*. Geological Society, London, 483–486.

Cormack, P. 1976. *Heritage in Danger*. New English Library, London.

Edmonds, R. P. H. 1996. The potential of visitor centres: a case history. *In*: Page, K. N., Keene, P., Edmonds, R. P. H. & Hose,

T. A. 1996. *English Nature Research Report No.176: Earth Heritage Site Interpretation in England: a review of principal techniques with case studies.* English Nature, Peterborough, 16–21.

Ham, S. H. 1992. *Environmental Interpretation: A Practical Guide for People with Big Ideas and Small Budgets.* North American Press, Golden, USA.

Hose, T. A. 1994a. Telling the story of stone – assessing the client base. *In*: O'Halloran, D. Green, C., Harley, M., Stanley, M. & Knill, J. (eds) *Geological and Landscape Conservation.* Geological Society, London, 451–457.

Hose, T. A. 1994b. *Interpreting Geology at Hunstanton Cliffs SSSI Norfolk – a summative evaluation.* Buckinghamshire College, High Wycombe.

Hose, T. A. 1996. Geotourism, or can tourist become casual rockhounds? *In*: Bennett, M. R., Doyle, P., Larwood, J. G. & Prosser, C. D. (eds) *Geology On Your Doorstep.* Geological Society, London, 207–228.

McKirdy, A. R. 1987. Protective works and geological conservation. *In*: Culshaw, M. G., Bell, F. G., Cripps, J. C. & O'Hara, M. 1987. *Planning and Engineering Geology (Proceedings of the Twenty-Second Annual Conference of The Engineering Group of the Geological Society, Plymouth, September 1986)*, Geological Society, London, 81–85.

Miller, J. S. 1991. Increasing visitor education through a tiered approach to interpretation. *Visitor Studies: Theory Research and Practice*, **3**, *Proceedings of the 1990 Visitor Studies Conference*, 144–151.

Page, K. N. 1992. *English Nature Research Report 24 – Site Information Boards for Geological and Geomorphological SSSIs.* English Nature, Peterborough.

Page, K. N. 1994. Information signs for geological and geomorphological sites: basic principles. *In*: O'Halloran, D., Green, C., Harley, M., Stanley, M. & Knill, J. (eds) *Geological and Landscape Conservation.* Geological Society, London, 433–437.

Page, K. N., Keene, P., Edmonds, R. P. H. & Hose, T. A. 1996. *English Nature Research Report 176 – Earth Heritage Site Interpretation in England: a review of principal techniques with case studies*. English Nature, Peterborough.

Page, K. N. & Wray, J. 1995. Our Earth Heritage: A perspective from English Nature, *Environmental Interpretation*, **10**, 2, 14–15.

Reid, C. 1994. 'The Time Trail': a lesson learned. *Geology Today*, **10**, 2, 68–69.

Stevenson, K. 1992. *Hunstanton Cliffs: A Geological Guide for Visitors*. Norfolk College/YHA, Kings Lynn.

Taylor, R. 1993. The influence of a visit on attitude and behavior toward nature conservation. *Visitor Studies: Theory Research and Practice*, **6**, Collected papers from the 1993 Visitor Studies Conference, Alburquerque, New Mexico. 163–171.

Toghill, P. 1972. Geological conservation in Shropshire. *Journal of the Geological Society, London*, **128** 513–515.

Wray, J. 1991. Interpreting geological sites. *Earth Science Conservation*, **28**, 27–29.

15 England's Earth Heritage Resource – an asset for everyone

Kevin N. Page

Summary

- Britain's geological heritage is incredibly rich and has consequently played a fundamental role in the historical development of geology as a science.

- Inland geological exposures are few in number and rapidly deteriorate. On the coast, however, natural processes can sustain such windows into the past.

- These coastal sites can be of regional, national or international importance for the following reasons: scientific, heritage, education, economic, engineering, coastal defence, ecological and cultural.

Introduction

Britain's geological heritage is incredibly rich and varied, a legacy of the area's position on the constantly evolving margins of one of the vast tectonic plates making up the surface of the earth. For hundreds of thousands of years our ancestors have used this geological resource to support an ever increasingly complex technology, from simple stone tools to more complex metal objects, the basic materials of which have to be chemically processed from their raw geological source. In parallel, the need for shelter necessitated the use of geological materials and features – from the earliest use of caves and rock shelters to the active manipulating of mud and rock to built structures.

Both these demands for tools and shelter created the science of civil engineering as the working of these deposits progressed from surface scrapings to simple bell shaped pits such as those to work flint at Grimes Graves, Norfolk (dating from around 2100 years BC) to more sophisticated mines and quarries. The use of geological materials for purely decoration or ceremonial purposes is probably almost as old as its technological use and in Europe, for instance in France, the use of fossils in this way was well established at least 35 000 years ago (although the collecting of fossils, presumably for reasons of curiosity goes back much earlier, to at least 80 000 years ago; Gayrard-Valy 1994, p.12).

It was not, however, until relatively recently that scholarly logic and study began to make sense of the occurrence of rocks, fossils and minerals. The philosophers of the Renaissance in the sixteenth and seventeenth centuries speculated on the true origins of geological materials (Gayrard-Valy 1994), but it was in the early nineteenth century that the fundamental framework of modern geological science was established in Britain through the work of pioneers such as William Smith (1769–1839), James Hutton (1726–1797) and Charles Lyell (1797–1875) (Gayrard-Valy 1994; Wilson 1994).

The demands of the early industrial revolution at this time forced scholarly philosophy to be translated into repeatable science. To fuel the developing economies it was necessary to know how and where to find the raw materials needed and gradually the geologist, as a professional, became established. In Britain the establishment of a national Geological Survey in 1835, under Sir Henry de la Beche (1796–1855) demonstrated a recognition by the state of the key role of the science in a developing industrial society (Rose 1996).

In a temperate lowland dominated country, such as England, however, exposures of this rich heritage are rare and rapidly deteriorate due to both natural processes (overgrowth) and human activity (dumping, infill, 'restoration' of former industrial works, etc). On the coast however, active natural processes produce ideal conditions for maintaining exposures – the 'windows into the past', so valuable and fundamental for access to this heritage of both national and international significance.

The justification for Earth Heritage conservation

When justifying the conservation of these sites, in the face of developments which may destroy or damage the features of importance, it is useful to invoke eight basic categories of significance. As discussed below, each provides a link between human society and features of nature conservation importance.

1. Scientific importance

Science is a process in which knowledge is gained by the empirical study of natural process, whether it be biological, chemical or physical. The knowledge gained is then applied for technological development. The raw materials for geological science are rocks and the minerals and fossils they contain. Access to these materials is crucial for the advancement of the science. Exposures, such as those so significantly seen in coastal areas, are therefore fundamental to the development of geological science. To lose an exposure is to stifle some small part of our developing understanding of the planet we live on.

The argument is often put forward that once sampling and measurement has taken place, an exposure is not 'needed' anymore. This is far from the truth; science is continually developing and new techniques and methods are always being developed. The application of these new techniques provides greater insight into geological materials and processes – but only if the original exposures remain. Such cycles of 're-discovery' occur around every 5–10 years or so and demand re-examination and re-assessment of previously established theories. Recent such advances in geological science include Plate Tectonics (from *c.* 1967; the realization that the earth surface is composed of moving plates which as a by-product produce earthquakes and volcanic eruptions with very direct human consequences; Press & Siever 1982, p. 441), sequence stratigraphy (from *c.* 1977; identifying packages of sediments as specific deposition phases – important for the detection and development of oil reserves; Wilson 1990) and the recognition of the periodicity of mass extinctions of life on Earth (from *c.* 1982; Hallam, Jablonski and Sepkoski *in* Briggs & Crowther 1990, pp. 161–179 including the effects of extraterrestrial impacts. The concept of a 'Nuclear Winter' was a spin-off from this research, as is the present USA interest in the possibilities of future impacts).

Fig. 15.1. Group examining geological exposures.

This scientific study underpins or gives rise to most of the following conservation justifications.

2. Heritage

The rocks record the history of the Earth and the origins and evolution of life. This is also our heritage, our own origins are recorded, as are those of all the animals and plants, with which we share the planet (International Declaration of the Rights of the Memory of the Earth *in* Martini and Pagès 1994). Such concepts of a shared heritage have given rise to organisations such as UNESCO and the development of *World Heritage* sites (Lyster 1985, p. 208). The Giant Causeway in the north of Ireland is a coastal site of geological importance where World Heritage status is already established and other coastal areas have been proposed.

The strong geological movement that developed in Britain in the nineteenth century also established the region's importance for subsequent global geological study – geological time is divided into named time periods, of which several were first named in Britain, following intensive study by pioneers. Time divisions such as Cambrian (after Cambria, the Roman name for Wales), Ordovician and Silurian (after the Ordovices and Silures Welsh borderland tribes) and Devonian (after the county of Devon) were first named in Britain. These time periods are divided into finer divisions known as stages – each typically around 2 to 6 million years in duration – these have geographical names commemorating their place of first recognition. Forty-eight of the 122 stages recognized by Harland *et al.* (1992) for the last million years of Earth history were first established in Britain (or 42 of the 66 for the first 280 million years of this 570 alone!). The definition of these stages is regulated by a UNESCO project, the International Stratigraphic Commission and each stage requires designation at a 'Global Stratotype Section and Point' or GSSP (Salvador 1994) – the only world designation for geological heritage – beyond more generalized 'World Heritage' status (Lyster 1985, p.208).

At least one GSSP has been established in England in a coastal location, near Holker Hall in Cumbria (George *et al.* 1976, p. 9) as a reference for the Holkerian Stage of the Carboniferous and candidates for several others exist (Melendez & Page 1995). The value of coastal locations as global references is that they are maintained indefinitely by natural systems and, excepting where coastal defences are constructed, will be available, in excellent condition in perpetuity for consultation and study by visitors from all over the world. It is only where deposits are of very limited extent that coastal erosion can remove them in their entirety, but such sites are unlikely to make good candidate GSSPs.

On a more local scale, the same superb exposures record in Britain at least 2900 million years of the history of the Earth, over 60% of the complete history of the planet. In England alone, the last 400 million years (Devonian Period to present day) is recorded in great detail, probably more completely than in any other comparably sized area on Earth.

3. Education

Education functions at many levels from basic primary introduction through to higher education and adult education. At all stages in Britain, geology is present in one form or another. The 'National Curriculum' itself requires pupils to be aware of some aspect of geological materials and processes at all stages from Key Stage 1 (age 5–7 years) onwards (Hawley 1996). Throughout this progress access to materials and sites becomes increasingly essential – and coastal sites with their typically open and free access (without the student age related controls of working minerals sites) are absolutely crucial. The large size of exposure – allowing the dispersal of student project groups – and relative safety of most sites (absence of machinery and availability of foreshore exposures away from more hazardous cliffs) makes coastal sites highly suitable and attractive for educational study.

At GCSE and 'A' level, the teaching is more closely related to the scientific development of the earth sciences and especially in higher education, HND and degree-level courses depend on precisely the same features that the scientific community is in the process of interpreting. Education does not of course finish once an individual leaves school or college, and the rise of adult education courses in geology – often linked to field study centres or university extra mural departments places further demands to find and utilize sites. Coastal sites have the added benefit that they are swept clean twice a day before the next class comes along!

Non-structured and informal education through passive inter-pretation of features or active guided walks is a form much valued in our society; both by those organizations responsible for site management (local authorities, national organisations such as English Nature, Wildlife Trusts, etc.) and by the visitors themselves. Site interpretation, involving sign-boards, self-guided trails and heritage centres (Page *et al.* 1996) informs and even attracts hundreds of thousands – maybe even millions – of people to geological sites every year in Britain. Coastal locations with their very obvious geological features and high recreational use can be particularly successful vehicles for raising public awareness – one small heritage centre on the Dorset coast for instance, recorded over 34 000 visitors in 1995 (Edmonds *in* Page *et al.* 1996) – the economic input of these visitors into the local economy can obviously be very significant.

Fig.15.2. Information plaque on the coast.

4. Economic

The scientific study of geological deposits of economic value or relevance, enhances the effectiveness and efficiency of subsequent exploration and production of such deposits. Recent relevant examples in Britain relate very directly to the oil industry and the development of oil fields in both the North Sea and also in Dorset. For instance, the coast of North Yorkshire shows the only extensive exposures anywhere around the North Sea of the type of geological environment in which the oil is produced from the deep wells. Much of this oil is contained in the spaces between the sand grains laid down by rivers during the Middle Jurassic (around 178–160 million years ago). These sands are excellently exposed around Scarborough in North Yorkshire as demonstrated by Nami & Leeder (1978) and often form sinuous bodies representing the constantly changing paths of meandering rivers. Understanding the geometry of these sand bodies is fundamental to the understanding and therefore prediction of where oil reserves may be found in similar deposits deep below the North Sea (Brooks & Glenure 1987). The floodplain muds which surround many of the sand bodies can provide an ideal 'cap' to hold in the oil.

These key surface exposures provide the only direct human access to features buried at depth and the most economically viable opportunity to increase exploration and production efficiency by improving the understanding of their formation (as boreholes are very expensive to drill). Comparable opportunities to improve survey and production efficiently have been provided by exposures of oil source rocks and reservoir sands in Dorset (Colter & Havard 1981), coal field exposures on the coast of NE England and also by exposures of metalliferous mineral deposits in Southwest England.

Very rarely are coastal mineral deposits actually worked themselves in Britain, planning controls restricting such developments in these sensitive coastal areas. Nevertheless, historically, good exposure has provided ready access to materials of economic value, examples including the Alum shales of North Yorkshire, the metalliferous mineral deposits of southwest England and the quality building stone deposits of South Dorset. The value of these old workings themselves is now primarily scientific or cultural (i.e. historical), but may still be of relevance for the development of inland or underground resources.

A much underrated economic justification for coastal site conservation links closely to the educational value of exposures – educational and recreational groups often have a high demand for site use – school and university parties, as well as extra-mural groups and innumerable amateur enthusiasts bring money to coastal towns and, in certain areas, actually help maintain a 'tourist' season well into the autumn and winter (including the 'Geotourists' of Hose 1996). Although nowhere quantified, it is certain that the economy of such locations significantly depends on the annual influx of such groups and in one Scottish example, hoteliers have been key players in trying to ensure continued access to geological features, so much do they depend on visiting groups out of season.

5. Engineering

The study of coastal exposures and processes is crucial to a number of engineering disciplines. In its simplest form the coast is a source of materials for assessment or study of their engineering properties, but by far more significant is the opportunity the coast provides, for the study of active geomorphological processes. Essentially, this study is scientific but it is frequently driven by geo-technical and engineering concerns.

Such features include the huge landslip systems of the West Dorset coast (Allison 1992) an understanding of which has direct relevance to road building schemes in the area, which others cross old landslip systems. Failure to understand the mechanisms of collapse can lead to the reactivation of such systems (Brunsden & Jones 1976) with obvious economic consequences.

The nature and mechanisms of cliff failure and sediment transfer and deposition are all very relevant to human activity and of fundamental relevance to coastal engineering. The maintenance and study of unprotected, naturally evolving systems is therefore absolutely crucial to the development of new and more efficient techniques for coastal protection in areas where human development has led to an artificial coast (and non-intervention would mean the loss of property and installations considered to be of sufficient importance or value that relocation is not presently a viable option).

6. Coastal defence

Closely linked to an increased understanding of coastal process as a result of scientific and geotechnical studies, is the realization that natural processes can actually achieve the aims of coastal engineering in a cheaper, more effective and sustainable manner. Coastal erosion provides sediment which is deposited as beaches which protect coastal developments. Prevention of erosion, leads to sediment starvation, beach scouring and damage or loss to such development (or to the increasing demand for ever more expensive engineering options). An excellent example of this is on the coast between Poole and Hurst Castle, in Dorset and Hampshire – coastal development and defence in the west of the bay and the construction of a groyne system, has starved the eastern part of the bay and led to increased coastal erosion. Attempts to control this recession around development near Highcliffe and Barton has cost tens of millions of pounds, and, further east, erosion of Hurst Castle threatens to destroy this historic feature and also threatens sites of cultural and wildlife importance (Bray *et al.* 1996). The chances of reinstating natural systems in this area are very unlikely considering the level of development, but elsewhere in Britain, realization of the importance of protecting sediment transfer systems can only reduce the possibility of creating such problems.

Very occasionally, however, it is possible to reinstate a natural system and the re-creation of salt marsh at Tollesbury in Essex, by removing a sea wall and allowing reclaimed agricultural land to return to its original condition, is an experiment based on the realization that natural systems such as these can provide alternative solutions to more expensive engineered coastal defences (Burd 1995).

7. Ecological

Rocky exposures and coastal soft sediment systems provide, in their natural condition, unique habitats for a vast diversity of living plants and animals (for example, see Duncan 1992). These range from salt and desiccation resistant dune and shingle plants, many nationally rare, to animals adapted to living either in soft moving sands and muds or attached to hard rocky surfaces. Birds, in particular, are a very obvious group with many species tied to a coastal existence, either for feeding or for nesting sites.

The intrinsic value of these species is not developed further here, but coastal areas provide ready access to a maritime world, not available to most people. This land–sea interface, is therefore of great educational importance and as discussed above, use by education groups can bring real economic benefits to coastal areas (beyond the obvious relevance to the demands and requirements of the educational system itself). The geological and geomorphological features of coastal sites underpin and-support these species and habitats and therefore to change or modify them can have significant biological knock-on effects.

8. Cultural

Coastal geological sites include features with a very long cultural significance; spectacular features such as Durdle Door and Lulworth Cove in Dorset are not only aesthetically appealing and draw hundreds of thousands of visitors each year but others may be associated with myth and legend, such as St Michaels Mount and King Arthurs Castle (Tintagel), both in Cornwall indicating a much older cultural fascination. Historically, such sites may have a long history of human use with archaeological deposits, occasionally in a geological context, such as at Brean Down on the Somerset coast.

Elsewhere, the remains of mineral workings including associated buildings and engine-houses are a testament to past economic exploitation of coastal mineral deposits. The West Cornish coast has many such features and elsewhere in Britain many old quarries remain, often showing features of significance to a man-made heritage such as buildings and machinery. The context of all these sites is intimately linked to geology – conservation of geology therefore conserves a built and a cultural heritage.

Science in fact is a cultural exercise and the strong links between geological features and the development of the science, raises the status of sites important in the history of the geology, to a status of cultural importance.

Conclusion

Inevitably the aesthetic, scientific, heritage, cultural and ecological importance of coastal sites, leads to recreational demands from millions of visitors each year, each attracted by the natural features a site possesses or the potential of these features for recreation. Such features are arguably valued in some way by the vast majority of people living in Britain today. The realization of the existence of such links with our own society and its development should encourage all decision makers with responsibilities for coastal areas, to work together to achieve more effective management of a rich and varied natural resource as an asset for everyone.

References

Allison, R. J. 1992. *The Coastal Landforms of the Dorset Coast.* Geologists' Association Guide, **47**.

Arkell, W. J. 1933. *The Jurassic System in Great Britain.* Clarendon Press, Oxford.

Bray, M. J., Carter, D. J. & Hooke, J. M. 1996. *Excursion Guidebook: Poole and Christchurch Bay.* Conference on Coastal Defence and Earth Science Conservation, 26–27 March 1996, University of Portsmouth.

Briggs, D. E. G. & Crowther, P. R. 1990. *Palaeobiology, a Synthesis.* Blackwell Scientific.

Brooks, J. & Glennie, K. W. (eds) 1987. *Petroleum Geology of North West Europe.* Graham & Trotman, London, 2 vols.

Brunsden, D. & Jones, D. K. C. 1976. The morphology of degraded landslide slopes in-South West Dorset. *Quarterly Journal of Engineering Geology*, **5**, 205–222.

Burd, F. 1995. *Campaign for a Living Coast. Managed Retreat: a Practical Guide.* English Nature.

Colter, C. S. & Havard, D. J. 1981. The Wytch Farm Oil Field. *In:* Illing, L. V. & Hobson, G. D. (eds). *Petroleum Geology of the Continental Shell of North-West Europe.* Heyden & Son, London, 494–503.

Darvill, T. 1987. *Prehistoric Britain.* B.T. Batsford, London.

Duncan, K. 1992. *An Introduction to England's Marine Wildlife.* English Nature.

Edwards, W. N. 1976. *The Early History of Palaeontology.* British Museum (Natural History), London.

Gayrard-Valy, Y. 1994. *The Story of Fossils: in Search of Vanished Worlds.* Thames and Hudson, London and Harry N. Abrams, New York (original French edition 1987, published by Gallimard).

George, T. N., Johnson, G. A. L., Mitchell, M., Prentice, J. E., Ramsbottom, W. H. C., Sevastopulo, G. & Wilson, R. B. 1976. *A Correlation of Dinantian Rocks in the British Isles.* Geological Society, London, Memoir, **7**.

Harland, W. B., Armstrong, R. L, Cox, A. V., Craig, L. E., Smith, A. G. & Smith, D. G. 1990. *A Geologic Time Scale 1989*. Cambridge University Press.

Hawley, D. 1996. Urban Geology and the National Curriculum. *In*: Bennett, M. R., Doyle, P., Larwood, J. G. & Prosser, C. P. (eds) *Geology on your Doorstep*. Geological Society, London, 155–162.

Hose, T. A. 1996. Geotourism, or can tourists become casual rock hounds? *In*: Bennett, M. R., Doyle, P., Larwood, J. G. & Prosser, C. P. (eds) *Geology on your Doorstep*. Geological Society, London, 207–228.

Lyster, S. 1985. *International Wildlife Law*. Corotius, Cambridge.

Martini, G, & Pagès (eds) 1994. Actes du Premier Symposium International sur la-protection du patrimonie geologique; Digne-les-Bains, 11–16 juin 1991. Mémoire Societé Géologique, France, **165**.

Melendez, G. & Page, K. N. 1995. Protecting the Jurassic: global boundary stratotypes and conservation. *Geology Today*, **11**, 226–228.

Nami, M. & Leeder, M. R. 1978. Changing channel morphologies and magnitude in the Scalby Formation (Middle Jurassic) of Yorkshire (England). *In*: Miall, A. D. (ed.) *Fluvial Sedimentation*, Canadian Society of Petroleum Geologists Memoirs, 431–440.

Nature Conservancy Council. 1990. *Earth Science Conservation in Great Britain. A strategy*. NCC.

Page, K. N., Keene, P., Edmonds R. P. H. & Hose, T. A. 1996 *Earth Heritage Site Interpretation in England. A Review of Principal Techniques with Case Studies*. English Nature Research Report 176.

Press, F. & Siever, R. 1982. Global plate tectonics: the unifying model. *In*: Press, F. & Siever, R. (eds) *Earth*. Freeman, New York, 441–463.

Rose, E. P. F. 1996. Geologists and the army in nineteenth century Britain; a scientific and educational symbiosis? *Proceedings of the Geologists' Association*, **107**, 129–142.

Salvador, A. (ed.) 1994. *International Stratigraphic Guide – a Guide to Stratigraphic Classification, Terminology and Procedure* (2nd edn). International Union of Geological Sciences and the Geological Society of America.

Shackley, M. 1977. *Rocks and Man*. George Allen and Unwin, London.

Wilson, R. C. L. 1990. Sequence stratigraphy: an introduction. *Geoscientist*, **1**(1), 13–23.

Wilson, R. C. L. (ed.) 1994. *Earth Heritage Conservation*. Geological Society, London and Open University, Milton Keynes.

Part Five

Case studies: Poole and Christchurch Bays, southern England

In this part the geology, geomorphology and management issues of a particular area are examined to illustrate many of the points made in the rest of the book. The area selected is that of Poole and Christchurch Bays on the central part of the south coast of England. This stretch of coast contains some prime conservation sites, including world stratotypes. Its geological exposures and the reasons for conservation designation are described in detail. The geomorphological setting is outlined, then the present management situation at three sites is presented. In each case the situation is described from the perspective of both the local authority management and the conservation agency through the SSSI documentation. This section provides up-to-date information on some key issues and demonstrates how potential conflicts and management problems are being addressed.

16 The importance of coastal sites in Palaeogene conservation, exemplified by the succession in Christchurch Bay

Brian Daley

Summary

- The unlithified nature of most British Palaeogene strata differentiates them in a conservation context from older better lithified rocks.

- With the demise of a variety of inland sections in such strata since the last century, coastal Palaeogene sections have become increasingly important as sources of data and understanding.

- The natural and often rapid recession of cliffs in Palaeogene strata has led to conflicts of interest which bear upon the quality of the sections.

- The Palaeogene GCR/SSSI sites in Christchurch Bay are described and interpreted as an example of the importance of coastal Palaeogene sections.

Introduction

In 1977, the Nature Conservancy Council initiated the Geological Conservation Review (GCR) to assess, document and publish accounts of a wide variety of sites representing Britain's geological heritage. The finally selected GCR sites have been notified as Sites of Special Scientific Interest (SSSIs) and are currently being written up in a series of thematic volumes in the Geological Conservation Review Series published by the Joint Nature Conservation Committee (JNCC).

In Britain, rocks assigned to the Tertiary Sub-era, are well represented. Igneous rocks of this age are mainly found in northwestern Britain (see the GCR volume by Emeleus & Gyopari 1992). Thick sedimentary deposits of Tertiary age occur offshore around Britain whilst onshore, such strata occur most extensively in two areas: the London Basin extending into parts of East Anglia and the Hampshire Basin.

In excess of 65 GCR sites have been chosen to represent these onshore Tertiary deposits. These include those selected for their importance regarding one or more fossil groups (mammals, fish, amphibia, reptiles, birds, plants) and/or their stratigraphical value. Of the latter, 33 are Palaeogene sites, 22 are of Neogene age, whilst one (Walton-on-the-Naze) represents both epochs.

Whilst there are lithified rocks of Tertiary age, such as the Bembridge Limestone in the Isle of Wight and the Hertfordshire Puddingstone in the London Basin, the generally unlithified nature of strata of this age in Britain gives rise to problems generally absent in older parts of the succession. With the demise of small brickpits and quarries in the present century, few inland Tertiary exposures remain. Even those which have been worked relatively recently soon degrade or become quickly overgrown whilst, in other cases, planning legislation frequently requires the restoration of a site once extraction has stopped. An example is the former ECC Ball Clays site known as Squirrel Cottage (southwest of Wareham, Dorset) where work ceased in 1993, backfilling was completed in 1995 and which is now landscaped and bereft of any exposure. Furthermore, the conservation of quarry faces in tandem with any refurbishment is not normally feasible with such weak unlithified strata (see appendices to Nature Conservancy Council 1990).

It is, therefore, not surprising that coastal sites have an enhanced importance in the conservation of Tertiary strata. Equally unsurprising is that conflicting interests have inevitably arisen as the cliff sections in these unconsolidated Tertiary rocks have been subject to natural recession and as various measures have been undertaken to protect and stabilize them.

In the Hampshire Basin, the Palaeogene strata extend for something like 2200 km^2 from just east of Dorchester in the west to Worthing in the east, with their maximum thickness developed in the Isle of Wight. Large areas, as in The New Forest, are present below a Quaternary cover whilst in places such as Portsmouth and Southampton, there is extensive urban development. Within this area there are 19 GCR sites chosen for their importance to Palaeogene stratigraphy and which have a considerable and indeed, in some cases, an international scientific value. Seven of these are in the Isle of Wight and 12 on the mainland of southern England. Of these 19, 13 (68%) are coastal sites, including the two most stratigraphically extensive sites of Palaeogene age in western Europe (Whitecliff Bay and Alum Bay). If one ignores the small and stratigraphically restricted western outliers at Blackdown, Bincombe Down and Creechbarrow, the relative importance of the coastal sites is even more apparent.

Of the 13 Palaeogene coastal sites in the Hampshire Basin, two (Wittering to Selsey Foreshore and Bognor Regis) are foreshore sites whose exposure is subject to variation in the distribution of the modern littoral sediments. Of the 11 remaining coastal sites, only five have escaped without some damage and/or the threat of damage. In the case of the remainder, there are some sites, such as Bournemouth Cliffs, where *bona fide* conflicting interests have resulted in compromise between need based on scientific value and that of local residents/businesses. Unfortunately, some sites have been seriously, perhaps permanently, damaged where this is not the case.

Christchurch Bay

Christchurch Bay is a particularly fine and scientifically valuable Tertiary coastal section and exemplifies some of the conflicting interests that arise with strata of this age. This paper presents a description of the Palaeogene geology and an evaluation of its importance, together with an historical review of research to illustrate how it has contributed over many years to improving our understanding of the Palaeogene, both locally and in a more international context.

Except at the entrance to Christchurch Harbour and at its eastern end, Christchurch Bay is bounded by cliffs comprising readily erodible, predominantly clastic strata. Three SSSIs, recognized for their stratigraphical importance, are present: Hengistbury Head to the west, Friars Cliff (just to the north of the entrance to Christchurch Harbour) and the laterally extensive section of 'Barton Cliffs' to the east of the latter (Fig. 16.1). All three are described in considerable detail and their SSSI status

Fig. 16.1. View westwards from the eastern part of 'Barton Cliffs' just to the west of Becton Bunny. The base of the cliff is protected here by rock armour, together with a number of rock groynes.

justified in the forthcoming Geological Conservation Review (GCR) volume on Tertiary Stratigraphy (Daley, in press).

Hengistbury Head

Hengistbury is a stratigraphically important Teriary site since it facilitates correlation of the more westerly exposures of strata adjacent to the Bracklesham Group/Barton Group junction with those further to the east. Palaeoenvironmentally, the site has helped geologists to better understand lateral changes in the Boscombe Sand and it is also the best exposure of the marginal sandy facies of the Barton Clay.

This stratigraphical SSSI comprises a sea cliff on the southern side of the Hengistbury Head peninsula (grid reference SZ 167907 to SZ 181906). Three lithostratigraphical units of Eocene age are present (Fig. 16.2). Historically, they have been referred to, in ascending order, as the Boscombe Sand (about 8 m), the Hengist-

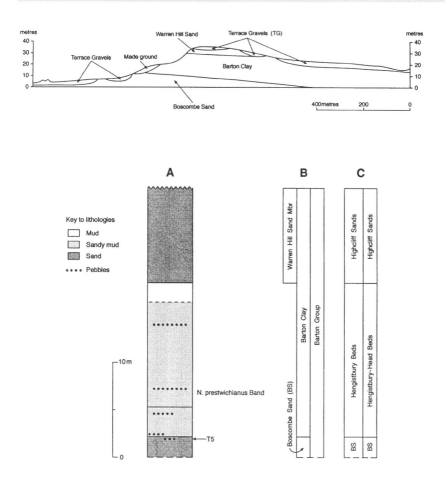

Fig. 16.2. The succession at Hengistbury Head (A), current lithostratigraphic usage (after Bristow *et al*. 1991) (B) and examples of earlier terminology (C).

bury Beds (about 16 m) and the Highcliffe Sands (9 m). The Boscombe Sand is now recognized as the lowest formation assigned by Edwards & Freshney (1987a) to their Barton Group. The other two correlate with the lowermost strata of the Barton Clay, exposed in 'Barton Cliffs' further to the east (Hooker 1975a; Curry 1976). Recently (Bristow *et al*. 1991), the highest of the three has been formally renamed the Warren Hill Sand Member of the Barton Clay.

The section has interested geologists since the early part of the nineteenth century. A great deal of attention has been paid to the stratigraphical position and correlation of the succession and this was a matter of considerable controversy over a number of years. Lyell (1827) assigned the strata at Hengistbury to the 'plastic clay formation' (i.e. the Reading Formation), stratigraphically *below* the 'London Clay' (*sic*) of Barton (i.e. what is now the Barton Clay). Prestwich (1849) took a contrary view, concluding that part of the succession represented a westerly reappearance of the Barton Clay. Only relatively recently (see particularly Curry 1976) has the matter been resolved and the 'Hengistbury Beds' recognized as the lower part of the Barton Clay.

Fossils present include molluscs, foraminifera including the zone fossil *Nummulites prestwichianus*, plant macrofossils and some vertebrate material. Costa *et al.* (1976) worked here on the dinoflagellate microflora as part of a broader correlative study.

A good stratigraphical account is given in Hooker (1975a), whilst Curry (1976, fig.1) also provides a useful summary of the sequence. Although Tylor (1850) considered the economic importance of the sideritic nodules in the section, it is only in recent years that the broader sedimentological aspects have been investigated. Plint (1983a,c) made a detailed study of the Boscombe Sands whilst the most up-to-date account of the overlying strata at Hengistbury is that of Bristow *et al.* (1991, pp. 66–7).

The Barton Clay below the Warren Hill Sand Member comprises some 16 m of sandy muds to muddy sands, its base being marked by a layer of well-rounded flint pebbles. The lowest 3 m are highly bioturbated and glauconitic. The remainder of the sequence includes five nodule bands of intermittent persistence. These are mainly sideritic ironstones, although the third set from the bottom comprises ball and pillow structures.

Lateral variation in the Barton Beds at Hengistbury Head has been referred to by Hooker (1975a). Whilst the nodule bands are less well-developed to the west, an increase in the sand and silt content in this direction is accompanied by an increase in the frequency of pebble bands within the sequence.

Microfaunal discoveries at the site have helped to resolve the Hengistbury Beds controversy. Curry (1937) found *Nummulites preswichianus* 4.6 m above the base of this unit. In a study of the dinoflagellate flora, Costa *et al.* (1976) found that the zone fossil *Wetzeliella draco* first appears immediately above the *N. prestwichianus* band, with their *Heteraulacacysta*? sp. A (*H. porosa*) about 1.5 m above. These two species define the base of Zone BAR-1 of Bujak *et al.* (1980), the oldest of the five 'Barton Beds zones' defined by these workers.

Good exposures of the Boscombe Sand occur at Hengistbury and comprise cross-bedded quartzose sands with flint pebbles, either scattered or in bands. The uppermost part of the Boscombe Sand comprises a clean, very well-sorted, fine-grained sand, up to 1.25 m thick, with a pebble bed locally developed at its base and which Plint (1983c) considered to mark the base of his T5 transgression. Body fossils are absent from the Boscombe Sand here but fossil burrows occur.

With the resolution of the correlation problem, the importance of the Hengistbury Head section in helping us to understand the palaeogeography of Barton Beds times becomes apparent. It has proved to be a key site palaeoenvironmentally, for it has contributed to our understanding of the lateral facies changes which characterises the Palaeogene rocks in this area. It in fact provides a valuable 'bridging' exposure between the more westerly sequences exposed around Bournemouth and beyond and those further eastwards on the mainland and in the Isle of Wight. It appears that the Hengistbury Beds represent a sandy, marginal marine facies compared with the contemporaneous muddy, off-shore Barton Clay facies found further to the east. Below, the palaeogeographical implications of the Boscombe Sand at this site cannot be ignored. Plint (1983b,c) considered that at Hengistbury, it comprises a lower estuarine tidal channel facies which correlates westwards with more up-river estuarine sediments and with distributary mouth bar facies to the east at Friars Cliff.

Friars Cliff, Mudeford

Immediately to the north of Christchurch Harbour is the SSSI of Friar's Cliff. This comprises a cliff section (Fig. 16.3) bounded to the west by a concrete sea wall and promenade (grid reference SZ

195927), with exposures continuing westwards above the later for a short distance. From the eastern end of the section (around SZ 199928), a well-vegetated cliff separates the site from Highcliffe and the long series of sections referred to as 'Barton Cliffs' *sensu lato*. The strata present comprise some 14 m of Boscombe Sands and the lowest part of the overlying Barton Clay and provide a link between the Bournemouth and Hengistbury sections to the west and those of the Isle of Wight to the east.

The earliest description of Friars Cliff is probably that of Prestwich (1849) in which he briefly surveyed the coastal geology from Christchurch to Poole Harbour and introduced such names as the Barton Beds and Boscombe Sands. Gardner (1879) gave the name Highcliff Sands to the sands below the Barton Clay at Friars Cliff although the term 'High Cliff sands and clays' had already been used by Wright (1851) for unit A3 of the Barton Clay. Fisher (1862) recognized a threefold division within the strata which he assigned to the 'Bracklesham Series' at this locality.

Fig. 16.3. Friars Cliff, Mudeford, Dorset. Boscombe Sand (Barton group), succeeded by the Barton Clay (greenish), below a cover of Quaternary Gravel at the top of the cliff.

The few metres of Barton Clay here, together with the much thicker sequence in 'Barton Cliffs' to the east, has attracted the attention of palaeontologists since the nineteenth century. Relatively recent work on the dinoflagellate zonation of the Palaeogene has established that the Barton Clay of Friars Cliff lies within the Zone BAR-1 of Bujak *et al.* (1980). In recent years, a study of the detailed sedimentology of Friars Cliff has been undertaken by Plint (1983b, 1988).

The Boscombe Sand at Friars Cliff comprises three 5–6 m thick, upward-coarsening sequences (Plint 1983b, 1988) where bioturbated silty sandy clay with abundant fine plant debris passes upwards into clean faintly laminated sand, overlain by cross-bedded fine to medium sand. At the western end of the section above the concrete promenade, the middle and upper-most of the three may be examined. Both sequences have been disturbed by contemporaneous soft sediment deformation with the resultant structures comprising an impressive feature of the section. 100 m eastwards from the promenade, the general bedded nature and tripartite division of the Boscombe Sands is lost and the whole unit is extensively deformed (Fig. 16.3).

The base of the overlying Barton Clay (about 3 m) is marked by an up to 30 cm thick pebble bed comprising well-rounded flint pebbles in a matrix of muddy glauconitic sand, overlain by green glauconitic muds very similar to the lowest part of the 'Hengistbury Beds' but less silty (Hooker 1975a).

From work on the dinoflagellate microfauna, Costa *et al.* (1976) suggested that the Boscombe Sands corresponded with the highest microplankton zone of the Bracklesham Beds (Zone B-5; see Bujak *et al.* 1980). Edwards & Freshney (1987a, p. 65) considered that it correlated with Prestwich Bed 28 of Alum Bay and that it ultimately passed eastwards into marine clays of the Barton Clay and that the pebble bed representing the initial Barton Clay transgression may be equivalent to that the top of Prestwich Bed 28.

Plint (1988) emphasized the importance of this site to our understanding of the palaeogeography of Boscombe Sand times. He considered that the coarsening-upwards cycles present here may represent pro-grading mouth-bars at the seaward end of a tidal channel system, with the tidal channels themselves represented further to the west in Bournemouth Cliffs. Plint (1988) believed that the Boscombe Sand of Friars Cliff correlates with lagoonal and coastal marine sediments in the Alum Bay section.

'Barton Cliffs'

Highcliffe, Barton, Beacon and Hordle Cliffs, which together comprise the SSSI referred to as 'Barton Cliffs', have provided a major contribution to the understanding of Middle to Late Eocene times in the southern British area. It includes the type sections for three formations within the Barton Group and is of international importance as the type section for the Bartonian Stage. Altogether, the section comprises cliffs extending from Highcliffe in the west (grid reference SZ 200930) to Milford-on-Sea (SZ 283915) some 8 km to the east (Fig. 16.4).

The strata present (Fig. 16.5) comprise, in ascending order, the Barton Clay (somewhat over 30 m, Fig. 16.6), the Chama Sand (around 5.5 m) and the Becton Sand (about 22 m) (all part of the Barton Group of Edwards & Freshney, 1987a), succeeded by more than 30 m of the Headon Hill Formation of Insole & Daley (1985) (= Headon Formation of Edwards & Freshney, 1987a) (Fig. 16.7). All beds dip eastwards at a very low angle. The oldest sediments occur at the western end of Highcliffe, whilst the youngest part of the Headon Hill Formation is exposed near Paddy's Gap to the west of Milford.

'Barton Cliffs' has a vast geological literature dating from the eighteenth century to the present day. In part, it is a catalogue of geological discovery, but also reveals some of the mistakes and some of the controversy that arose both in terms of classification and correlation. Early difficulty in correlating the mainland sections with those of the Isle of Wight is exemplified by Bowerbank's (1841) assignment of the beds at Barton to the London Clay. As an understanding of the stratigraphy developed, Prestwich (1847a) recognized the Barton Beds and Bracklesham Sands as separate formations and suggested (1847b) that the Barton Beds of Hampshire correlate with part of the Bagshot Sands succession in the London Basin. The earliest detailed, reasonably accurate descriptions of the succession in Barton, Beacon and Hordle Cliffs were published by Wright (1851) and the Marchioness of Hastings (1848, 1852, 1853). Towards the latter part of the nineteenth century, a large number of papers of a stratigraphical nature were published. Judd (1880) correlated the 'Lower Headon Beds' of Hordle with those of Headon Hill, largely on faunal evidence. Fisher (1882) correlated the thin Lower Headon Limestone and 'Upper Marine Bed' of Hordle with the How Ledge Limestone and the Middle Headon Beds of the Isle of Wight but his paper led to a furious controversy involving a large number of protagonists.

A few years later, Gardner *et al.* (1888) published an account of the complete succession of the Barton Clay and overlying Barton Sand. An important twentieth century study was that of Burton (1929) and his lettering system, by which he labelled the principal units of the Barton Beds, is still in use today. More recent work on the stratigraphy has been undertaken by Hooker (1986), Plint (1984) and Edwards & Freshney (1987a).

Notwithstanding the importance of stratigraphical matters, the abundance of well-preserved fossils was without doubt the principal factor which attracted an early interest in 'Barton Cliffs' and ultimately led to its becoming a classic British Tertiary locality. There is no disputing that palaeontologically 'Barton Cliffs' is one of the most important sites in the British Palaeogene succession. In the eighteenth century, a number of fossils from Barton were figured in Brander (1766). In the nineteenth century, many lists of fossils were published (e.g. Wright 1851). Many references to specimens collected from Barton Cliffs were made in a series of memoirs documenting the British Tertiary biota published by the Palaeontographical Society in the second half of the century, including works on the echinoids, bivalves, cephalopods, gastropods and fossil flora. Twentieth century work on the palaeontology includes studies of the Bryozoa, the molluscs, Foraminifera (including *Nummulites*), brachiopods, on asteroids and ophiuroids, decapod crustaceans and the echinoids. It is perhaps particularly famous for its molluscan fauna, the quality and preservation of which is unrivalled in the Hampshire Basin. Burton (1933) listed some 480 species, most of which occur in large numbers. Vertebrate studies include those on fish otoliths, small amphibians, reptiles and mammals. Plant macrofossils (leaves, fruits and seeds) described

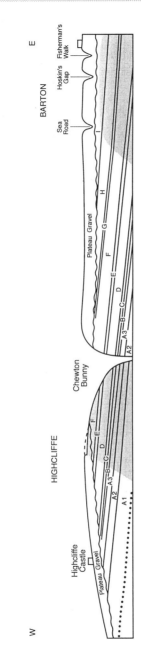

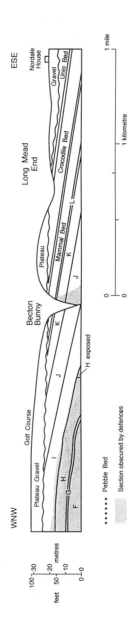

Fig. 16.4. Profile of 'Barton Cliffs' (after Melville & Freshney 1982).

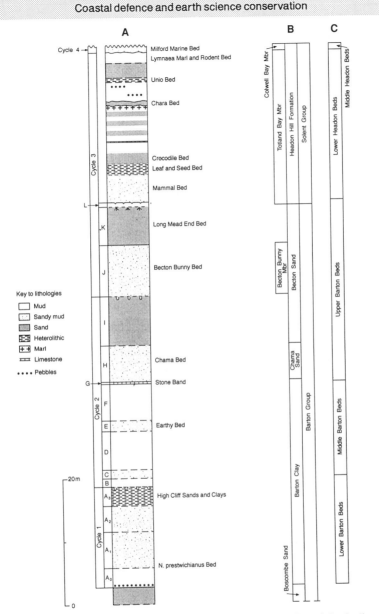

Fig. 16.5. The succession in 'Barton Cliffs' (after various authors), including the bed lettering system of Burton (1929) and cycles recognized (Hooker 1976) (A), current lithostratigraphic usage (Edwards & Freshney 1987a; Insole & Daley 1985) (B) and former terminology (Curry & Wisden 1958) (C).

Fig. 16.6. Barton Clay to the east of Chewton Bunny, below a cover of Quaternary Gravel at the top of the cliff.

Fig. 16.7. Cliff to the east of Becton Bunny, showing the Becton Sand and a thin development of the succeeding Headon Hill Formation, overlain by Quaternary Gravel.

from 'Barton Cliffs' have made important contributions to our understanding of contemporary geography and climate (Chandler 1925, 1926, 1961).

Micropalaeontological studies feature in relatively recent work on 'Barton Cliffs'. Bujak *et al.* (1980) recorded a hundred species of dinoflagellate from the Barton Beds and it is significant that the first three of their 'Barton Beds Zones' (BAR-1, BAR-2, BAR-3) have 'Barton Cliffs' as the type section. Calcareous nannoplankton from the section enabled Aubry (1986) to approximate the NP 16/17 boundary in Bed E of the Barton Clay.

Below Highcliffe Castle, the junction of the Barton Clay with the underlying Boscombe Sand is marked by a thin pebble bed. From here, a conformable, gently dipping succession extends to Milford-on-Sea. Although at one time a continuous and mainly well-exposed section, it is now interrupted by sea defence works, where exposures are poor or non-existent (see Melville & Freshney 1982) whilst the Hordle Cliff section is much obscured by talus. The long section displays what were for a long time simply called the 'Barton Beds' and, above them to the east, the 'Lower and Middle Headon Beds'. The Boscombe Sand is also exposed below Highcliffe Castle, but is best seen further to the west in Friar's Cliff, Mudeford and beyond. The stratigraphical sequence has been described on a number of occasions, but Burton's (1929) system of labelling the principal units of the 'Barton Beds' with letters is still widely used. Tawney & Keeping (1883) divided the 'Lower Headon Beds' into 33 numbered beds whilst Edwards (see Edwards & Daley in prep.) assigns the latter (= Totland Bay Member of Insole & Daley 1985) to nine lithologically distinctive subdivisions, each containing a number of individual beds.

With the recognition of the need to regulate and standardize stratigraphical terminology (cf. Hedberg 1976), new terms have been introduced at formation level and above. As referred to earlier, Edwards & Freshney (1987a) recognized three formations within the 'Barton Beds': the Barton Clay (up to and including Burton Bed G); the Chama Sand (Burton Bed H); and the Becton Sand (Burton Beds I, J, K). The lithostratigraphic importance of Barton Cliffs is apparent in its choice as stratotype for all three. With the Boscombe Sand, these three formations comprise the

Barton Group of Edwards and Freshney (1987a). These authors
included the remainder (younger) part of the 'Barton Cliffs' section
in their Headon Formation, although this part of the succession
had earlier been assigned to the Headon Hill Formation of Insole &
Daley (1985). The formerly named 'Middle Headon Beds' of this
part of the succession were assigned to the Colwell Bay Member by
these authors and called the Lyndhurst Member by Edwards &
Freshney (1987a).

The section is very important chronostratigraphically as the type
section for the Bartonian Stage (Mayer-Eymar 1857). The 'Barton
Cliffs' section is also the type locality for nannoplankton Zone
NP17 (Martini 1971), whilst from glauconites in Burton Bed A_1
(containing *N. prestwichianus*), Odin *et al.* (1969) obtained a date of
42.0 ± 2 million years BP for the basal part of the succession.

The sediments of 'Barton Cliffs' represent a diverse suite of
sedimentary environments: offshore and inshore shelf, littoral beach
or barrier, lagoon, lake, river, marsh and swamp conditions. The
sequence in fact reflects alternating transgressions and regressions.
Hooker (1976) interpreted the succession as representing four
transgressive-regressive cycles, although the youngest (represented
by the Colwell Bay Member) is incomplete. The first two cycles are
coarsening-upwards sequences in which highly glauconitic muds
pass up through non-glauconitic muds, then sandy muds to sands.
Cycle 1 (Beds A_0 to A_3) begins with a basal pebble bed representing
a transgressive lag. Bed A_3 contains abraded fossils indicative of
considerable reworking as regressive-phase shallowing developed.
Cycle 2 (Beds B to I) has no basal pebble bed, but there is a sharp
burrowed junction and some rolled shells probably derived from
Bed A_3. Glauconitic silty clays at the base represent a transgressive
phase. An ultimate upwards shallowing is reflected in the highly
winnowed lag of Bed G, whilst the sands with *Ophiomorpha* of Bed
I (the bottom part of the Becton Sand) represent shoreface
conditions (Edwards & Freshney 1987b, p 66).

Cycle 3 comprises Beds J, K and the Totland Bay Member of the
overlying Headon Hill Formation. A break occurs at the base of
Bed J (the Becton Bunny Member of Edwards and Freshney 1987a)
and there is an upwards transition into the clean sands of Bed K,
perhaps reflecting the development of beach or barrier island

conditions. The remainder of Cycle 3 differs from earlier cycles in the succession in that regressive facies are better represented. This part of the succession represents a range of brackish and freshwater conditions and comprises several minor transgressive and regressive cycles and a major palaeochannel fill. The significance of this part of the sequence is emphasized by a number of named beds: the 'Mammal Bed', the 'Leaf and Seed Bed', the 'Crocodile Bed', the 'Chara Bed', etc.

Cycle 4 is incomplete, comprising the transgressive phase ('Milford Marine Bed') of the Colwell Bay Member more fully developed in the Isle of Wight.

Conclusions

Despite the coastal protection works, the Palaeogene SSSIs in Christchurch Bay continue to be of considerable geological importance. The absence of quarry or other inland sections in the strata exposed here emphasizes their unique scientific value. Hengistbury and Friars Cliff provide a valuable link between the more westerly facies of Bournemouth and the west with those of the Isle of Wight to the east, whilst 'Barton Cliffs' comprises a classic site which, as the subject of geological interest for over 200 years, has greatly enhanced our understanding of Middle to Late Eocene times. As a type section for three formations and the type section for the Bartonian Stage, it is undoubtedly important but it is best known for its prolific fauna, including as many as 600 molluscan species, together with other invertebrates, vertebrates and fossil plants. It exemplifies the importance of the coastal section as a source of data and consequently our understanding of Tertiary geology. Furthermore, it illustrates the importance of the need to protect such exposures and the valuable role played by the Geological Conservation Review in the achievement of this end.

References

Aubry, M.-P. 1986. Palaeogene calcareous nanno-plankton bio-stratigraphy of northwestern Europe. *Palaeogeography, Palaeo-climatology, Palaeoecology*, **55**, 267–334.

Bowerbank, J. S. 1842. On the London and Plastic Clay Formations of the Isle of Wight. *Transactions of the Geological Society, London*, **6**, 169–172.

Brander, G. 1766. *Fossilia Hantoniensia collecta, et in Musaeo Britannico deposita*, London.

Bristow, C. R., Freshney, E. C. & Penn, I. E. 1991. Geology of the country around Bournemouth. *Memoirs of the Geological Survey of the United Kingdom*, Sheet 329 (England and Wales).

Bujak, J. P., Downie, C., Eaton, G. L. & Williams, G. L. 1980. Dinoflagellate cysts and acritarchs from the Eocene of Southern England. *Palaeontology Special Paper*, **24**, 1–100.

Burton, E. St. J. 1929. The horizons of Bryozoa (Polyzoa) in the Upper Eocene Beds of Hampshire. *Quarterly Journal of the Geological Society of London*, **85**, 223–239.

Burton, E. St J. 1933. Faunal horizons of the Barton Beds in Hampshire. *Proceedings of the Geologists' Association*, **44**, 131–167.

Burton, E. St J. & Curry, D. 1950. Field meeting at Barton and Milford-on-Sea, Hants. *Proceedings of the Geologists' Association*, **61**, 161–162.

Chandler, M. E. J. 1925. *The Upper Eocene flora of Hordle, Hants, 1*. Palaeontographical Society (Monograph).

Chandler, M. E. J. 1926. *The Upper Eocene flora of Hordle, Hants, 2*. Palaeontographical Society (Monograph).

Chandler, M. E. J. 1961. Flora of the Lower Headon Beds of Hampshire and the Isle of Wight. *Bulletin of the British Museum (Natural History) Geology*, **5**, 91–158.

Clasby, P. S. 1972. Field meeting to the Barton-on-Sea district of Hampshire 22 V 1971. *Tertiary Times*, **1**, 115–116.

Clasby, P. S. 1974. Report of field meeting to Barton-on-Sea, Hampshire. *Tertiary Times*, **2**, 51–52.

Costa, L. I., Downie, C. & Eaton, G. L. 1976. Palinostratigraphy of some Middle Eocene sections from the Hampshire Basin (England). *Proceedings of the Geologists' Association*, **87**, 273–284.

Curry, D. 1937. The English Bartonian Nummulites. *Proceedings of the Geologists' Association*, **48**, 229–246.

Curry, D. 1968. Excursion en Angleterre 25–29 avril. *Colloque sur l'Eocène.*

Curry, D. 1976. The age of the Hengistbury Beds (Eocene) and its significance for the structure of the area around Christchurch, Dorset. *Proceedings of the Geologists' Association*, **87**, 401–408.

Curry, D. & Wisden, D. E. 1958. *Geology of the Southampton Area; Including the Coast-sections at Barton, Hants and Bracklesham, Sussex.* Geology Association Guide, No. 14.

Daley, B. *Tertiary Stratigraphy.* Geological Conservation Review Series, Chapman and Hall, London, in press.

Daniels, M. C. 1970. Report of Easter Field Meeting to Barton, Hants and surrounding regions. *Tertiary Times*, **1**, 27–28.

Edwards, N. 1971. Report of field meeting to Milford-on-Sea, Hampshire. *Tertiary Times*, **1**, 50–52.

Edwards, N. & Daley, B. 1996. Lithostratigraphy of the Totland Bay Member (Headon Hill Formation, Late Eocene) at Hordle Cliff, Hampshire, Southern England. *Tertiary Research*, in press.

Edwards, R. A. & Freshney, E. C. 1987a. Lithostratigraphical classification of the Hampshire Basin Palaeogene Deposits (Reading Formation to Headon Formation). *Tertiary Research*, **8**, 43–73.

Edwards, R. A. & Freshney, E. C. 1987b. Geology of the country around Southampton. *Memoirs of the Geological Survey of the United Kingdom*, Sheet 315 (England and Wales).

Emeleus, C. H. & Gyopari, M. C. 1992. *Tertiary Volcanic Province* (Geological Conservation Review Series, 4). Chapman and Hall, London.

Fisher, O. 1862. On the Bracklesham Beds of the Isle of Wight Basin. *Quarterly Journal of the Geological Society of London*, **18**, 65–94.

Gardner, J. S. 1879. Description and correlation of the Bournemouth Beds. Part I. Upper Marine Series. *Quarterly Journal of the Geological Society of London*, **38**, 209–228.

Gardner, J. S., Keeping, H. & Monkton, H. L. 1888. The Upper Eocene comprising the Barton and Upper Bagshot Formations. *Quarterly Journal of the Geological Society of London*, **44**, 578–635.

Hastings, Marchioness of (1848) *On the Freshwater Eocene Beds of Hordle Cliff, Hampshire.* Report of the British Association for the

Advancement of Science. Transactions of Sections, 63–64.

Hastings, Marchioness of 1853. On the Tertiary beds of Hordwell, Hampshire. *Philosophical Magazine*, **6**, 1–11.

Hastings, Marquise d' 1852. Description géologique des falaises d'Hordle, sur la côte du Hampshire, en Angleterre. *Bulletin de la Société Géologique de France*, **9**, 191–203.

Hedberg, H. (ed.) 1976. *International Stratigraphic Guide: a Guide to Stratigraphic Classification, Terminology and Procedure.* Wiley Interscience, New York.

Hooker, J. J. 1975a. Report of field meeting to Hengistbury Head and adjacent areas, Dorset; with an account of published work and some new exposures. *Tertiary Times*, **2**, 109–121.

Hooker, J. J. 1975b. Report of field meeting to Barton Hampshire. *Tertiary Times*, **2**, 163–167.

Hooker, J. J. 1976. Joint Tertiary Research Group/ Geologists' Association meeting to Barton, Hants. Unpublished field handout.

Hooker, J. J. 1986. Mammals from the Bartonian (middle/late Eocene) of the Hampshire Basin, southern England. *Bulletin of the British Museum of Natural History, (Geology)*, **39**, 191–478.

Insole, A. and Daley, B. (1985) A revision of the lithostratigraphical nomenclature of the Late Eocene and Early Oligocene strata of the Hampshire Basin, southern England. *Tertiary Research*, **7**, 67–100.

Judd, J. W. (1880) On the Oligocene strata of the Hampshire Basin. *Quarterly Journal of the Geological Society of London*, **36**, 137–177.

Lyell, C. 1827. On the strata of the Plastic Clay Formation exhibited in the Cliffs between Christchurch Head, Hampshire and Studland Bay, Dorsetshire. *Transactions of the Geological Society, London* (Series 2), **2**, 279–286.

Martini, E. 1971. Standard Tertiary and Quaternary calcareous nannoplankton zonation. *In*: Frinacci, A. (ed.) *Proceedings II Planktonic Conference, Roma*, 739–785.

Mayer-Eymar, K. 1857. Versuch einer neuen Klassifikation der Tertiär Gibilde Europas. *Verhandlungen der Schweizerischen naturforschenden Gesellschaft*, **42**, 165–199.

Melville, R. V. & Freshney, E. C. 1982. *British Regional Geology.*

The Hampshire Basin and adjoining areas. HMSO, London.
Nature Conservancy Council 1990. Earth science conservation in
Great Britain. A strategy. Appendices. *A Handbook of Earth
Science Conservation Techniques.* Nature Conservancy Council,
Peterborough.

Odin, G. S., Curry, D., Bodelle, J. Lay, C. & Pomerol, C. 1969.
Geochronologie de niveaux glauconieux tertiaires des bassins de
Londres et du Hampshire (méthode potassium–argon). *Som-
maire des Séances Société Géologiques de France*, **8**, 309–310.

Plint, A. G. 1983a. Sandy fluvial point-bar sediments from the
Middle Eocene of Dorset, England. *Special Publication International Association of Sedimentologists*, **6**, 355–368.

Plint, A. G. 1983b Facies, environments and sedimentary cycles in
the Middle Eocene, Bracklesham Formation of the Hampshire
Basin: evidence for global sea-level changes? *Sedimentology*, **30**,
625–653.

Plint, A. G. 1983c. Liquifaction, fluidization and erosional
structures associated with bituminous sands of the Bracklesham
Formation (Middle Eocene) of Dorset, England. *Sedimentology*,
10, 107–145.

Plint, A. G. 1984. A regressive coastal sequence from the Upper
Eocene of Hampshire, southern England. *Sedimentology*, **31**,
213–225.

Plint, A. G. 1988. Sedimentology of the Eocene Strata exposed
between Poole Harbour and High Cliff, Dorset, UK. *Tertiary
Research*, **10**, 107–145.

Prestwich, J. 1847a. On the probable age of the London Clay and
its relation to the Hampshire and Paris Tertiary systems.
Quarterly Journal of the Geological Society of London, **3**, 354–
377.

Prestwich, J. 1847b. On the main points of structure and the
probable age of the Bagshot Sands and their presumed
equivalents in Hampshire and France. *Quarterly Journal of the
Geological Society of London*, **3**, 378–399.

Prestwich, J. 1849. On the position and general characters of the
strata exhibited in the coast section from Christchurch Harbour
to Poole Harbour. *Quarterly Journal of the Geological Society of
London*, **5**, 435–454.

Tawney, E. B. & Keeping, H. 1883. On the section at Hordwell Cliffs, from the top of the Lower Headon to the base of the Upper Bagshot Sands. *Quarterly Journal of the Geological Society of London*, **39**, 566–574.

Tylor, A. 1850. On the occurrence of productive iron ore in the Eocene Formations of Hampshire. *Quarterly Journal of the Geological Society of London*, **6**, 133–134.

Wright, T. 1851. A stratigraphical account of the section of Hordwell, Beacon and Barton Cliffs, on the coast of Hampshire. *Annals Magazine Natural History*, **72**, 433–446.

17 Geomorphology and management of sites in Poole and Christchurch Bays

Malcolm Bray & Janet Hooke

Summary

- Poole and Christchurch Bays in southern England, exemplify some of the key issues involving the management and practice of coastal defence in areas of geological and geomorphological importance.

- For almost its entire length, the coast consists of sand and shingle beaches backed by cliffs rising to between 20 and 35 m in height with the exception of Christchurch Harbour. To the east, the low shingle Hurst Castle spit forms a boundary with the western Solent. Many valuable geological exposures and dynamic landforms are present within the Bay.

- The attractive environmental and amenity qualities of this same area have resulted in widespread residential and tourist development of the shoreline over the past 100 years. Patterns of development tended not to respect or accommodate natural processes forming and maintaining this coast.

- The local authorities have applied a diverse range of management techniques in attempts to control the problems of coastal erosion and flooding. These interventions have modified significantly the natural coastal processes, often to the detriment of neighbouring areas creating self-perpetuating tendencies to extend measures (Bray & Hooke 1995).

- These management activities have put pressure upon the geological and geomorphological sites of the area, both through the artificial stabilization of dynamic features or exposures, and the adverse impacts resulting from modifications of natural processes. Remaining sites are thus valuable assets needing sensitive managment to ensure the continuation of process activity essential to their integrity.

Geomorphological setting

The physical environment of Poole and Christchurch Bays (Fig. 17.1) needs to be understood in terms of its formative geomorphological history, the operation of its contemporary natural process systems and its management history. Continued operation of natural processes is essential both for maintenance of dynamic landforms and for geological exposures, although this has not always been viewed as a management priority. Traditionally, management has been imposed upon the landscape and knowledge of physical characteristics served only to assist in the technical design of the various engineering structures adopted. More recently, improved understanding of the natural process systems and the desire to conserve environmental qualities has led to widespread incorporation of the physical characteristics into coastal defence strategies as well as in key decisions of where, when and how specific schemes should be implemented. A sound knowledge of the geomorphological setting is therefore essential if sustainable management is to be achieved. The underlying natural processes are outlined prior to examination of the modifications and impacts upon earth science resources that have resulted from coastal defence activities.

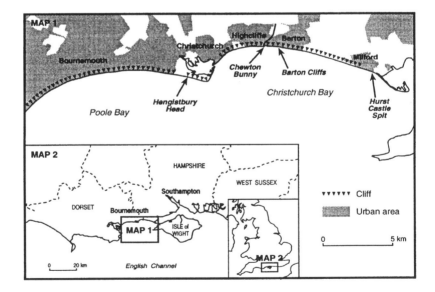

Fig. 17.1. Location of sites in Poole and Christchurch Bays.

Geomorphological history

During the Devensian (late Pleistocene) cold stage when sea-level was up to 120 m below present), an ancient Solent River (Fig. 17.2) flowed across south east Dorset and southern Hampshire and into a major 'English Channel' river through what is now the Solent (Allen and Gibbard 1993). An elevated Chalk ridge was previously continuous between the Foreland of the Isle of Purbeck and the Needles (Isle of Wight) and would have formed the southern limit of this ancestral drainage basin. Poole and Christchurch Bays were opened up by rapid marine erosion of the soft Tertiary strata following the breaching of this Chalk ridge. Rapid sea-level recovery and marine erosion during the Holocene transgression, 15 000–5000 years BP (Devoy 1982) would have completed removal of the ridge and facilitated excavation of the bays (Nicholls & Webber 1987). The plan shape of the Poole Bay coastline is approximately zetaform, fixed by the 'anchoring' presence of Hengistbury Head. The headland was previously much larger, but was substantially eroded during the late-Holocene and only remains as the submerged shoal of Christchurch Ledge extending several kilometres further southeast. Removal of this point of resistance triggered the erosion of Christchurch Bay, which is therefore younger than Poole Bay (Nicholls & Webber 1987). The remaining headland is critical to the stable configuration of both embayments.

Inundation and erosion of Christchurch Bay eventually led to the connection of a tidal channel through the western Solent to isolate the Isle of Wight at between 8400 and 6500 years BP (Nicholls & Webber 1987). River terrace gravels released by the eroding cliffs in Poole and Christchurch Bays drifted eastward to form a spit extending across part of the west Solent entrance (the ancestral Hurst Castle spit). Fine sediments were deposited and saltmarshes formed to the north east within the shelter afforded by the spit. Subsequent 'rollover' of the spit has occurred to shift its position to the northeast.

Hydrodynamic regime

The wave climate of Poole and Christchurch bays is determined by a dominant southwesterly approach that is significantly modified by

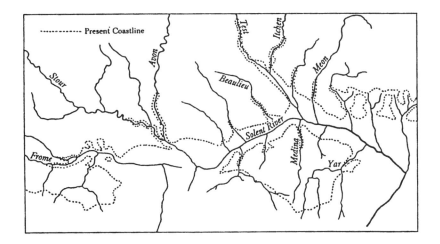

Fig. 17.2. Hypothesized pattern of drainage during the last glacial period (after West 1980).

interaction with the eastern Purbeck coastline. Storm conditions can be energetic and a maximum wave height of 8.8 m has been recorded near Bournemouth (Henderson & Webber 1978). Tidal range is small, thus concentrating wave action within a relatively narrow beach zone. Tidal currents are generally weak except in extreme eastern parts, where flows are constricted within the Hurst Narrows channel.

Natural sediment circulation system

The contemporary geomorphology comprises a dynamic littoral sediment transport regime involving sand and shingle beaches receiving sediments directly from local eroding cliffs. Poole and Christchurch bays operate as the main sub-cells within a larger sediment circulation cell extending between Durlston Head and Hurst Spit (Bray *et al.* 1995). The dominant littoral drift path is from west to east in Poole Bay and Christchurch Bay and delivers large quantities of sand and shingle, to Hengistbury Head and thence into Christchurch Bay. Although there is an increase in transport potential eastward from Bournemouth Pier to Hengist-bury, sand is progressively transported offshore in the more energetic conditions. Thus, the beach sediments coarsen towards Hengistbury where only shingle and coarse sand are stable. The overall transport pattern in Christchurch Bay is a distinct clockwise net sediment circulation that has historically been sustained by coast erosion. Similarly, sediments are coarser towards Hurst Spit which is almost entirely shingle. Material drifting along Hurst Spit is lost offshore entrained by strong tidal currents in Hurst Narrows and preferentially transported seaward to the Shingles Bank.

Effects of management

Commencing in the mid-nineteenth century, progressive extensions of sea-walls, cliff stabilization schemes and groynes along the Bournemouth frontage substantially reduced littoral drift sediment inputs to Hengistbury Head from Poole Bay (Lelliott 1989; Bray & Carter 1996). Major beach replenishments at Bournemouth in 1974 and 1988 provided new beach materials and effectively maintained the littoral sediment circulation system (May 1990; Harlow & Cooper 1995; Bray & Carter 1996). Sediment inputs from eroding cliffs remain significant in central and eastern parts of Christchurch Bay, although several long sections of cliffs at Highcliffe, Barton and Milford have also been stabilized and protected with consequent loss of inputs (Lacey 1985). Since the 1970s, installation of several fields of rock groynes have intercepted beach drift and caused artificial compartmentalization.

Budget analysis has shown that these practices and their process impacts have caused a downdrift sediment deficit which has had serious implications for Hurst Spit, the terminal beach storage unit of the pathway (Nicholls & Webber 1987).

Where cliffs remain open to wave attack, their morphology is controlled strongly by the nature of their materials. The cliffs are of geomorphological value as an example of a dynamic landform as well as of geological value (Chapter 16). Some cliffs at Bourne-mouth and Milford are protected at their toes by sea-walls, but otherwise continue to degrade by weathering and minor falls so that some geological exposures remain until basal scree slopes develop.

At one site on the northeast of Hengistbury Head, scree is removed periodically by the local authority so as to uncover geological exposures. Most of the Bournemouth cliffs and all of the Highcliffe and central Barton cliffs have been artificially regraded to stable slopes of lower angle, with various drainage measures installed and growth of vegetation has been assisted so that all exposures are covered.

There have been significant changes in attitudes towards the management of coastal defence within the study area. In addition to the shift away from traditional 'hard' engineering (structural) schemes towards 'soft' methods that accommodate natural processes, there are now established mechanisms to facilitate strategic management, most notably in the form of the coastal group SCOPAC (Standing Conference on Problems Associated with the Coastline) and the development of Shoreline Management Plans (SMPs) (Hooke & Bray 1995). Understanding of the interdependencies in recent years has led to the adoption of strategies and schemes designed to permit operation of natural processes.

For the four major sites designated as SSSIs on Poole and Christchurch Bays (Fig. 17.1) extracts from statements by the local authority and English Nature follow. These exemplify well the debates, contrasting attitudes and difficulties of decision-making in relation to these coastal problems.

Hengistbury Head: the local authority perspective

Neal Turner, Bournemouth Borough Council

Introduction
Located at the eastern extremity of Poole Bay and composed of an elevated (up to 36 m O.D.) outlier of predominantly sandy materials, Hengistbury forms a prominent headland of steep eroding cliffs and is the only such site remaining unprotected within Poole Bay. It affords valuable protection to Christchurch Harbour and the surrounding lowlands as well as being important for its environmental and geological qualities.

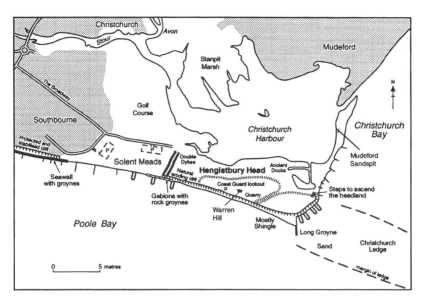

Fig. 17.3. Hengistbury Head and coastal defences.

In the two decades after 1852, the Hengistbury Mining Company stripmined the foreshore below Warren Hill for the huge masses of Siderite ironstone boulders which formed a natural breakwater at the foot of the cliffs and the resulting erosion from this activity virtually reshaped the whole of the northern and western flanks of Warren Hill. This initiated the phase of rapid coastal erosion that drew alarm from the citizens of Christchurch and Mudeford who relied on the Headland for protection against the sea in Poole Bay. In some 80 years, from 1852 to 1932, about half of the Headland was lost to the sea, the eroded products contributing to beaches on either side of Christchurch Harbour entrance and beaches further east in Christchurch Bay. Hengistbury Head and its environs were purchased by Bournemouth County Borough Council in 1930.

The breaching of the Mudeford Sandspit (Fig. 17.3) located at the southern side of Christchurch Harbour entrance, in 1935 caused great alarm in the vicinity. This was because the spit and Hengistbury Head afford valuable protection to an extensive low-lying hinterland around Christchurch Harbour. For example, levels taken on 14 February 1911 showed that the surface of the sea off Double Dykes was 1.22 m higher than the surface of the waters in Christchurch Harbour, opposite, on Spring Tides. More significant was the loss of cliff in this area indicated by the resetting of a monument erected in 1870 originally some 40 m from the cliff edge, and by 1907 it was only 8 m from the cliff edge – a loss in 37 years of 32 m.

Bournemouth Borough Council, whilst advancing its own programme of coast protection works in the form of promenades and groynes eastwards through Boscombe and Southbourne towards Hengistbury Head, commenced consultations over the construction of a barrier groyne to manage material on the beaches at Hengistbury Head in order to reduce the risk of a breakthrough by the sea into Christchurch Harbour. Since its construction in 1938, the main benefits of the Long Groyne (Fig. 17.3) have been the accumulation of material in front of the vulnerable cliffs of the eastern end of Warren Hill, valued for its mixed archaeology, the protection of Christchurch Harbour, and the stabilizing of the Harbour Entrance.

The main problems associated with the Long Groyne have been the starving of the beaches of the Mudeford Sandspit in the period 1938–1986, lying in the lee of the Hengistbury Head Long Groyne, with a consequential removal of material from the southeastern faces of Warren Hill. This resulted in very large slips of material from the coastal slopes and destruction of sites for Royal Fern (*Osmunda regalis*) and nesting sites for Sand Martins (*Riparia riparia*). The balance in maintaining a safe access for all beach users and coastal walkers was placed in peril with the burying of a party of Girl Guides in 1976 by a mudslide during a period of heavy rainfall.

Management philosophy
In 1977, Bournemouth Borough Council set up a Working Party to define the management needs of Hengistbury Head and its environs following a period of substantial erosion, both by nature and by humans. The Working Party represented all interested groups, in

particular representatives from the various earth science community and the various academic institutions and museums. The outcome of this work, after various reports and consultation, was a Management Plan formally adopted by the Council in 1985.

The valuable contribution to the formulation of the Management Plan of the earth science interest groups quickly identified the need to protect interests such as the geological record at Solent Beach and Warren Hill. Accordingly, the Council was notified in 1983, after consultation by the Nature Conservancy Council, of the Order to create the Christchurch Harbour Site of Special Scientific Interest (SSSI) that embraced the valuable geology. The SSSI was extended in 1985 to include the low lying cliffs and sand dunes west of Double Dykes up to the beach access from the Solent Meads Car Park.

All schemes for protection of the Headland required consultation with the Statutory Authorities and resulted in the adoption of Management Agreements with English Nature for the geological record in the cliffs northeast of the Long Groyne. The whole programme of these works has been subject to monitoring by aerial photography, hydrographic and topographic surveying, and sediment sampling and analysis.

The proposed final phase of this programme includes the provision of short low crested rubble rock groynes to maintain efficient beach levels below Warren Hill without endangering the maintenance of the valuable geological exposures. Geologists have identified the significant and sensitive sections where skilful management is required, and the proposed rock groynes have been relocated to enable the sections and exposures to be maintained as well as providing access for equipment for management of the lower cliffs after cliff falls. Other works include the creation of a reinforced earth embankment to support the sensitive archaeology in the cliff edge immediately above the Long Groyne.

The Council is presently negotiating a comprehensive agreement with English Nature over the implementation of the proposed coast protection works and the management of the geological exposures, under the auspices of a newly constituted Monitoring Group reflecting earth science interests.

Christchurch Harbour (Hengistbury): extracts from SSSI citation

English Nature

Description and reasons for notification of site

The site comprises the drowned estuary of the Rivers Stour and Avon and the peninsula of Hengistbury Head. The varied habitats include saltmarsh, wet meadows, drier grassland, heath, sand dune, woodland and scrub, and the site is of great ornithological interest. Hengistbury is a stratigraphically important bridging exposure, linking the Tertiary formations outcropping around Poole and Christchurch Bays. It will also provide an important comparative locality in the eventual correlation of the Eocene sediments of St. Catherines Hill. The Boscombe Sands, exposed at the base of the cliff are important not only in the cnvironmcntal and geographical reconstruction of very late Aurversian (Upper Bracklesham) time, but also contain a unique type of bituminous sand. The upper part of the cliff exposes an unusual, 'marginal' variety of the Barton Beds.

In addition, the site is designated for its flora and fauna, outlined in the SSSI citation and notification.

Principles of conservation

The principle of conservation for the site is to maintain representative sections through the strata currently exposed in the cliff face for further research. There should be a regular monitoring of the site to ensure its present condition is maintained. In particular, the section should be observed for unauthorized coastal protection measures, the establishment of vegetation or slumped material at the cliff base over large sections of the site and vegetation obscuring sections of the upper cliff. Access to the site should be maintained.

Highcliffe-on-sea: the Local Authority perspective

Frank Tyhurst, Christchurch Borough Council

Introduction

The coast of Highcliffe-on-Sea (Fig. 17.1) has been the subject of the most intensive coastal protection activity for nearly 30 years, arising from a perceived need by the Local Authority to preserve its interests in the face of accelerating erosion by the sea. From the late nineteenth century this portion of Christchurch Bay was protected by Mudeford Sandbank, then the extended seaward spit of the Christchurch Harbour entrance configuration. In 1939, the Hengistbury Long Groyne was constructed, effectively cutting off the natural sedimentary supply to the spit and within 20 years, this protective feature had shrunk to roughly its current truncated length, exposing Highcliffe to the direct attack of waves generated by the prevailing westerlies. The Local Authority has developed a progression of coastal defence measures so that much, but not all, of its frontage is protected in some manner (Fig. 17.4).

Coastal land use: recent changes

In terms of development, the coastal strip of Highcliffe was once in the ownership of a few large estates and remained largely undeveloped. In the early 1930s, much of this land was sold off for development, mostly for retirement homes and much of Highcliffe is now built up to the coastal margin. This development trend has had significant effects upon coastal stability, e.g. urbanization has increased drainage problems, formal defences have become necessary to protect housing and a greater resident and visitor population has led to demands for enhanced amenity qualities.

Shoreline management response

Christchurch Council's response to the relatively rapid deterioration of the coast from the 1950s onwards was initially purely reactive. At that time, a large colony of beach huts on the cliffs represented the Council's most important capital asset and it was

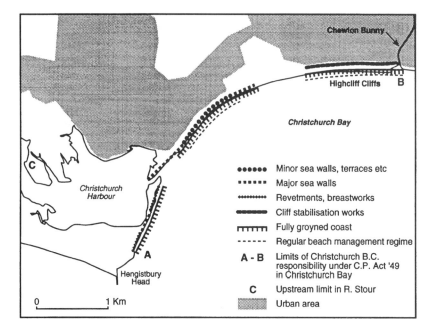

Fig. 17.4. Coastal defences on Christchurch Borough Council frontage (after Christchurch Borough Council).

the accelerating loss of this amenity which prompted action. Labour intensive ditching amongst the huts had kept the land drainage problems under control, but direct attack by the sea could not be resisted and towards the end of the 1960s, the colony had all but disappeared. Together with the residential development of potentially vulnerable cliff top land, this prompted the Council to be more proactive and the first of a long series of major engineering projects was started in 1970.

During the next 22 years twelve schemes costing between £6000 and £636 000 each were carried out, representing an investment of £2.5 million at contemporary prices, perhaps around £4 million today. These include carefully considered engineering responses using both well known techniques as well as site specific measures developed by experience over the years. At first the schemes tended to be emergency measures to cope with cliff slips, but as the various

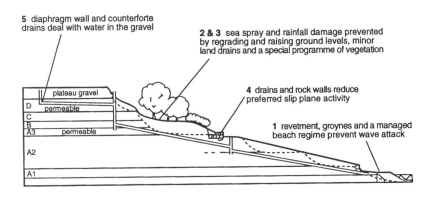

Fig. 17.5. Cliff stabilization measures at Highcliffe, Christchurch Bay.

measures started to achieve results, schemes became part of a planned rolling programme of improvements with definite targets. A graphical representation of the main features of recent slope stabilisation and coast protection is shown in Fig. 17.5.

The justification for this investment was based entirely on financial value of threatened assets and the Council used its powers under the Coast Protection Act 1949 as the vehicle. It is fair to say that the works at Highcliffe have sterilized much of the SSSI by modifying the landform and covering up the fossil bearing horizons with vegetation. However, in the absence of any formal comments by the Nature Conservancy Council at the planning stage, Christchurch Borough Council saw no reason not to proceed.

The situation at present

The long-term package of defence works at Highcliffe were completed in 1985 and have since been declared a success in engineering terms, based upon the lack of erosion and low maintenance requirements.

Much has been learned about the stabilization of soft eroding cliffs on this site, Highcliffe having been the test-bed for a number of new techniques. The concept of 'counterforte drains' and 'engineering swards' are examples, as are soft engineering on beaches including low cost nourishment and 'low-tech' rock groynes. The treatment of the cliffs has also been considered successful on amenity grounds, since Highcliffe has once again become a popular site, especially for day visitors.

Highcliffe and Barton to Milford Cliffs: extracts from SSSI citation

English Nature

Reasons for site notification

The Highcliffe to Milford Cliffs Site of Special Scientific Interest extends for some 9 km along the cliffs of Christchurch Bay. Its entire length comprises steep coastal slopes and cliffs which are locally dissected by deeply incised 'bunnies' or ravines.

This coastal site provides access to the standard succession of the fossil rich Barton Beds and Headon Beds. Various exposures within the Site are considered important both in a national and international context.

Friars Cliff, Dorset, is a key Tertiary Site providing an opportunty to study the marginal marine sediments desposited during the terminal, regressive phase of the Auversian (Upper Bracklesham) and the earliest, marine transgression phase of the Bartonian.

Within the sands of Friars Cliff and Highcliffe there is a particularly fine assemblage of plant fossils.

The coastal section from Friars Cliff to Milford on Sea is the world type locality (stratotype) for the Barton Beds and is also the best exposure of the Lower Headon Beds. This is one of Britain's most important stratigraphic and palaeontological sites.

The cliffs in the vicinity of Chewton Bunny are the only sites to yield fossil plants from Lower Barton Beds. Lying between Chewton Bunny (Hampshire) and Beckton Bunny the Barton Beds of Barton Cliff are well known for their reptile remains. To the east of Beckton Bunny lies Hordle Cliff which is a locality for the Headon Formation, strata containing a diverse fossil mammal fauna. Hordle Cliff is also a key site for fossil birds: so far 13 families (representing 8 orders) have been identified. In addition to birds and mammals Hordle Cliff is one of Britain's best known Tertiary reptile sites.

The fossilized animals are complemented by fossil plant remains. This is a key locality for palaeobotanical studies and it includes the most important locality for plants from the Lower Headon Beds.

At the extreme east of the site lies Paddy's Gap at Rook Cliff. This site shows the thin *Limnocarpus* Band, within the Headon Beds, crowded with the fruits of an extinct pondweed relative, to the exclusion of almost all other plant fossils. This is the only site now exposing this horizon. This is a famous plant locality with abundant fossil fruit remains.

The Bartonian facies is not represented in some other parts of Europe because there is a hiatus at the top of the Bracklesham Beds caused by a drop in sea level at the end of the Eocene. At Barton there is a complete section with a continuation of marine rocks which contain a unique fish fauna. The nearest assemblage with similar fishes is in Georgia, North America. Like all these Eocene fish sites the faunal assemblage consists of great numbers of species, based on disarticulated remains of fish, particularly teeth and otoliths. However, these species are in the main unique to this site.

Throughout the SSSI the Cliffs are capped with a flight of Pleistocene terrace gravels. At the cliff tops these gravels are exposed in cross-section. The cliffs around The Solent are the only place in Britain where large continuous exposures of Pleistocene terrace gravels are available for study. Furthermore, the gravel at Barton is one of the richest sources of Palaeolithic (Old Stone Age) artefacts in the Hampshire Basin.

In addition to the geological interest the cliffs and coastal slopes of this site are of contemporary biological interest.

Principles of conservation

Highcliffe to Milford SSSI is one of the most important stratigraphical localities in the world as it includes a reference section for a time division – the Bartonian Stage of the Eocene. This site is also of international importance palaeontologically as various levels have yielded good vertebrate and invertebrate faunas and other plant floras.

Unfortunately, however, due to the clayey or silty nature of the sediments, the cliffs are prone to slumping and erosion. This is exacerbated by hard coastal defence works to the west which trap otherwise protective beach sediment. This leads to end effects and enhances erosion beyond groynes or promotes wave scour.

Under the guise of coast protection works or 'emergency works' large areas of the site have now been badly damaged, often excessively so, often with little regard for nature conservation and especially for the international importance of the site.

That these works have not actually succeeded in preventing slipping or controlling erosion is demonstrated by continued slumping in supposedly stabilized areas and have a continual requirement for beach feeding and toe protection. The result is massive site damage for little or no longer-term gain – allegedly around £10 million have already been spent on the works and more may be required if stabilization is to be achieved. Clearly the whole context of works on the SSSI requires reassessment and practical longterm alternative measures or options investigated.

As it stands now, the condition of this extremely important site represents the greatest ever disaster for earth science conservation in Great Britain. What is now required is a strategy to attempt to revive the site – this can be achieved by both controlling future coastal works and by recreating key exposures at appropriate locations within the extent of existing defences.

The ultimate aim would be to establish a strategy for management of the site which the relevant Local Authorities can sign up to. This strategy would allow for permanent exposure of a complete geological sequence for the SSSI in a context of appropriate, effective and essentially nondamaging coastal protection works.

Barton-on-Sea: the local authority perspective

Doug Wright, New Forest District Council

Coast protection works in Christchurch Bay are believed to have begun about 1840 with a groyne scheme at Highcliffe. Serious protection works began in 1938 when the Long Groyne at Hengistbury Head was built, which intercepted the movement of shingle from Poole Bay into Christchurch Bay. There followed a denudation of the beaches downdrift and subsequently an acceleration in the rate of cliff erosion between Hengistbury Head and Barton-on-Sea. This prompted a series of protection works at Mudeford, Highcliffe, Barton and Milford on Sea, beginning in 1944. The most extensive works were constructed between 1964 and 1969 at Highcliffe and Barton, and extended in the 1970s and 80s. By reducing or halting cliff erosion, these works enormously reduced sediment inputs to the beaches and hence the eastward movement of beach material. Between Barton and Milford (down-drift), beach levels have fallen alarmingly over the last 10–20 years, particularly to the west of Milford where a previously buried seawall is now suffering undermining of its foundations, the beach level having fallen by more than 2 m in five years.

Scheme specific surveying and monitoring of beach profiles and natural processes has taken place since the early 1960s, but since 1988 New Forest District Council has undertaken long term beach monitoring which includes the measurement of wave conditions, the measurement of beach performance, aerial surveys and sediment sampling. This programme has identified a consistent downward trend in beach volumes throughout the frontage, and a rapid and accelerating rate of cliff recession.

The Barton-on-Sea frontage divides into two distinct sections. To the west are the unprotected Naish Cliffs stretching for three kilometres between Barton and the culverted stream course of Chewton Bunny near Highcliffe, whilst to the east is the 1.75 km protected section in front of the main developed area of Barton. Chewton Bunny forms the boundary between the counties of Hampshire and Dorset, between New Forest District Council and Christchurch Borough Council, and between MAFF's southeast and southwest regions.

Naish Cliffs
The Naish shoreline is dominated by the low, slumping cliffs, with a variable, but often depleted mixed sand and shingle beach at their base. Cliff erosion at this site provides one of the few remaining natural sources of beach sediment in Christchurch Bay. The major clifftop land use is the Naish Farm Holiday Village complex. The cliffs are of international geological importance forming part of the

Highcliffe to Milford Cliffs SSSI and containing outcrops of fossil-bearing strata. Continued exposure of the fossil beds through erosion is an intrinsic part of their special interest.

Naish Cliffs are located at the pinch point between the two heavily defended sections of coastline at Highcliffe and Barton-on-Sea, with the updrift end of the site coinciding with the administrative boundary between the neighbouring coast protection authorities of Christchurch Borough Council and New Forest District Council. Emergency works have already been carried out by Christchurch, to prevent outflanking of their defences, on the New Forest side of the boundary. From New Forest District Council's beach monitoring programme there is clear evidence that the effects of these and earlier works have resulted in increased beach erosion and focusing of wave attack downdrift along the undefended Naish Cliff shoreline. This site therefore suffers from *ad hoc* coast protection policies adopted since the early part of this century, which have allowed coast protection works to take place without proper assessment of their effects on the downdrift shoreline. The result has been that Naish beach has become starved of shingle and the rate of cliff recession has increased. Cliff-top recession rates vary, but are generally in the range 1.5–3.0 m per year.

If left unchecked the current rate of cliff erosion may eventually outflank the western end of the current Barton coast protection works and cause further problems for Christchurch Borough Council at Chewton Bunny. However, erosion of the cliff provides a continuing supply of beach material and ensures that fresh fossil beds are being continually exposed. Cliff stabilization would halt this process, leading to further denudation of the beach and the exposed fossil beds becoming obscured by vegetation. The fossil resource though is limited due to the inland dip of the strata (progressively younger beds exposed as recession proceeds in the long term), and it is argued without some form of protection, the international stratotype exposure will eventually be lost.

Between 1968 and 1985, a number of conventional, large scale coast protection and cliff drainage schemes were planned for stabilizing Naish Cliffs, but all failed at the cost benefit hurdle because of the low economic value of the cliff top land, even before any of the environmental dis-benefits were taken into account. The current policy is to develop a scheme in consultation with English Nature which is designed to reduce the rate of erosion and to provide environmental enhancement of the beach without degrading the geological value of the site.

A beach recharge scheme has been designed, utilizing a novel shingle groyne concept developed by New Forest engineers. The recharge material would be used in two ways, part of the material would be spread on the beach and graded in a conventional manner; the remainder would be formed into 'dynamic' free-standing shingle groynes to a design tested by physical models in the wave tanks at HR Wallingford Ltd. The design has been optimized by mobile bed physical model testing. Implementation of the scheme now depends upon sourcing shingle at a price which meets cost/benefit criteria.

Barton Cliffs

Barton Cliffs, extending from Naish Farm Holiday Village to Barton Golf Course, are backed by predominantly residential suburban development, with a small cluster of shops and other facilities. The beach and the cliff top are popular recreation areas, offering excellent views of Christchurch Bay and the Needles, and attracting many seasonal visitors. There are approximately 150 beach huts along the under-cliff.

Coast protection measures began in earnest in the late 1930s, but these early works were allowed to fall into disrepair during World War 2, when access to the beach was prohibited. By the 1960s the frontage was virtually unprotected and cliff recession was taking place at 0.6–0.9 m per year. In 1960, the then Lymington Borough Council commissioned Sir William Halcrow and partners to draw up proposals to renew the protection works, and in 1964 timber groynes and a cliff drainage system were installed along 300 m of the frontage. These works were designed to limit toe erosion due to wave action, and to control groundwater and gully erosion of the cliff face. The results were encouraging and stage two followed on between 1965 and 1968 comprising a flexible timber revetment backed by rock, an extension to the drainage system, additional rock groynes and regrading of the undercliff to a slope between 1 in

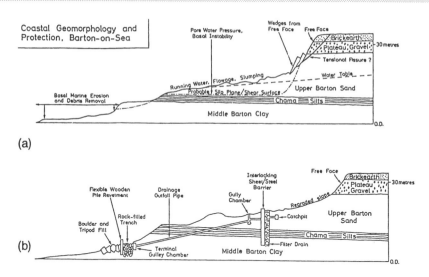

Fig.17.6. (a) Cliff form and processes promoting erosion before 1960 (after Phillips 1975). **(b)** Section of coast protection works 1980–60.

3 and 1 in 4, bringing the total protected length to 1750 m. The key component of the drainage system was a 7 m deep sheet piled wall which was driven parallel to the cliff line, through the gravel strata and into the underlying clays to cut off the flow of groundwater along the gravel clay interface. A steel Armco pipeline at the base of the piles on the landward side collected the water for discharge to the beach (Fig. 17.6b). However, these measures were only partially effective in the long term, for deep seated failures in the undercliffs in the winter of 1974–75 penetrated beneath the sheet piling causing rotation, bowing and splitting of the barrier (Fig. 17.6c). It is probable that these failures occurred along previously undetected slip planes deep within the Barton Clay. The result was two-fold; first, mudslides surged over the sea-cliff and revetment and onto the beach; second, the cliff-top receded 5–10 m over a 150 m front in 1975 (Clark *et al.* 1976).

Since 1968, various additions and improvements have been made, notably the construction of five large rock groynes to replace the existing timber ones, replacement of the timber revetment with a rock structure, and the extension of the revetment eastwards by 200 m to combat the formation of an erosion pocket just beyond the

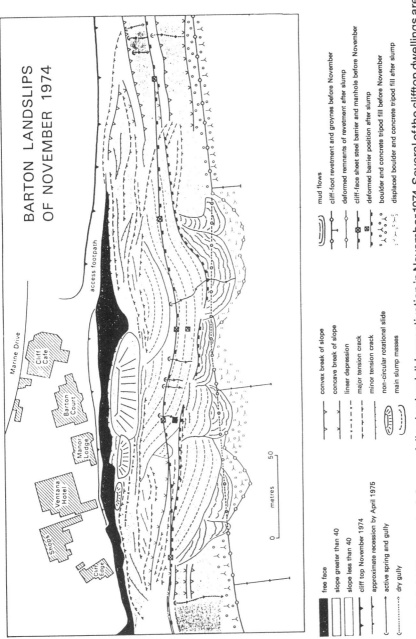

Fig. 17.6. (c) Damage to defences, following landslide reactivation in November 1974. Several of the clifftop dwellings are now demolished.

final rock groyne. Often referred to as 'terminal groyne syndrome' this phenomenon is a result of the abrupt termination of hard defence works constructed on a soft coastline.

More recently, extensive emergency works had to be undertaken following a major cliff slip at the western end of the frontage in December 1993. Small scale, superficial slips along the upper cliff slip planes occur quite frequently and are relatively easy to deal with. However, the 1993 slip was of a different magnitude and displaced the cliff toe revetment by up to 8 m. A stability analysis commissioned from Rendel Geotechnics indicated a complex multi-plane failure with substantial movement along the Highcliffe Sand bed deep below the cliff, and passing under the revetment and nearshore seabed (Fig. 17.7).

Implementation of full scale remedial works, estimated to cost over £3 million, has been put on hold until the Shoreline Management Plan for Poole and Christchurch Bays is finished. In the meantime, the area has been tidied up, the broken drains repaired and some limited regrading undertaken to allow vehicular access to the beach, and to improve public safety.

In spite of the coast protection works constructed to date, the cliff top continues to recede slowly, and will do so until its natural angle of repose is reached (assuming continued protection of the cliff toe). Buildings in the Barton Court area will probably be lost in the next 10–20 years; a number of them are already within 20 m of the cliff edge, with some as close as 3 m. The only effective alternative to this is to regrade the cliff slope artificially, which would further damage the geological SSSI, and result in the immediate loss of the buildings and part of the cliff top open space. An area at risk from erosion has been identified in the District Local Plan and is defined by the line to which the cliff could recede in the next 60 years, assuming no further maintenance of the protection and drainage works. In practice, some maintenance of the works is likely to continue, and the rate of erosion could be slower. No further development will be permitted within this zone.

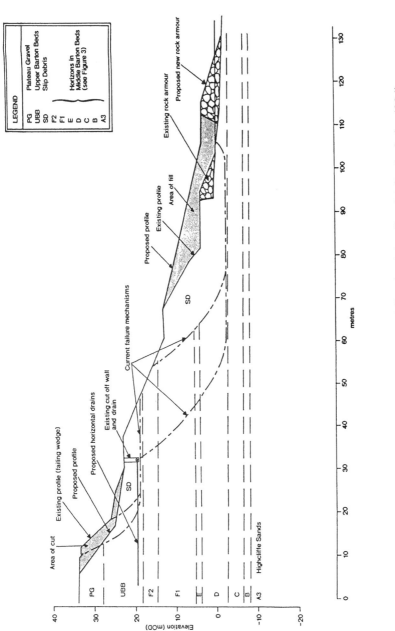

Fig. 17.7. Barton cliffs: failure mechanisms and options for stabilization (after Rendel Geotechnics 1994).

Hurst Spit: the local authority perspective

Doug Wright, New Forest District Council

Introduction

The eastern end of Christchurch Bay is dominated by Hurst Spit, and the well known coastal landmark of Hurst Castle. The Spit is a naturally formed shingle bank which extends 2.5 km from the end of Milford beach and effectively divides Christchurch Bay from the Solent. Although 600 m of its landward portion have been covered by a rock revetment, and despite extensive emergency repair works undertaken over the last 30 years, the spit has retained its classic form and is a well known example of a multi-recurved spit. It is also an integral and critical geomorphological element of the wider coastline.

The Western Solent coastline, to the east of the Spit, is low lying and particularly susceptible to flooding. The Spit and the Lymington to Keyhaven sea-wall are the first line of defence against the sea, but both have been breached or over-topped in recent years. Following extensive damage and flooding during the winter storms of 1989/1990, the sea-wall has been rebuilt and raised in height. However, the new wall has not been designed to withstand significant wave attack, this function being performed by the Spit.

An extensive area of saltmarsh and mudflats has developed in the lee of Hurst Spit, extending as far as the Lymington River. The Spit and saltmarsh system lie within the Hurst Castle and Lymington River Estuary Site of Special Scientific Interest (SSSI). This is of particular importance because it contains a remarkable assemblage of salt, brackish and fresh water habitats supporting a great variety of wildlife, in particular, birds and certain rare invertebrates and plant species. In recognition of this it is currently being reviewed by English Nature as a proposed National Nature Reserve. It also forms an important part of the wider review of the North Solent and Southampton Water as a candidate Special Protection Area under the EC Birds Directive, and as a Wetland of International Importance (Ramsar Site). The Lymington-Keyhaven marshes also contain archaeological relics of what was once a thriving sea salt industry. This area is also of considerable historic and archaeological interest. Hurst Castle is the principal historic feature of the Spit.

Processes
There are three main depositional processes which control the profile and rate of transgression of the Spit as follows (Fig. 17.8):

- *Berm formation* at the limit of wave runup on the seaward face of the Spit. The swash percolates back to the sea through the porous shingle structure.
- *Overtopping* which is similar to berm formation, but occurs when the swash reaches the crest of the Spit without spilling over onto the back face. Overtopping can therefore raise the crest level by pushing shingle from the front face onto the top of the Spit.
- *Overwashing* is the next stage beyond overtopping, and occurs when the swash passes over the crest and runs down the back face of the Spit. Overwashing can therefore push shingle over the Spit, from the front face to the back, but in storm conditions it can also knock over the crest, reducing the height of the Spit.

Once the crest level has been lowered the swash can pass over the Spit more easily, and the frequency of overwashing greatly increases. This is the basic mechanism of 'rollover', and it is the most important process affecting the Spit because it makes possible the wholesale transfer of shingle from the front face to the back in the course of a single severe storm.

Hurst and Milford beaches have been receding since the Spit formed, nineteenth century records showing an average rate of recession of 1.5 m per year (Fig. 17.9). From the late 1960s the rate of recession increased to 3.5 m per year caused by the construction of protection works to the west, particularly at Milford where erosion of the terrace gravel beds was completely stopped and the main source of fresh shingle inputs curtailed. Recession of the beach has been accompanied by a steady loss in volume, which has been offset partially by the local authority through regular nourishments with imported material.

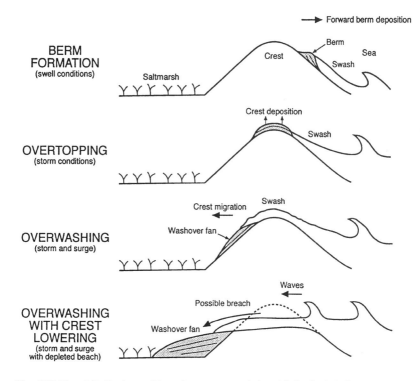

Fig. 17.8. Hurst Spit: depositional processes (after Nicholls 1985).

According to historic records and maps North Point, at the end of the active recurve, remained stable for over 150 years until the early part of this century. Since 1908 though, the tip of the recurve has grown rapidly, extending across the mouth of the Keyhaven River and deflecting it northwards into the saltmarshes, resulting in substantial erosion of the saltmarsh and restriction of the navigable channel (Fig. 17.9).

Recent history
Hurst Spit has probably been declining in volume since the early part of this century when coast protection works first began to interrupt the erosion and transport of shingle around Christchurch Bay, although there is no historical evidence of the Spit breaching

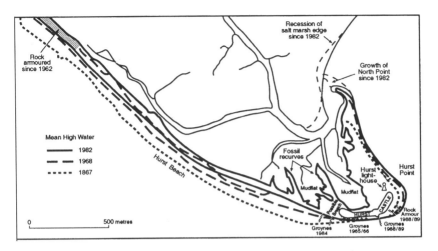

Fig. 17.9. Hurst Spit: recession of MHW 1867–1987 and coast protection (after Nicholls 1985).

before 1954. However, since then the Spit has been breached repeatedly, most notably in January 1962 when the recently constructed timber groynes were outflanked and rendered useless. Between 1965 and 1966, rock armouring was placed along a 600 m length at the western end of the Spit from the Milford seawall. This revetment has performed reasonably well, preventing breaches along this length but needing regular rebuilding itself after severe storms.

Another event attributable to human activity which has affected the Spit was the arrival of *Spartina anglica* in 1895. Spartina growth raised the level of the marsh considerably, which in turn artificially raised the crest level of the Spit and masked the decline in volume until the 1960s. Also, the raised marsh, which is trapped beneath the Spit as it rolls back, is subject to rapid settlement and erosion which encourages further recession.

Hurst Point has receded in parallel with Hurst Beach, with the result that Hurst Castle is developing into a headland. To protect the castle wing walls against wave attack a series of timber groynes joined together by zig-zag timber breastwork were built in the mid-1960s, supplemented by two more groynes, built to prevent breaching west of the castle, in 1984 (Fig. 17.9). However, the new groynes caused starvation and recession of the downdrift beaches, and in 1988 the defences had to extended westwards by 120 m. Since then the beaches around the castle have continued to be unstable and further work has been necessary.

In June 1984, following a particularly severe winter when the Spit was severely damaged on nine occasions, consulting engineers were commissioned to undertake a desk study and to recommend short term measures that could be taken to improve the stability of the Spit, pending consideration of a long term solution. It was concluded that a 450 m length of the Spit beyond the rock armouring should be widened and strengthened to achieve a 6 m wide crest and side slopes of 1 in 3, and, in addition, a small rock groyne should be built at the end of the rock armouring. Work was completed at the end of 1985 at a cost of £215 000. These measures proved effective for five years although a lot of material was lost from the recharged area over this period.

In 1986, in response to a consultation on the future of Hurst Spit, the County and District authorities, land owners and those with interests in the Spit were in unanimous agreement that it was an extremely important feature in need of some form of environmentally acceptable stabilization scheme to secure its future. As a result of this decision New Forest District Council, in consultation with the Ministry of Agriculture, embarked upon a research and monitoring programme to measure and record the natural forces and processes at work on the Spit, and to monitor the Spit's responses. The information would be used to design an environmentally sensitive scheme which would retain as far as possible the natural appearance of the Spit, and interfere as little as possible with the natural processes acting upon it.

On 21 October 1989, a south westerly storm caused severe and damaging over-washing of the Spit over a length of 100 m, lowering the crest level by one metre. About 4000 tonnes of gravel rejects were used to replace shingle lost or displaced during the storm. These repair works cost £50 000. On 16 and 17 December 1989 southwesterly storms combined with a tidal surge in excess of 1 m flattened an 800 m length of the Spit. In a matter of hours the Spit was rolled back up to 80 m and 50 000 tonnes of shingle were pushed into Mount Lake ('rollover' process) or lost offshore. Before repairs could be started the flattened remains of the Spit were cut through by channels down to low water level and large areas of saltmarsh were eroded by wave action. About 25 000 tonnes of material were recovered and used to rebuild the Spit, together with 20 000 tonnes of imported gravel rejects. Due to the rapid erosion of the underlying saltmarsh deposits when the Spit was flattened it was not possible to rebuild on the pre-storm line. Later surveys showed that the rebuilt section of the Spit had been set back by about 12 m. Repair works took four months to complete at a cost of £450 000.

Following these events, the monitoring programme was accelerated in order to identify, as quickly as possible, a long term strategy for the stabilization and maintenance of the Spit. However, there were no conventional models in existence which would allow an appropriate design to be formulated, and the only technically sound option available was to utilize mathematical and physical modelling to help develop and test an original design.

A mathematical model which simulated wave action in Christchurch Bay was first developed, using measured and predicted deep water wave data to examine the effects of the seabed on waves as they progress towards the shore. This model was used to calculate wave conditions at various points along the Spit.

Following discussions with HR Wallingford Ltd., a large scale physical model study was then commissioned into the processes and management options.

The stabilization scheme
The chosen strategy, developed from very extensive model testing involved the following actions:

- recharge of the most vulnerable 800 m length of the Spit with 300 000–400 000 cubic metres of shingle, matching as closely as possible the size grading of the natural beach material;
- construction of a small nearshore rock breakwater at the junction between the rock armoured and unprotected sections to smooth out the abrupt transition and refract wave energy,
- construction of a rock groyne west of Hurst Castle to limit the

loss of shingle from Hurst Point;
- construction of a rock revetment and perched beach around the castle wing walls to replace the existing inadequate defences;
- restoration and strengthening the rock armoured western section of the Spit by placing a second layer of armourstone over the existing structure.

Of all the options and combinations of options tested, this strategy is the one which best satisfied the engineering, environmental and economic criteria determined through consultation with all the bodies with interests in the Spit and its surroundings.

The resulting scheme, which was constructed between August 1996 and January 1997, doubled the volume of the Spit by building up its landward side and raising the crest height by an average of 13 m. The model testing showed that strengthening the Spit in this way would allow it to resist a combination of storm wave heights and surge levels with a statistical probability of occurring once every 200 years. Before the start of the works, the Spit was vulnerable to storms and surges with a return period of only once a year. It is not possible, or desirable, to completely stop the natural loss of shingle from the end of the Spit, and topping up with about 50 000 cubic metres of shingle will be needed every 10–15 years. The cost of the scheme was £6.5 million.

Three possible sources of shingle for the scheme were identified:

- land-based gravel pits;
- licensed marine aggregate dredging areas; and
- the Shingles Bank in Christchurch Bay.

There are advantages and disadvantages associated with each, but the Shingles Bank source was estimated to offer the most satisfactory shingle size grading at an economical price. The Shingles Bank lies in very shallow water close to the New Forest and Isle of Wight shorelines and would not normally be licensed for commercial aggregate extraction. However, consultations with the licensing authority, the Crown Estate, led to an agreement that a dredging licence application from New Forest District Council would be considered if the material was used solely for rebuilding

Fig. 17.10. Hurst Spit: replenishment in action, September 1996.

Hurst Spit, and no detrimental effect on the Isle of Wight shoreline, or on the long term stability of the Bank itself, could be demonstrated.

Following extensive computer modelling of wave data and wave refraction patterns in Christchurch Bay, and the completion of an in-depth environmental impact assessment, it was shown that these conditions could be met and an application for a dredging licence was made. After much delay this was approved (Fig. 17.10).

Hurst Spit and Lymington Estuary: extracts from SSSI citation

English Nature

Reasons for notification
This Site of Special Scientific Interest comprises the intertidal muds, cord-grass *Spartina anglica* marshes and high level mixed saltmarsh along 9 km of the northwest Solent shore, including the estuaries of

three substantial streams and a belt of fresh and brackish marsh protected by sea walls. The intertidal marshes terminate at the southwest in a well developed shingle spit with terminal recurved shingle ridges (Hurst Spit). The outer margins of the *Spartina* marshes, which occupy much of the intertidal area, are marked by numerous further ridges of shells and small pebbles. The SSSI is of national importance for its breeding populations of terns and supports concentrations of waders and wildfowl in autumn and winter which are part of the nationally important concentration of birds in the West Solent as a whole. The site embraces a wide range of coastal habitats of limited distribution on the south coast.

Within the citation, details follow on the flora and fauna of the site.

Hurst Castle Spit is a key site for coastal geomorphology. It is the classic shingle spit upon which W. V. Lewis based his seminal paper outlining the relationship of beach alignment to the direction of approach of dominant waves. Although much weakened at its proximal end by the steady retreat of cliffs at Milford and their protection by walls and groynes, Hurst Spit still retains its characteristic form. The present interest of the beach lies in its classic form.

Principles of conservation
The site should be allowed to evolve as naturally as possible. However, if left totally alone, breaching of the spit will occur, and this could lead to the possible permanent inundation of the marshlands. This would mean that Hurst Castle itself could become an island, and Keyhaven could become flooded. Valuable plant life and the breeding grounds for birds will also be lost. Thus there is need for some type of balance between leaving Hurst Castle Spit alone, and totally protecting it.

Without very detailed scientific investigations it is very hard to determine what the response of the spit is going to be to sea level rise. It is likely, however, that increased breaching will occur unless the spit can receive more shingle. Thus the dumping of shingle on the spit from that dredged from the nearside of the Shingles Bank should reduce the likelihood of it occurring.

At Barton and Milford sea defence construction is occurring at present and this is further reducing the sediment received by Hurst Castle Spit.

At present the site is used frequently for educational purposes.

Acknowledgements

The following have very kindly provided primary source information used in the text and diagrams: M. E. Barton, B. J. Coles, A. P. Bradbury, M. J. Clark, P. J. Ricketts, P. S. Clasby, R. J. Nicholls, Rendel Geotechnics and Sir William Halcrow and Partners.

References

Allen, L. G. & Gibbard, P. L. 1993. Pleistocene evolution of the Solent River of southern England. *Quaternary Science Reviews*, **12**, 503-528.

Bray, M. J. & Carter, D. J. 1996. Poole Bay and Hengistbury Head. *In*: Allison, R. J. (ed.) *The Coastal Landforms of East Dorset*. Geologists' Association, London.

Bray, M. J. & Hooke, J. M. 1995. Strategies for conserving dynamic coastal land forms *In*: Healy, M. G. & Doody, J. P. (eds) *Directions in European Coastal Management*. Samara, Cardigan, UK, 275–290.

Bray, M. J., Carter, D. J. & Hooke, J. M. 1995. Littoral cell definition and budgets for central southern England. *Journal of Coastal Research*, **11**, 381–400.

Clark, M. J., Ricketts, P. J. & Small, R. J. 1976. Barton does not rule the waves. *Geographical Magazine*, **48**, 580–588.

Devoy, R. J. N. 1982. Analysis of the geological evidence for Holocene sea-level movements in southeast England. *Proceedings of the Geologists' Association*, **93**, 65–90.

Harlow, D. A. & Cooper, N. J. 1995. Bournemouth beach monitoring: the first twenty years. *In*: *Coastal Management '95 – Putting Policy Into Practice*. Conference Proceedings, Institution of Civil Engineers.

Henderson, G. & Webber, N. B. 1978. Waves in a severe storm in the central English Channel. *Coastal Engineering*, **2**, 95–110.

Hooke, J. M. & Bray, M. J. 1995. Coastal groups, littoral cells, policies and plans in the UK. *Area*, **27**, 358–368.

Lacey, S. 1985. *Coastal Sediment Processes in Poole and Christch-urch Bays, and the Effects of Coast Protection Works*. Unpub-lished PhD Thesis, Department of Civil Engineering, University of Southampton.

Lelliott, R. E. L. 1989. Evolution of the Bournemouth defences. *In*: *Coastal Management*. Thomas Telford, London, 263–277.

May, V. J. 1990. Replenishment of Resort Beaches at Bournemouth and Christchurch, England. Journal of Coastal Research, **6**, 11–15.

Nicholls, R. J. 1985. *The stability of shingle beaches in the eastern half of Christchurch Bay*. PhD Thesis, Department of Civil Engineering, University of Southampton.

Nicholls, R. J. & Webber, N. B. 1987. The past, present and future evolution of Hurst Castle Spit. *Progress in Oceanography*, **18**, 119–137.

Rendel Geotechnics, 1994. *Barton on Sea Cliff Stabilisation: Recommended Stabilisation Measures*. Consultants Report to New Forest District Council.

West, I. M. 1980. Geology of the Solent Estuarine System. *In*: *The Solent Estuarine System: an Assessment of Present Knowledge*. NERC Publications Series C, No. 22, 6–18.

Index

Page numbers in *italics* refer to Figures or Tables